AIDS: A Guide to the Law

A second, thoroughly revised and updated edition of the first ever guide to the legal aspects of AIDS. Written by experienced legal professionals, many of whom are advisers, or have advised, at The Terrence Higgins Trust in London, *AIDS: A Guide to the Law* provides clear, straightforward guidance through areas of the law affected by AIDS. Some of the most controversial and challenging topics are addressed, including:

- Insurance
- Housing
- Employment
- Children and young people
- Immigration
- Criminal law

The second edition accounts for legal changes, practices and experience to August 1994, including two new chapters on children and young people and on criminal law. The children's chapter includes important advice to parents with HIV infection involved in custody or care disputes and a legal explanation of the 'need to know' argument that often concerns local authorities and social workers.

The second edition provides coverage of general legislative change affecting people with HIV infection, which includes the Access to Health Records Act 1990 and Access to Medical Reports Act 1988 as well as the Children Act 1989, which changed and codified the law relating to children and parental responsibility.

Concise and accessible, *AIDS: A Guide to the Law* is indispensable to health and social workers, counsellors, lawyers, welfare agency advisers and indeed anyone who needs a legal rights guide to AIDS.

Richard Haigh is Artists' Manager at Performing Arts in London and since 1983 has worked as a volunteer at The Terrence Higgins Trust. **Dai Harris** is Legal Services Officer for the National Association of Citizens Advice Bureaux (London Division) and was previously at The Terrence Higgins Trust as Legal Officer (1987–92).

AIDS: A Guide to the Law

Second Edition

Edited by
Richard Haigh and Dai Harris
for The Terrence Higgins Trust

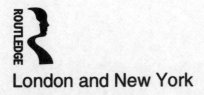

London and New York

First published 1990
Reprinted 1990
Second edition published 1995
by Routledge
11 New Fetter Lane, London EC4P 4EE

Simultaneously published in the USA and Canada
by Routledge
29 West 35th Street, New York, NY 10001

© 1995 The Terrence Higgins Trust

Typeset in Times by Michael Mepham, Frome, Somerset

Printed and bound in Great Britain by
Mackays of Chatham PLC, Chatham, Kent

British Library Cataloguing in Publication Data
A catalogue record for this book is available from the British
Library

Library of Congress Cataloguing in Publication Data
A catalogue record for this book has been requested

ISBN 0–415–11511–6 (hbk)
ISBN 0–415–09699–5 (pbk)

In memory of Lauren Jackson and of Colin d'Eça

Contents

Contributors

Jackie Bates is Housing Section Manager at The Terrence Higgins Trust.

Nigel Clarke is a solicitor and since 1975 a partner with Bradley & Clarke Solicitors, Chesterfield. He deals with the day-to-day problems of those no longer able, physically or mentally, to deal with their own affairs and with the preparation of wills and administrations of estates. In 1986 he became a member of the Legal Services Group of The Terrence Higgins Trust. More recently he has also been involved as a volunteer to his local HIV and AIDS advice service in North Derbyshire.

Timothy Costello is a solicitor at Eversheds, London. For eight years he has been a voluntary legal adviser helping people affected by HIV and AIDS.

Wesley Gryk is a member of the New York Bar and a solicitor qualified to practise in England and Wales. He has recently established his own firm based in Central London, specialising in criminal law and civil liberties.

Angus Hamilton is a solicitor in private practice working at J.P. Malnick & Co., London. He specialises in criminal litigation and actions against the police. He is a volunteer member of The Terrence Higgins Trust Legal Services Group and on the Board of Trustees of the National AIDS Manual.

Lauren Jackson was Housing Section Manager at The Terrence Higgins Trust.

Una Padel is the co-ordinator of London Prisons Links. She was Deputy Director of the Prison Reform Trust from 1985 to 1989 and wrote the PRT publication *HIV, AIDS and Prisons*. She then became Assistant Director at SCODA where she organised a project designing HIV education in prisons and wrote *HIV Education in Prisons: A Resource Book* with Rose Twidale and John Porter.

Bernard Richmond is a practising barrister specialising in crime and immigration work; he has been interested in HIV-related employment law for some time. He is a trainer and public speaker for The Terrence Higgins Trust.

Peter Roth is a barrister in professional practice specialising in commercial law and was the chairman of the Insurance Working Party of The Terrence Higgins Trust from 1989–94.

Simmy Viinikka is a solicitor with a background in family and childcare law. She is currently employed at The Terrence Higgins Trust providing legal services for people affected by HIV. She has developed a particular interest in medico-legal issues arising from the joint THT/King's College Living Will project which she helped to develop.

Acknowledgements

The editors would like to acknowledge the outstanding contributions made by the authors of this second edition of *AIDS: A Guide to the Law* who have cheerfully undertaken numerous revisions to their chapters. Thanks are also due to the staff and volunteers of The Terrence Higgins Trust; to Alice Holt, solicitor at the THT, our editors at Routledge and Dr Andrew Grubb of King's College, London.

Introduction

Dai Harris

AIDS: A Guide to the Law provides a legal guide to Acquired Immune Deficiency Syndrome (AIDS). Written principally for advisers, the book deals with fundamental legal and advisory issues for people affected by the Human Immunodeficiency Virus (HIV) and AIDS. Legal issues such as whether it is lawful to test a patient for HIV without their specific consent, whether transmission of HIV by consensual sex is a criminal offence, or whether it is lawful to sack someone who has HIV infection are examined. Advice issues include the likely effect of disclosing HIV status in criminal cases, the importance of making wills to provide for partners and children, what factors determine the suitability of housing for a person with HIV infection and time limits in employment and immigration cases.

Its ten chapters cover medico-legal matters, housing, children, crime, wills and probate, immigration, employment, prisons and prisoners' rights, insurance and the legal issues concerning voluntary organisations. All the contributors are advisers, or have advised, at The Terrence Higgins Trust in London. For this reason it reflects the legal experience in England and Wales, and not necessarily in Scotland or Northern Ireland where the law can be different. The Terrence Higgins Trust Advice Centre is the largest and longest-established specialist centre providing legal, welfare rights and housing advice in the UK. There is a full-time staff of eight (including two solicitors) and over fifty dedicated volunteers who provide free and confidential advice and representation to affected individuals on all the areas concerned in this book and many others.

This book is a unique resource on AIDS. An adviser can find, in one textbook, the relevant law and practice having a bearing on an AIDS-related legal issue. This might include unreported or recent legal cases, regulations made under primary legislation and policy guidelines or statements issued by ministers, government departments and medical or other professional bodies.

The second edition accounts for legal changes, practices and experience from 1988 to August 1994. Reflecting increasingly important legal issues, there are two new chapters in this edition, one on children and young people and the other on criminal law. The children's chapter includes important advice to parents with HIV infection involved in disputes concerning their children, and a legal explanation of the 'need to know' argument that often concerns local authority social workers.

Practical advice on the legality of health education materials and disclosure of HIV status to the police is provided in the criminal law chapter. The immigration chapter has been completely revised, and the employment and housing chapters updated by new authors. Welfare rights advice is now covered in its own separate, annually revised book published by and available from The Terrence Higgins Trust, *Benefits for People with HIV* by Colin Nee.

Except for the HIV Testing Kits and Services Regulations (1992) and provision on sex education in the Education Act 1993, there has been no specific AIDS-related legislation passed since the last edition, but there has been important government guidance on antenatal testing of pregnant women, HIV-infected health care workers, and sex education in schools. The second edition also provides coverage of general legislative change affecting people with HIV infection. This includes the Access to Health Records Act 1990 and Access to Medical Reports Act 1988 that afford rights of access to medical records and reports (see medico-legal, insurance, and children's chapters of the book), and also the Children Act 1989, which changed and codified the law relating to children and parental responsibility. It has also created a duty for local authorities to provide for children in need (and therefore, by argument, for children with HIV). The Asylum and Immigration Appeals Act 1993 has adversely affected the rights of overstayers and people seeking asylum.

Case law is the other means by which UK law changes. In the last six years only a few court decisions directly concerning HIV have been reported. These are referred to and discussed in the children and crime chapters. That said, none of the authors suggest that these cases set definitive precedents about how future cases should be handled or decided.

Certainly there has been little change in the legislative or judicial field directed solely at people with HIV infection or AIDS. What we have seen are both good practices towards people with HIV infection which are an improvement on the law, and bad practices which so far appear to be within the law.

The police practice of recording people's HIV status on the Police National Computer is due to stop within the next two years. Despite recent improvements in practice, insurance companies still classify people in 'at risk groups' and then discriminate against them. As the authors of the insurance chapter say, this was understandable as a panic reaction in the early 1980s. But as they note, even the Institute of Actuaries says that insurance underwriting should now be based on the risk of sexual practices rather than sexuality.

It is encouraging to hear of more humanitarian responses. As noted in the immigration chapter, the Home Office has carefully considered applications from people with HIV or their carers, who are unwell, for compassionate leave to remain in the UK. Another example is in the employment field where major employers have signed up under a voluntary scheme called 'Companies Act' to support a more sympathetic policy towards employees with HIV infection. The medico-legal chapter contains a discussion of the importance of Living Wills or advance directives, for people who become too ill to make decisions about their medical treatment. The Terrence Higgins Trust can claim credit for its ground-breaking work in developing a Living Will form which has achieved acclaim both from people affected by HIV and the medical and legal establishment. At the same time, developments in case law have given legal recognition to the advance refusal of medical treatment.

The Association of British Insurers recently announced that it was recommending the withdrawal of standard questions about prior HIV tests on life insurance proposal forms. This is a long overdue development for which The Terrence Higgins Trust has campaigned for many years and can again claim credit for its involvement.

Notwithstanding these positive developments, many AIDS-related problems are not helped by the law. For example, it is problematic that laws exist which prohibit direct safer sex information being provided to adults and young people. It is also wrong that health educators are liable to prosecution for trying to encourage changes in sexual practices that might prevent people from becoming infected. The law permits employers and others to ask people questions about their medical condition. At the same time the law offers no remedy if they are refused a job or suffer discrimination.

The UK is far behind states in the US and Australia that have introduced AIDS-specific laws protecting the rights of people with HIV infection as well as legislation protecting people with disabilities (including AIDS) and European countries such as the Netherlands who have adopted provisions of the European Convention on Human Rights into their own law. By contrast, there is as yet no antidiscrimination legislation in the UK on grounds of HIV status or disability, and this country has not incorporated the principles of the European Convention into domestic law. Whilst it is possible to pursue a complaint under the Convention, this takes time and money – commodities that may not be available to a person with AIDS or HIV infection.

To date, the legal restrictions on the publication of safer sex information and the non-availability of legal remedies for discrimination remain as much a political issue as a legal one. Consequently, the legal needs of people affected by HIV and AIDS may best be met by a combined strategy of individual case work (especially in areas such as wills and employment advice) and active campaigning for change on a broader level. If this book makes the task of giving legal advice on AIDS easier it will have served its purpose.

Dai Harris
August 1994

Chapter 1

Children, young people and HIV infection

Simmy Viinikka

Some parts of this chapter were published in 'Children looked after away from home: some legal implications', by Simmy Viinikka in Batty (ed.) *HIV Infection and Children in Need* (BAAF 1993).

INTRODUCTION

This chapter discusses how family law and the law relating to children and young persons may be relevant to those infected with HIV. It will look at treatment and consent to testing for HIV and confidentiality, the resolution of disputes over children, and the provision of local authority services including education. The law on consent to treatment is particularly complex in relation to young people. It is also at present subject to change by the courts and cannot be regarded as static.

Child care and children's law were entirely restated by the Children Act 1989 which came into force in October 1991. The Act incorporates a clear public policy agenda. It is formulated on the premises that children are normally best looked after within their family of origin, and that, where they are obliged to intervene, local authorities should work in partnership with parents. Local authorities are required to see that services are available for families, rather than necessarily to provide them themselves. The Act places greater priority than previous legislation on children's voices and needs. However, despite its good intentions, it is clear that cash constraints are having a severe impact on service planning and delivery.

The Department of Health has published useful guidance specifically on the subject of children and HIV (*Children and HIV: guidance for local authorities*, December 1992) which anyone interested in this field is advised to read.

In 1991, the United Kingdom ratified the United Nations' Convention on the Rights of the Child. This was developed during 1989 and has been ratified by over 160 states. Monitoring procedure requires that member states report on implementation two years after ratification and thereafter every five years. It is not incorporated into domestic law and therefore not enforceable in this country. It is effective mostly as a statement of intent and a basis from which to pursue legislative change. Key articles in the context of children and HIV include Article 3 (all actions concerning the child should take full account of his or her best interests); Article 12 (the right to express an opinion and have it taken into account); Article 16 (the right to privacy) and Article 24 (the right to the highest level of health possible, and access to health and medical services).

All references in this chapter are to the Children Act 1989 unless stated otherwise.

HIV TESTING AND MEDICAL TREATMENT

The right to consent: children and young people

Children and young people under the age of 18 have limited legal powers in relation to medical treatment. A young person of 16 or over may consent to 'any surgical, medical or dental treatment which, in the absence of consent, would constitute a trespass to the person' (Family Law Reform Act 1969, section 8). As the provision relates to 'treatment', any medical procedures would need to be therapeutic. The consent of a person with parental responsibility or the permission of the court is required where the proposed treatment is non-therapeutic or where a young person lacks the mental capacity to consent (Re E. (a minor) [1991] BMLR). Whilst a young person of 16 or over may consent to treatment, a refusal to accept treatment has been held not to be binding and may be overridden by the Court. This happened in a well-publicised case concerning a young woman with anorexia nervosa who was treated against her wishes following a court hearing (Re W. (a minor) [1992] 4 AER 627) (formerly known as 'Re J.').

The legal position regarding those under 16 was given extensive consideration in 1985 by the House of Lords in the Gillick case (*Gillick* v. *West Norfolk and Wisbech Area Health Authority* [1985] 3 AER 402; [1986] 1 FLR 224) and was revisited in Re R. (a minor) [1991] 4 AER 177.

Gillick concerned an application to the Court by a mother who wanted to ensure that contraceptive facilities would not be made available to her daughters, who were all under 16, without her consent. The Court held that, provided a young person is, in the doctor's opinion, of sufficient maturity to understand what is proposed and to make up his or her own mind, she or he is entitled to consent to medical treatment despite being under 16. Accordingly a young person under 16 may in certain circumstances lawfully consent to undergo an HIV-antibody test without parental or other consent. Two qualifications to this are set out in the Gillick decision. First, treatment without parental knowledge is exceptional, and it is the doctor's duty in every case to try and persuade the young person to allow his or her parents to be informed. Secondly, the young person has to be seen to understand not simply the medical advice offered but where relevant its wider social and moral implications in order to give fully informed consent. For example, a young person who can lawfully consent to the setting of a broken arm may lack the capacity to give valid consent to an HIV-antibody test.

Unfortunately the 'Gillick' principle suffered a setback in the Court of Appeal in Re R. at a time when it appeared to be settled law. Re R. was concerned with the medical treatment of a 15-year-old girl with psychiatric problems. At least one of the judges in Re R. appears to have held that, whilst a young person with sufficient capacity may consent to treatment, if he or she vetoes it, treatment may, nevertheless, lawfully be given with the consent of a parent, guardian or local authority if the child is in care. This flies in the face of the spirit of the Children Act and of the Gillick decision itself, where Lord Scarman said that 'as a matter of law the parental rights to determine whether or not their minor children below the age of 16 will have medical treatment terminates if and when the child achieves sufficient understanding and intelligence to enable him or her to understand what is proposed'. Both Re R. and by implication Re W. have cast doubt on this principle, and a further House of Lords' decision is needed to restate the law.

The Gillick decision is given statutory recognition in the Children Act where a court, when making an emergency protection or child assessment order or interim care or supervision order, may direct that a child be psychiatrically or medically examined. The child, if of sufficient understanding, has a statutory right to refuse such an examination (ss. 38[6], 43[8], 44[7]). Once again, this apparently clear principle has been judicially undermined by recent decisions. In *South Glamorgan County Council* v. *W. and B.* [1993] 1 FLR 574 it was held that the inherent jurisdiction of the High Court can be used to override a refusal of assessment under s.38[6]. In another case involving a direction under s.38[6], magistrates, on making an interim care order, directed that children (whose parents were HIV-positive) be tested for HIV despite the objection of the local authority concerned (Re O. [1993] 1 FLR 860). One of the issues in this case was the extent (which is unclear) to which the magistrates heard expert evidence on the advantages and disadvantages of testing children for HIV before making that decision.

The law concerning consent to testing and treatment for babies and young children who do not have sufficient capacity to consent on their own behalf, has been considerably revised by the Children Act. Consent to testing in all such cases must be given by a person with *parental responsibility*.

Parental responsibility is defined to include 'all the rights, duties, powers, responsibilities and authority by which law a parent of a child has in relation to the child and his or her property'(s.3). Parental responsibility extends to the child's mother in every case. A father has parental responsibility if he is married to the mother or if he acquires it by means of a court order or a formal agreement with the mother. A person caring for a child under a *residence order*, a guardian and a local authority (or voluntary organisation) looking after a child who is *in care* under a *care order* will also have parental responsibility during the currency of the order. Where a local authority is looking after a child at the request of a parent ('accommodating the child') the local authority does not acquire parental responsibility.

Local authorities and consent

Whether a local authority may consent to testing or treatment on behalf of a child therefore depends on whether or not it has parental responsibility for that child. It is important to note that the parent of a child in care does not lose his or her parental responsibility on the making of a care order and may continue to exercise it provided that he or she does not do so in a way which is incompatible with the terms of any order. In theory, such parent could arrange an HIV-antibody test for his or her child in care. A local authority may act to limit the exercise of parental responsibility if it considers that to do so is in the interests of the welfare of the child (s.33[3](b)).

Any decision to test a child in care for HIV infection must be made by a local authority in the context of its general duty under section 22[3] of the Act to safeguard and promote the welfare of the child. A local authority is also subject to legal duties to have due regard to the child's religious, racial, cultural and linguistic background and to ascertain the wishes and feelings of the child, his or her parents and any other person who has parental responsibility, or whose wishes and feelings the authority consider to be relevant. In order properly to fulfil all these duties, and in the absence of a medical emergency, it would appear desirable for any decision to seek an HIV-antibody test to be made at a statutory review or case conference. Legal advice should be taken in every case as an application to the court may be necessary. Notwithstanding its obligation to consult, the ultimate decision to test a child in its care rests with the local authority. The Children Act reinforces the well-established principle whereby the wardship jurisdiction cannot be invoked to interfere with the local authority's exercise of its discretion in relation to the upbringing of a child in its care (*A.* v. *Liverpool City Council* [1982] AC 363; [1981] 2 AER 385).

The Arrangements for Placement of Children (General) Regulations 1991 provide for the medical examination and the preparation of a written assessment of the state of health of every child who is looked after by a local authority or voluntary organisation. In arranging a placement, a local authority is to have regard to a wide range of considerations in respect of the child's state of health and health history. A local authority could, subject to its duty to safeguard and promote the welfare of such children, decide to test for HIV antibodies under these regulations (provided that it has the consent of those with parental responsibility). Local authorities are advised by the Department of Health (*Children and HIV: guidance for local authorities*) that testing should never be carried out solely at the request of foster parents or as a matter of routine.

Limits of parental powers

A parent, in consenting to testing or medical treatment on behalf of a child for whom he or she has parental responsibility, is not subject to the statutory duty of the local authority to *safeguard and promote* the child's welfare. However, a parent has nevertheless an enforceable legal duty in making a decision on behalf of a child, to do so in accordance with the interests of the welfare of that child. This duty was discussed in the Gillick case and was confirmed in Re B. (a minor) [1991] 2 FLR 426. This was a case where the mother of a 12-year-old girl refused to allow her to have an abortion and the local authority made the child a ward of court. The Court granted leave for the abortion, holding that the interests of the ward were first and paramount and therefore the wishes of the mother could not be said to be conclusive.

A clear analogy can be made to a situation where there is a dispute as to whether or not a child should have an HIV-antibody test. Such a dispute could arise where a local authority is accommodating a child at the request of the child's parents, and therefore does not have parental responsibility for that child. The local authority, or any other interested party, may apply to the court under section 8 of the Children Act for a *specific issue order* and this procedure has been held to be appropriate where medical treatment is sought against the wishes of parents (*Camden LBC* v. *R.* [1993]). Any person who can demonstrate sufficient interest in the child's welfare or, for example, a hospital trust or health authority, may, as an alternative, apply to make the child a ward of court, and wardship may also be appropriate where there is a dispute over the child's capacity to make a decision (Re R.). Wardship is not available in respect of children in care but a local authority may apply with leave of the Court for the exercise of the High Court's inherent jurisdiction in specific cases of dispute or difficulty.

It is for the person with parental responsibility for a young child to decide whether and when the child is to be told of his or her antibody status. The issue has arisen in practice in the cases of haemophiliac children with HIV infection whose parents have taken various different attitudes towards telling their children, and health professionals and social workers have had to respect these views. A serious dispute may be brought before the Court as described above.

CONFIDENTIALITY AND ACCESS TO INFORMATION

Health services

A doctor treating a child or young person is bound by the same professional and legal obligations of confidentiality which protect adult patients. In the majority of cases, a parent will give consent for a child to be tested and he or she will also be given the result. However, where a young person over 16 or younger, if sufficiently mature, has an HIV-antibody test and will not tell his or her parents or allow a doctor to do so, his or her wish should normally be respected. Helpful guidance has been issued by the British Medical Association (BMA), Family Planning Association (FPA) and other organisations (*Confidentiality and people under 16*, 1993).

The medical duty of confidentiality is not absolute and there has been considerable debate about whether a doctor has the power or indeed the duty to disclose a young person's antibody status to a sexual partner or other third party. These issues are discussed in Chapter 7.

Young people may request access to health records compiled about them under the Access to Health Records Act 1990. Access may be given if the record holder is satisfied that the young person is capable of understanding the nature of the application.

Social services

Social services departments in many districts have developed policy on dealing with HIV/AIDS, stressing the need for confidentiality. Useful advice is provided in the Department of Health's *Guidance on Children and HIV* which discusses client confidentiality in some detail.

A local authority or voluntary organisation looking after a child has a duty of confidentiality in respect of the affairs of that child. Regulations provide for the maintenance of comprehensive records in respect of each child being looked after by a local authority. Such records are normally to be retained for a period of 75 years from the child's birth and steps should be taken to ensure their safekeeping and to restrict access to them to authorised persons.

Young people have the right of access to information held in their case files compiled from April 1989 under the Access to Personal Files Act 1987 and the Access to Personal Files (Social Services) Regulations 1989 provided that the authority is satisfied that the young person understands the nature of the request. Because of the particularly sensitive nature of this information, some local authorities have taken steps to ensure that information relating to a child's HIV status is kept off the case file and retained separately at Assistant Director or equivalent level.

A local authority or voluntary organisation is obliged to enter into a 'foster placement agreement' in respect of each child whom it is arranging to place with a foster parent. This agreement must include a statement containing all the information which the authority considers necessary to enable foster parents to care for the child and, in particular, information regarding the child's state of health and need for health care and surveillance. Where any significant information is withheld, the reason should be recorded on the child's case file. Department of Health guidance confirms that where a child has HIV infection, the foster parents will normally need to be fully informed of this. Where there is HIV infection in the child's family, it would have to be established that any disclosure is in the interests of the child's welfare (and that consent has been obtained). Foster carers are required to treat any information so given to them as confidential and should receive training on the maintenance of confidentiality and of safe-keeping of documentation relating to a child.

Policy and good practice have varied over time. For example, in Lothian where there are a number of HIV-infected children in foster care, social services were initially advised that the parents of other children should be told when an HIV-infected child came into a foster family. This advice has now been rescinded. In Lothian and most other areas disclosure of antibody status is restricted initially to a very limited number of people within the social services department and the child's primary health and general care givers only. Any disclosure has to be justified in accordance with the Council's policy on what is termed a 'need to know' basis. The National Foster Care Association's advice is that any disclosure should be authorised by the child's social worker on a similar basis. In most cases it advises that there is no 'need to know' in the case of a healthy child where schools, nurseries and other organisations operate a good general standard of hygiene. This considerably reduces the need for their principals and staff to be told of an individual child's status.

Under the Adoption Agencies Regulations (1983), the adoption panel's medical adviser must obtain a full health history of the natural parents, up-to-date medical reports on the prospective adopters, and prepare a full report on the child's health, arranging such examinations and screenings as he or she considers necessary. The reports on the child and the prospective adopters are expected to be very detailed and to include any relevant information which may assist the adoption panel in reaching a decision, including, in the case of adoptive parents, details of their daily consumption of alcohol, tobacco and any habit-forming drugs. If a placement is approved, it is the medical examiner's responsibility to provide the prospective adopters and their family doctor with information on the child's health and to notify the Local Education Authority and District Health Authority of the placement. The adoption panel and prospective adopters should be given any information about a child's HIV status.

The routine screening for HIV infection of all children who are to be placed for adoption is discouraged by most agencies and the Department of Health. Children should only be tested for HIV infection on medical advice where a clear risk exists, and prospective adopters should be advised that it is not possible to guarantee that a child, particularly a baby, is free from HIV infection.

The 'need to know' can be interpreted extremely widely and contrary to popular belief does not eliminate the need for consent prior to disclosure. In some cases, other considerations may prevail, for example a social services department may decide to breach confidentiality for child welfare reasons if a known HIV-infected child in care is having a sexual relationship with another child also being looked after by the authority. The department would have to consider, among other factors, the other child's antibody status if known, the HIV-positive child's knowledge and practice of safer sex, the parents' and the young person's own wishes. In legal terms the authority must balance its duty to safeguard and promote the welfare of both children with its duty of care towards those, including the second child, who might have a claim against it for negligence if it does not disclose, and its duty of confidence towards the first child. Legal advice should be sought, and if disclosure is contemplated, every effort made to discuss the matter and to obtain consent.

Where a child is felt to be at risk of abuse, *Working Together* constitutes recognised good practice to be followed by the social and health services and the police. It recommends that information about children at risk should be shared between professionals and that the child's views should be made known at a case conference, usually through a social worker. Such advice is in potential conflict with many typical local authority policies on HIV and confidentiality. In the case of an older child it is also in potential conflict with his or her right, following the decision, in Gillick, to seek independent advice and counselling in confidence. The conflict can be readily reconciled in relation to HIV status if the child or parent consents to disclosure. Department of Health guidance states that discussion of HIV status should only take place at a case conference if absolutely necessary for a full consideration of the need to protect the child.

It also states that 'non-infected children using daycare services are unlikely to be at any risk from an infected child'. It is therefore not necessary for staff working in daycare settings to be informed about a child's HIV status or that of his or her parents although parents may choose to give the agency this information. Guidelines in *HIV and AIDS: a Guide for the Education Service* (DES 1991) emphasise the reduction of risk through good hygiene, the need for confidentiality and the possibility of discrimination against a child whose antibody positive status becomes known.

DISPUTES OVER CHILDREN

A diagnosis of HIV disease or AIDS can precipitate a crisis in the lives of a child's carers or HIV/AIDS may be an added complication to pre-existing difficulties. This section will look at ways in which the law can be used to resolve these disputes.

Disputes can arise if a parent with HIV infection/AIDS finds that he or she is suddenly not allowed to see his or her children, or that he or she is only allowed to see them in the presence of a third party acting as 'supervisor'. His or her capacity to care for the children on a long-term basis may be questioned by relations or the other parent. If all else fails either party may decide to apply to the Court for a resolution of the dispute.

An individual, primarily a parent (but the Act also authorises applications by non-parents), who wants the Court to make a decision about a child must apply for a *Section 8 order*. There are four kinds of Section 8 order: a *residence order* (defining with whom a child is to live); a *contact order* (which states who the child may visit or stay with); a *specific issue order* (a decision over any specific question relating to the child's upbringing); and a *prohibited steps order* (restricting the exercise of parental responsibility in a specific way). Any person with whom a child has lived for at least three years may apply for a residence or contact order. Such a person could be, for example, a former partner.

Any other person may apply for an order with the consent of those with parental responsibility or if the Court gives leave. This could, for example, be a friend or relation who is being prevented from seeing the child, or the child him or herself. Joint orders may also be made, enabling a residence order to be sought by a parent with HIV disease jointly with his or her cohabitee who is not a parent, although recent decisions have held that a shared residence order will only be made in exceptional circumstances (Re H. [1993] 1 FLR 671 CA).

In making a decision, the Court must give paramount consideration to the child's welfare (s.1). A checklist of specific aspects of the child's welfare to which the Court is to have regard is set out in section 1[3] of the Act and reproduced below:

Section 1

(a) the ascertainable wishes of the child concerned (considered in the light of his age and understanding);
(b) his physical, emotional and educational needs;
(c) the likely effect on him of any change in his circumstances;
(d) his age, sex, background and any characteristics of his which the court considers relevant;
(e) any harm he has suffered or is at risk of suffering;
(f) how capable each of his parents, and any other person in relation to whom the court considers the question to be relevant, is of meeting his needs;
(g) the range of powers available to the court under this Act in the proceedings in question.

The Court must only make an order if it considers that doing so will be better for the child than making no order at all. Thus, for example, it may be that in a divorce a court may decide that there should be no formal order and that the parents should sort things out for themselves. The intention behind this is to promote the idea of continuing parental responsibility for both parents and to prevent the child being seen as a prize in a legal dispute.

The outcome of any case involving children depends very much on its individual facts, rather than on the precedent or 'case law' set by previous reported cases. Only cases heard in the Court of Appeal are regularly reported, and the opportunity to appeal in children's cases is restricted to those where it can be shown that the original decision was 'plainly wrong'. Only one reported Appeal Court decision appears to have been taken involving HIV and children in a private law context (as opposed to public law where a local authority is involved) (Re T. (Lexis 26.6.89)). This is an unusual case of peripheral relevance but illustrates an HIV-positive mother suffering direct discrimination. Following a dispute she had brought her child into the UK from the USA where the family had been living; the father successfully applied under an international convention for the return of the child to the USA so that the courts there could make a custody decision. This is standard procedure to discourage 'child snatching'. The Court here did not accept the mother's argument that US immigration law, which restricts entry to HIV-anti-body-positive individuals, would prevent her from staying in New York to fight her case and care for the child in the interim. The mother in that case has now apparently been reunited with her child following further litigation.

Despite the individual nature of each case it might be useful to take a practical look at some of the issues which might arise in a case involving HIV/AIDS. Anyone proposing to go to court should carefully think through the strengths and weaknesses of their case with their lawyer, in the light of the checklist of factors listed above, and should also decide why it is important that the Court should be asked to make any order at all on the facts of their particular case.

The Court may, and almost certainly will in a case of any difficulty, order a welfare report to be prepared by a probation officer or social worker. It is likely to carry significant weight with the judge or magistrate but he or she is not bound to follow its recommendations. In some cases the judge or magistrate may decide to see the child, but in any event the court has a duty to consider the child's preference and is likely to look to the welfare officer to give evidence of this. The child may be able to apply to be made a party to the proceedings or bring the case him or herself, thereby ensuring his or her views are put.

If the parent or other applicant is HIV-infected, but is non-symptomatic, the case against him or her may focus on the fear of transmission of HIV. If so, it is advisable to provide the Court with expert evidence of the minimal risks of transmission of HIV in ordinary household contact. It is generally advisable to produce up-to-date medical evidence, from a consultant specialising in HIV, of the applicant's own health. The parent or other applicant can also expect to face questions about how he or she would cope if they become ill, what arrangements they would make to see or care for the child and what, if anything, they would tell the child.

If the parent already has HIV disease all of the above considerations will apply but there will be a greater emphasis on his or her prognosis and symptoms, on the emotional impact on the child, and on his or her physical ability to care for the child. Medical evidence will obviously be very important, in particular to convey to the court that the parent is 'living with' HIV disease and not necessarily facing imminent death. One of the issues which is likely to concern the Court is the child's ability to deal with illness and death. Expert evidence from a child psychologist, counsellor or religious adviser may be very useful to supplement the parent's own evidence on this. If the parent is also gay or lesbian, other arguments may also be encountered, for example, that the child could be stigmatised at school, or that she or he may suffer psycho-sexual damage and gender disorientation as a result. Even if the other parent is sympathetic to these issues, they may be raised by the judge or the welfare officer. Case law relating to lesbian mothers states that a mother's lesbianism does not disqualify her from having care of her child, but that it is a factor which the Court will put into the balance (Re C. (a minor), December [1991] Fam. Law 524). A gay father may choose to refer to these cases and he may also face gender-specific questioning regarding his parenting ability. Recent cases have now firmly established that there is no automatic presumption in law that a mother is more fitted by virtue of her sex than a father to take care of small children.

Questions of financial provision on relationship breakdown and the workings of the Child Support Act 1991 are outside the scope of this chapter.

PARENTS WITH HIV DISEASE – WILLS, AND THE APPOINTMENT OF GUARDIANS

A parent with HIV disease will need to make arrangements for the children including choosing who will be responsible for them if he or she dies. This person is known as a guardian and he or she acquires parental responsibility once the appointment takes effect. The Children Act has revised the law relating to guardians but it remains quite complicated.

A guardian may only be appointed by a parent with parental responsibility, by a previous guardian, or by the Court. An appointment may therefore be made by a mother, or by a father if he is married to the mother or if he has acquired parental responsibility. It may be made in a will or in any signed statement. Normally a guardian is appointed in a will. It is sensible to check first that the person is willing to act.

When the parent dies, if there is no other surviving parent with parental responsibility the appointment (unless refused by the guardian) will take effect immediately. This will apply for example on the death of a single mother where the father has not acquired parental responsibility, or if the father is already dead.

If, however, on the death of a parent, there is a surviving parent with parental responsibility, a guardianship appointment will not take effect during the surviving parent's lifetime, unless the deceased parent had a residence order in his or her favour. In this case the guardian's appointment takes immediate effect, but parental responsibility is shared between the guardian and the surviving parent. Any dispute between the guardian and the surviving parent can be brought before the court, which can terminate a guardian's appointment.

Practical points to note are that an appointment made in a will is revoked if the will is revoked, and that it is advisable to take legal advice to ensure that the proposed arrangements will work as envisaged. In particular, it will be necessary to have a residence order if there is a surviving parent who has parental responsibility and the parent with care of the child wants the guardian's appointment to take effect immediately on his or her death. It is an open question whether or not a court would grant a residence order for this purpose alone. If not, the 'would be' guardian could consider seeking a residence order instead on the parent's death. This would require leave of the Court.

If no one appears willing to take responsibility for a child on the death of one or both parents the local authority has a duty to look after him or her by providing accommodation and maintenance. This is discussed in the next section. The Court may also be asked to appoint a guardian.

If the parent dies without leaving a valid will any property will be distributed according to the 'rules of intestacy' (see chapter on wills for further details). If there is a surviving husband or wife he or she will inherit a certain amount according to a set formula under which the children may also get a share. Where there is no husband or wife it is divided between the children, usually equally but with some complicated provisos. Moreover where there is no will, the people who administer the property on behalf of the children are appointed from a list of relatives, and any money or property inherited by the children can only be used or invested according to cumbersome and restrictive rules. It is possible in a will to specify a later age than 18 at which children may inherit. As children cannot generally inherit under the age of 18, it is best to have a will involving a gift to a child drawn up by a solicitor. A lone parent or a person with a disability who receives income support, family credit or disability working allowance with savings of (usually) under £1,000 may have a will prepared by a solicitor under the Green Form Legal Aid scheme. Straightforward wills are prepared free of charge at The Terrence Higgins Trust Advice Centre and Immunity Legal Centre.

A child who has not been properly provided for in his or her parent's will (for example where everything is left to a new partner or to a charity) may be able to apply to the Court under the *Inheritance (Provision for Family and Dependants) Act 1975* for reasonable financial provision. This is discussed further in the chapter on wills.

Local authority support for children and families

Local authority support and services are summarised in Part III and Schedule 2 of the Act. The Department of Health has issued a series of volumes of *Guidance and Regulations* which supplement the Act and which are essential reading for service providers and clients' representatives as they define the standard of service to be provided.

The ideological premise of this part of the Act is that children are best looked after in their own families, and that where a local authority becomes involved, it should act in partnership with the parents. Whilst the Act imposes on local authorities certain specific duties and responsibilities, it is drafted to give them wide discretion in implementation and prioritisation. This may make it more difficult to challenge a local authority which is failing to provide a service, or is interpreting its responsibilities in a restrictive way.

Every local authority has a general duty, in relation to all of the children in its area, to take reasonable steps (through the provision of services) to prevent them from suffering ill-treatment or neglect, and to reduce the need to bring care or other proceedings. There is also a general duty to encourage children not to commit criminal offences, and to avoid the need for their placement in secure accommodation.

Most local authority services are likely to be targeted towards 'children in need'. Children in need are defined as children who are unlikely to achieve or maintain a reasonable standard of health or development (or to have the opportunity of so doing), or whose health or development are likely to be significantly impaired (or further impaired), without the provision of local authority services, or who are disabled (s. 17[10]). 'Health' and 'development' are broadly defined, and 'health' means physical or mental health, and 'development' means physical, intellectual, emotional, social or behavioural development.

A child is considered to be disabled if he or she is 'blind, deaf or dumb or suffers from mental disorder of any kind or is substantially and permanently handicapped by illness, injury or congenital deformity' (s.7[11]). It is suggested that this definition encompasses a child with AIDS. He or she may also be failing to 'achieve or maintain a reasonable standard of health or development'. Whether a child with HIV infection, or whose parents are infected with HIV, is considered to be 'in need' will depend on an assessment of the individual circumstances of the family and the interpretation of the definition made by each local authority. It is suggested that such a child in most circumstances may properly be defined as 'in need'. Whether a child with HIV infection is, or should be, additionally described as 'disabled' is another matter.

Every local authority is required to take reasonable steps to identify the extent of children in need within its area, and to publish information about available services. The assessment of a child as being 'in need' is the key to local authority services; the procedure for making the assessment is up to the individual authority.

Local authorities have the discretion within the broad parameters of the Act, and the various regulations, to provide whatever services they consider appropriate to children in need and their families. There are, however, specific requirements to provide certain services, of which the following are amongst the most significant:

to provide appropriate day care for pre-school children;
to provide after school and out-of-hours care for school-aged children (s. 18);
to provide a family centre (Schedule 2, para. 9);
to make such provision as they consider appropriate for children in need living with their families in the form of:
advice, guidance and counselling,
home helps,
help with travel and to take a holiday (Schedule 2, para. 8).

Every local authority is required to publish a review and to make proposals upon the availability of child-minding and any care facilities for children under the age of 8 and generally within their area (s.19). There is also a duty to provide accommodation for children in need which is dealt with below.

In relation to children with disabilities, the stated aim of the Act is to integrate, as far as possible, the local authority services for such children with general services for children in need. The Act imposes a clear and positive duty on local authorities to provide services to minimise the effect of their disabilities on children and to give them the opportunity to lead lives which are as normal as possible (Schedule 2, para. 6). The duty is not further defined and may be freely interpreted but a local authority should have full regard to volume 6 of Guidance, 'Children with Disabilities', in implementing this requirement.

So as to avoid multiple assessments, the Act provides that a child may be assessed as 'in need' for the purposes of the Children Act at the same time as an assessment of special needs is made under the Education Act 1981 or the Chronically Sick and Disabled Persons Act 1970. Every local authority is required to establish and maintain a register of disabled children (Schedule 2, para. 2). Guidance states that registration should be voluntary and confidential and that parental participation should be encouraged. This is an area of potential concern to families with children with HIV disease and, as yet, the benefits of registration to individual children and families are not clear, but registration is intended to assist in planning and providing services.

As under the previous law, assistance to families with children in need may be given in kind or, exceptionally, in cash (s. 17(b)). However, the Act confers a broad power on local authorities to charge parents for any such assistance, or for the provision of services other than advice, guidance and counselling. The effect of this is that families may now be charged for services which they previously enjoyed without charge. Families receiving Income Support or Family Credit are excepted.

The provision of accommodation

Section 20 deals with the duty to provide 'accommodation' for certain children. 'Accommodation' is to be arranged by a local authority in partnership with the person with parental responsibility; it replaces the term 'reception into care'. A local authority does not acquire parental responsibility for the child or young person who is being accommodated. There is a duty to accommodate any child in need who appears to require accommodation because there is no one with parental responsibility for him or her (for example, in the event of illness) to provide suitable care or accommodation. The duty also arises if the child is lost or abandoned. A local authority may also accommodate a child if it considers that to do so will safeguard and promote the child's welfare (s. 20[4]). For example, if a child is failing to thrive and his or her parents agree to the plan, he or she may spend some time with a foster carer as part of a child protection strategy.

Before offering accommodation to any child or young person, a local authority is required to ascertain and to give due consideration to the child's wishes, and may not accommodate a child where there are objections by a person with parental responsibility who is willing and able to accommodate the child him or herself (s. 20[7]). A child who is being accommodated may be removed at any time by a person with parental responsibility. Nevertheless, regulations require that the length of any placement and a period of notice should be agreed in writing between the authority and the parents.

Children who are being accommodated, and children who are in care under a care order, are both described as being 'looked after' by the local authority. The legal duties of the authority towards both groups of children are identical and are summarised below:

to safeguard and promote the welfare of any child being looked after (s. 22[3](a));

to make use of the services normally available to children being cared for by their parents in the area (s. 22[3](b));

before making any decision in relation to the child, to ascertain and give due consideration to the wishes and feelings of the child, the child's parents and anyone else who has parental responsibility or whose wishes the local authority consider relevant (e.g., a grandparent or a co-parent);

to give due consideration to the child's religious persuasion, racial origins and cultural and linguistic background in any decision-making (s.22[5](c));

to provide accommodation and maintenance for children who are being looked after by placing them with a family, a relative or other suitable person or in one of a variety of residential establishments.

So far as is practicable and consistent with their welfare, children are to be placed with a parent or other person with parental responsibility, or with a relative or friend, and near to their homes and with any other siblings who are also being accommodated.

A disabled child should be placed in accommodation which is 'not unsuitable to his particular needs' (s.20[9]);

to promote contact between the child, his or her parents and any other person who has parental responsibility and any other relative or friend unless it is not reasonably practicable or consistent with his or her welfare (Schedule 2, para. 15). A local authority is empowered to make payments to assist in promoting contact (Schedule 2, para.16).

In the case of children who are not in touch with their parents or visited by them, a local authority may appoint an independent visitor for the child. The role and appointment of independent visitors is dealt with in *Guidance and Regulations*.

A local authority is required to consider whether it should seek a financial contribution from the parents of the child it is looking after unless the parents are receiving Income Support or Family Credit (Schedule 2, part III).

A parent who has HIV disease and is sometimes unable to care at all for his or her children and at other times needs regular support should ideally find that these new provisions make it possible for flexible and effective arrangements to be made with the local authority. The reality is likely to vary widely depending on a local authority's resources and commitment and The Terrence Higgins Trust Advice Centre would be very interested to hear of people's experiences.

YOUNG PEOPLE

Young people, particularly those in residential accommodation, may be at risk of HIV infection through abuse by adults, including prostitution, unsafe sex or risky drug use. It is clearly important that they receive adequate sex education and the opportunity to learn about HIV infection. Department of Health guidance on preparing children for leaving care provides specifically that they should be enabled to build and maintain relationships, including sexual relationships, with others and that practical issues such as contraception and the transmission of HIV should be covered. The guidance also refers to the specific needs and concerns of gay young men and women who, it says, should be enabled to accept their sexuality and to develop their own self-esteem.

A young person of 16 or over may request accommodation in his or her own right which should be provided if the authority considers that his or her welfare is otherwise likely to be severely prejudiced (s.20[3]). In addition a local authority may provide accommodation for young people between the ages of 16 and 21 in a community home if this would safeguard and promote their welfare (s.20[5]). This and other provisions of the Act concerning young people in housing need is being monitored and are likely to be challenged if (as is anticipated) local authorities attempt to avoid their responsibilities.

The Act puts 'safe houses' or refuges for young people who are on the run from home or care on to a statutory basis. Easier access to safe houses should benefit young people with HIV or at risk of infection, such as those who are homeless or are escaping sexual abuse or prostitution. There is also a duty placed on a local authority to assist 'any young person between the ages of 16 and 21 who has at sometime between the ages of 16 and 18 been looked after by them if the young person requests and appears to be in need of help'. Such assistance may take a broad form and includes help in cash or in kind. Children or young persons may be placed in secure accommodation if they have a history of absconding and, if they do so again, are likely to suffer significant harm, or else if they are likely to injure themselves or others if not kept in secure accommodation. It does not appear impossible that it could be sanctioned in order to restrict liberty, in a case where a local authority knew or believed that a young person had HIV, although the use of secure accommodation for such a purpose would be quite wrong and has been officially denied.

EDUCATION

Every child between 5 and 16 must attend school or otherwise receive appropriate full-time education. Particular issues in relation to AIDS and HIV are discrimination in school, special educational provision and sex education in schools.

Discrimination in schools

Government guidance on HIV and AIDS states that HIV-infected children should be allowed to attend school freely and should be treated in the same way as other pupils. It advises that information concerning a child's antibody status should be 'rigorously confined to those that need to know', and recommends improvements in general standards of hygiene to minimise the risk of transmission and hence the 'need to know' (DES 1991).

None the less there have been some examples in this country, and very many in the USA, of prejudice against infected school children. In one or two known instances in the mid-1980s in the UK, children were withdrawn from schools in protest at the presence of haemophiliac HIV-infected children. These incidents were resolved through public education via meetings and without recourse to the courts. A similar approach was taken in April 1991 when controversy arose in Kirklees over the presence of a child with the Hepatitis B virus in a state school. By way of contrast, there is now a string of cases in the USA, some brought on behalf of HIV-infected children, seeking to enforce their right to attend school, and others brought by other parents trying to exclude them.

Special education

Special education provision is relevant to HIV in several ways; children who have HIV disease may have special educational needs; other disabled children with disabilities may be at risk of HIV infection (for example, through sexual abuse), and infants who have HIV infection may develop neurological problems and learning difficulties. The Department of Education and Science advice on such children is that developmental delay and handicap, together with HIV infection, will be taken into account in an assessment of the child's special educational needs. This involves a lengthy and cumbersome procedure colloquially known as 'statementing' which should result in the issue of a statement of Special Educational Needs under the 1981 Education Act. Appropriate education should then be offered. This assessment can now be combined with any undertaken under the Children Act or other legislation to avoid multiple assessments. Problems arise in delays in statementing and then, once 'statemented', in the provision of appropriate services. There may be legal remedies by way of judicial review in these instances.

Sex education and learning about HIV and AIDS

If we believe in the importance of good health education to reduce the rate of HIV transmission, it is necessary to consider whether and how the subject is dealt with at school. For a brief period, education on HIV and AIDS formed part of the national curriculum in science lessons. Following the 1993 Education Act, education about HIV and AIDS is now included only in sex education lessons. Sex education lessons are governed by the Education (No. 2) Act 1986 and the Education Reform Act 1988 (as amended by the Education Act 1993). The governors of maintained primary schools must decide whether sex education should be taught, and provide a written sex education policy. Sex education must be taught in all maintained secondary schools. The syllabus is the responsibility of the governors, who must provide a policy document for parents. A survey published in June 1992 found that only 4 per cent of local education authorities in England and Wales had information regarding these education policies within schools in their area. Of these 69 per cent of schools had a policy, 25 per cent had no policy and 6 per cent had adopted a policy against sex education teaching. Wherever sex education is provided, governors must ensure that it 'is given in such a manner as to encourage those pupils to have due regard to moral considerations and the value of family life' (Section 46, Education Act 1986).

Parents have an absolute right to withdraw their children of whatever age from sex education lessons (Section 241, Education Act 1993).

Chapter 2

The criminal law and HIV infection

Angus Hamilton

DISCLOSURE OF HIV STATUS AT A POLICE STATION

For solicitors who advise on the telephone or who attend detainees at a police station a question may arise as to whether an HIV-infected detainee should disclose their status to the police.

In some circumstances the decision may be taken away from the detainee – for example, if another person at the scene of the arrest discloses the fact to the arresting officers, or if the arrested person has medication on them from which HIV infection or disease can be inferred.

A detainee may be eager to disclose their status if they need access to medication. On arrival at a police station all medication and indeed most other property will be removed from the detainee. Access to medication will not be permitted without the sanction of a Divisional Surgeon.

It is generally inadvisable for an HIV-antibody-positive detainee to disclose their status to the police. In the first place, general experience has shown that HIV-infected detainees are treated less considerately during the course of their detention. Secondly, adverse inferences relating to the alleged offence for which the person has been arrested may be drawn – for example, if a man has been arrested for an alleged offence of sexual misbehaviour and discloses that he is HIV-infected he may suffer an attitude of 'Oh well, he must be gay and must therefore have committed the offence'. Thirdly, it would appear to be routine police practice for an individual's HIV status to be recorded on the police national computer (PNC).

This practice has been a source of considerable disquiet, since it means that HIV-infected people who have come into contact with the police and whose status has been ascertained – not necessarily with their consent – can be readily identified. When there are regular calls for controls on 'irresponsible people with AIDS', it is clear why the central recording of 'criminals or semi-criminals' who are HIV-infected causes so much concern. In mid-1991 there were press reports (for example, *The Independent*, 15 June 1991) that the police in Cleveland took the recording of detainees' HIV status one step further by displaying photographs of people suspected of being HIV-infected on a police station notice-board.

The practice of recording HIV infection on the PNC was the subject of a complaint in 1992 by, amongst others, The Terrence Higgins Trust, to the Data

Protection Registrar (DPR) – the public official who is responsible for the regulation of storage and use of personal data (information about living individuals) on computer. The basis of the complaint was that the information was excessive and irrelevant and therefore held in breach of the Fourth Data Protection Principle which provides that:

> Personal data held for any purpose or purposes shall be adequate, relevant and not excessive in relation to that purpose or those purposes.

The Registrar, in his eighth annual report, concluded:

> It appears to me that there is a small, but foreseeable, risk of infection with HIV/AIDS which could arise in connection with policing activities. Accordingly, I am satisfied that, in general, the holding of a factual warning signal, including an indication of HIV/AIDS status in the PNC conviction records, is neither excessive nor irrelevant to policing purposes.

In practice an individual's HIV status should have no relevance at all to their arrest or detention. The police should already have in place procedures to reduce the risk of contracting infections during arrest and detention without such procedures being dependent upon ascertaining the detainee's health status. Furthermore, even if such procedures are not implemented the information that an individual is HIV-infected invariably becomes available after a 'risk' situation has passed. For example, if the police are dealing with someone injured and bleeding after a fight or car accident it is very unlikely that personal details sufficient to carry out a PNC check and ascertain health details will be obtained until after the immediate emergency has passed.

For these reasons The Terrence Higgins Trust, amongst others, made further representations to the DPR after the publication of his eighth annual report arguing against permitting the police to record individuals' HIV status on the PNC. These representations were instrumental in achieving a change of view on the part of the Registrar, who in his ninth annual report stated:

> I have reviewed the position which I took last year. The new factor is that there is now a firm policy on procedures, which should be adopted by police forces, to avoid the risk of HIV infection. Once these procedures are in place, whilst I would look at the facts of each particular case, the holding of HIV markers would seem to be irrelevant. Such markers would also possibly be excessive in view of the danger that they may encourage a false sense of security. This might undermine the hygiene procedures and put police officers at risk.

> I have concluded that I should hold to my original view until there has been sufficient time for the necessary training and education activities for police officers to be put in place. . . . I would expect an early development of the required courses and materials.

It is not yet clear when such training will have been satisfactorily established and when the Registrar will, consequently, require the removal of HIV markers from the PNC.

In the situation where a detainee wishes to disclose their HIV status with a view to obtaining access to medication it is recommended that the detainee be advised to request the attendance of the Divisional Surgeon, explain the circumstances to them, insist that they treat the disclosure of HIV status as confidential, and ask them to authorise access to medication. As a matter of practice Divisional Surgeons routinely disclose information about a detainee's health to the police and indeed an officer may be present or nearby when the examination is carried out. However, Divisional Surgeons are not, despite their common title of 'police doctors', employed by the police, but are independent general practitioners, and as such, it is submitted, subject to the same rules of confidentiality as if they were the detainee's own doctor. If a detainee specifically forbids disclosure, therefore, this will serve to remind the doctor of the duty of confidentiality and to emphasise the possible disciplinary consequences if disclosure occurs.

One final note of caution needs to be sounded with respect to advising an HIV-infected detainee at a police station and trying to ensure that their status is not needlessly disclosed. Very few telephone conversations between a detainee and their advising solicitor are confidential and, indeed, many outgoing telephone lines from a police station are routinely taped. Consequently, such matters should not be discussed over the telephone but only during a personal attendance at the police station.

DISCLOSURE OF HIV STATUS DURING CRIMINAL PROCEEDINGS

A defendant's HIV status is a factor that is potentially relevant in all prosecutions. It may be directly relevant to the commission of the alleged crime – for example, inadequate state benefits or financial support have, on more than one occasion, been the impulse for the commission of an offence of dishonesty.

Furthermore, the HIV status of a defendant may provide grounds, particularly in less serious cases, for an approach to the Crown Prosecution Service (CPS) to see if they will deal with the defendant either by withdrawing the charge altogether or by coupling such a withdrawal with a non-conviction option such as a caution or a bind-over. (Binding over is a general power the criminal courts have. To bind over a defendant means, effectively, to require them to give an undertaking to the court to be of good behaviour for a stated period [normally a year]. A sum of money is also specified and if the defendant breaches the bind-over they become liable to forfeit the sum or part of it.)

It is of course fundamental that the defendant consents to and co-operates with such an approach, or indeed any disclosure of their health status (for example, for the purposes of mitigation) which may take place during criminal proceedings. It is advisable for information relating to HIV status to be volunteered by the defendant rather than asked for. If sought, the questions should be qualified with an explanation as to how the disclosure of the information may assist the client and an assurance that the questions need not be answered if that is the client's wish.

As mentioned in the preceding section, HIV infection may unfortunately be established during criminal proceedings without a defendant's co-operation and consent, for example, when a search is conducted at a police station and medication or a medical appointment card is discovered, which indicates that the detainee is infected by HIV. This information is then likely to be recorded on the detainee's Custody Record (the record of a detainee's detention at a police station). In such a case the proper course is to establish with the client whether any further, beneficial use can be made of the information.

Having established HIV infection and the client's informed consent to disclosure, the next consideration is whether disclosure is likely to be of benefit to the client – that is, whether it is likely to lead to the discontinuance of the prosecution and the avoidance of a criminal conviction. Such a resolution is less likely where the offence is serious or indeed where the defendant is, relatively, healthy.

It is also important to take into account the nature of the alleged offence and the possible ignorance of the prosecutor with whom you are dealing. The latter factor is, of course, quite unpredictable. For example, where the allegation is one of sexual misbehaviour, disclosure may have the wholly undesirable result of encouraging rather than discouraging a prosecution on the basis that the defendant's behaviour may have transmitted the virus and put others at serious risk. This is an attitude that has been displayed in cases of alleged sexual misbehaviour even where the activity complained of is not capable of resulting in HIV transmission. An attempt can, of course, be made to counter such attitudes by providing the prosecutor with more realistic information, but this type of prejudice and misinformation is not easy to tackle.

The CPS has certain criteria to consider in establishing whether to charge a potential defendant or to proceed with a prosecution. These are set out in The Code for Crown Prosecutors which is published on behalf of the Director of Public Prosecutions. These criteria place an obligation on the prosecuting authorities to consider, amongst other points, the defendant's health and also whether the pursuit of a prosecution may lead to the worsening of the defendant's state of health. The latter consideration is important given that it is well established that stress can result in a deterioration in the health of a person who has HIV infection or disease.

The criteria explicitly state that more weight should be given to such factors in less serious cases – especially where the defendant's health is likely to lead a court to impose a purely nominal penalty if the prosecution is pursued.

An approach to the prosecuting authorities suggesting that, through reasons of health, a prosecution ought not to be continued, should be in the form of a letter referring the prosecutor to the criteria relied on and any additional points of assistance relating to the particular defendant (age, previous good character, etc.). It should be accompanied by a medical report confirming a diagnosis of HIV infection, describing the defendant's current state of health and treatment and – if the supervising doctor is willing – expressing the likely adverse effect of continuing the prosecution. On the issue of confidentiality, it is important to state in the letter that the information disclosed about the defendant is not to be passed to any other party under any circumstances.

The approach will either be met with a refusal to halt a prosecution, an agreement to do so (possibly coupled with a bind-over) or a request for further information (clarification of the defendant's state of health or, in exceptional cases, a request for an independent medical examination).

If the initial approach is met with a refusal, it is always worth considering a further appeal later in the proceedings, especially if there have been developments in the defendant's state of health which can be attested to in a further medical report. Further approaches will, of course, only be possible if the case is continuing for some time and not, for example, being dealt with by way of a guilty plea at the first hearing.

A DEFENDANT'S HIV STATUS AS A POINT OF MITIGATION

If there seems to be no possibility of the prosecution discontinuing the case, then the material gathered for the purposes of making the relevant representations to the CPS can be used, in the event of a guilty plea or conviction, for the purposes of mitigation.

There is a strong, but encouraging, distinction between the regular experience of practitioners who are presenting details of their client's HIV infection as a point of mitigation and the few Court of Appeal authorities on the relevance of a defendant's HIV diagnosis.

The general experience is that sentencing judges and magistrates are prepared to give considerable weight to the consequences of HIV infection or disease for either the defendant or their partner in terms of the likely impact on their life expectancy and quality of life and, as a result, to reduce substantially the 'usual' penalty. It must be mentioned at this point that although the HIV status of a defendant's partner can be relevant for the purposes of mitigation it does not appear to be a point which the CPS are obliged or ready to take into account in considering whether to drop a case.

There are three leading Court of Appeal authorities which specifically consider the relevance of HIV infection as a point of mitigation.

R. v. Moore [1990] 12 CrAppR(S) 384 was a case in which the appellant pleaded guilty to two counts of burglary and asked for three other offences to be taken into consideration. The burglaries were carefully planned attacks on substantial houses and involved the theft of property worth over £40,000. The appellant had been diagnosed in 1986 as HIV-infected and the lower court apparently found that there was a likelihood that he would develop AIDS within about two years. The Court of Appeal accepted that his treatment would be more difficult in prison, but Lord Lane CJ ruled as follows:

We . . . are asked in this case to mitigate the penalty of five years' imprisonment imposed upon the appellant because this man is HIV infected and it is suggested, but not based upon any medical evidence apart from second hand evidence via the defendant himself, that his life expectancy may thereby be diminished. As I say, we have no medical evidence as to the length of life expectancy.

Nevertheless, assuming that such evidence does exist, we do not consider that it is the function of this court to base its decision upon possible medical considerations of this sort . . .. We do not know what the future may hold with regard to medical science and medical expertise. We do not know what the future may hold with regard to this particular appellant. If the time should come when it is no longer possible, for practical reasons, or for reasons of humanity, to hold this appellant in prison because of his physical condition, then that is the job of the Home Office . . . [it] is not for this court.

A very similar line was taken by the Court of Appeal in *R. v. Stark* [1992] CrimLR at 384. In this case the defendant pleaded guilty to possessing heroin with intent to supply. The defendant had been in possession of 27 grams of heroin with an estimated street value of £2,500. He was sentenced to four years' imprisonment. Before the Court of Appeal it was emphasised that the appellant had been diagnosed as being HIV-infected some time previously and more recently AIDS had developed. His life expectancy was estimated at between twelve months and two years. It was accepted that his condition made life in prison 'particularly hard'. The Court was asked to reduce the sentence to allow the appellant to be released and to die with dignity, but declined to do so, holding that the appellant's record clearly indicated that there was a grave risk that the appellant would continue to traffic in drugs as long as he would be able to do so. As in *Moore*, the court held that it was not their function to manipulate a sentence in such circumstances – it was a matter for the exercise of the Royal Prerogative of mercy.

The third authority also called, rather confusingly, *R. v. Moore* [1993] 15 CrAppR(S) 97, confirmed the approach taken by the Court of Appeal in *Stark* and held that it was not for the Court to 'alter an otherwise proper sentence to achieve a desirable social end'. The latter part of that phrase possibly reflects a more compassionate view of the appellant's circumstances and certainly the Court directed that all the medical reports before them should be forwarded to the prison authorities to effect a consideration as to whether the Royal Prerogative should be exercised in the appellant's favour.

In the latter *Moore* the appellant had pleaded guilty to possessing a class A drug with intent to supply – namely 84 grams of heroin. The appellant had been diagnosed as HIV-antibody-positive but had not received an AIDS diagnosis. He was sentenced to five years' imprisonment which was reduced, on appeal, for reasons other than his health, to three-and-a-half years.

The earlier *Moore* might be excused on the basis of ignorance about the medical issues involved. Certainly Lord Lane emphasised the rather surprising lack of professional medical evidence before the Court. The decisions in *Stark* and the latter *Moore*, however, were reached after the Court heard medical evidence. Given this series of decisions it is difficult to argue that the cases should be confined to their own particular facts although in *Stark* it is clear that the concern of the court was to 'control' a defendant who, despite his illness, was continuing to offend and who had already had one previous prosecution for drugs offences halted on grounds of his illness.

These Court of Appeal authorities do not appear to be being followed by the lower courts and it may be that other more general sentencing guidelines are being applied. There are authorities, for example, that urge leniency where it can be established that an offence was committed in circumstances of severe emotional stress (*R. v. Law Court of Appeal*, 24 April 1975), or where an offence of dishonesty is committed as a result of severe financial difficulties (*R. v. Oakes Court of Appeal*, 4 November 1974; and note this was a case of the defendant's partner's overspending causing the financial difficulties). The courts may also take into account any physical disability or illness which would subject the defendant to an exceptional degree of hardship if sent to prison (*R. v. Herasymenko*, Court of Appeal, 12 December 1975) and the possibility that a defendant may be placed in a segregation unit under Rule 43 of the Prison Rules if imprisoned (*R. v. Holmes* [1979] 1 CrAppR(S) 233, but note the conflicting decision in *R. v. Kirby* [1979] 1 CrAppR(S) 214). This latter point may be of significance to an HIV-infected defendant at risk of imprisonment as such a person is likely to be segregated if their health status is known to the prison authorities.

In very general terms the courts will not take into account the possible adverse effects on immediate family if a defendant receives a custodial sentence (*R. v. Ingham*, Court of Appeal, 3 October 1974). This would appear to cause difficulties with mitigation for a defendant who is the partner or carer of a person with HIV infection or disease. However, leniency is shown where a custodial sentence would clearly cause an unusual measure of hardship, for example, *R. v. Renker* (Court of Appeal, 29 June 1976), where the defendant was the carer of a child with leukaemia or *R. v. Halleth* ([1982] 4 CrAppR(S) 178), where the defendant was the sole surviving parent of a child with kidney disease.

THE TRANSMISSION OF HIV AS A CRIMINAL OFFENCE

In June 1992 there was an outcry in the British press over the alleged behaviour of a young HIV-infected haemophiliac, Roy Cornes. It was suggested, although never verified, that he had, following a diagnosis of HIV infection, deliberately sought to infect a number of women who were unaware of his status, with the virus through consensual, but unprotected, sexual intercourse.

The alleged facts of the case prompted wide consideration of whether there were any criminal charges which could have been brought in such circumstances. The preoccupation of the press with the concept of controlling the 'irresponsible' person with HIV infection meant that other issues, such as the irresponsibility of the press itself in constantly promoting HIV as an infection which was of no risk to heterosexuals and the responsibility of any couple to engage in safer sex practices, were largely ignored.

However, there remains the possibility of criminal charges being brought in similar circumstances in the future and that possibility must, therefore, be considered.

There are a number of late-nineteenth-century authorities on the question whether the knowing or reckless infection of a sexual partner with a venereal disease constitutes rape or indecent assault on the basis that concealment of the defendant's health status constitutes a fraud on their partner and, consequently, the fraud vitiates the partner's consent. Consensual sexual contact would thereby become non-consensual.

In the case of *R. v. Bennett* ([1866], 4 F & F, 1105 followed in *R. v. Sinclair* [1867], 13 Cox, CC 190), the defendant had sex with a girl of 13. He was infected with a venereal disease but did not tell the girl this. She contracted the disease and Bennett was subsequently convicted of indecent assault. Because of her age the girl could not have been regarded as consenting in any event, even if Bennett had not been infected. Despite this, the case appears to have been decided on the basis of Bennett's concealment of his health status from the girl. This was held to constitute a fraud and the fraud to vitiate the girl's consent.

However, in the later case of *R. v. Clarence* ([1886–90] AER Rep at 135) the analysis in Bennett was disapproved. In *Clarence* the defendant was, to his knowledge, suffering from gonorrhoea and had intercourse with his wife without informing her of his condition. As a result she too contracted gonorrhoea. The defendant was, at first instance, convicted of offences under s.47 and s.20 of the Offences Against the Person Act 1861.

The Court of Crown Cases Reserved overturned the convictions and held:

> That consent obtained by fraud is no consent at all is not true as a general proposition either in fact or in law. If a man meets a woman in the street and knowingly gives her bad money in order to procure her consent to intercourse with him, he obtains her consent by fraud, but it would be childish to say that she did not consent.
>
> (per Wills, J. at 135)

The court held that the concept of a fraud vitiating consent could only apply to a fraud as to the nature of the act (for example, pretending that an act of sexual intercourse was a surgical operation (*R. v. Flattery* [1877] 2 QBD 410)), or possibly to a fraud as to the identity of the person involved.

Clarence also considered whether the transmission of an infection could amount to an assault *per se*. The majority held that it could not. An infection was analysed as a kind of poisoning lacking in the 'immediate and necessary connection between a cut or a blow and the wound or harm inflicted' (per Stephen, J. at 143) that an assault requires.

It is submitted, however, that the definition of assault adopted in *Clarence* is rather particular. Assault is more ordinarily defined 'as an act by which a person intentionally or recklessly causes another to apprehend immediate unlawful personal violence or to sustain unlawful personal violence' (see *R. v. Kimber* [1983] 77 CrAppR 225 at 228).

If this definition is considered it is rather more difficult to see why the transmission of an infection cannot amount to an assault *per se*, although a great deal would depend on the interpretation of 'violence'. It is well established that 'violence' includes the application of only slight force.

Certainly in his dissenting judgment in *Clarence*, Hawkins, J. expressed the view that 'wilfully to place his diseased person in contact with hers without her express consent amounts to an assault' [p.148].

There may also be difficulties arising from the particular wording of s.20 of the Offences Against the Person Act 1861. This states that it is an offence to 'unlawfully and maliciously wound or inflict any grievous bodily harm upon any other person, either with or without any weapon or instrument'.

The term 'assault' is not, therefore, used in the provision. Instead the concept of 'infliction of harm' is used. These words also appear in s.23 of the Offences Against the Person Act 1861, which deals, along with s.24, with the administration of poison. The majority in *Clarence* considered the transmission of an infection to be similar to poisoning.

The meaning of 'infliction of harm' was considered in *Clarence* and it was held that the meaning of the word 'inflict' suggested an immediate and necessary connection between the accused's conduct and the harm suffered by the victim (per Stephen, J. at 143) and that, consequently, the transmission of an infection could not constitute an 'infliction' of harm. It is respectfully submitted, however, that the analysis here is seriously at fault. Stephen, J. refers in his judgment in *Clarence* to poisoning not constituting an 'infliction of grievous bodily harm', because, amongst other reasons, the provisions of s.24 of the Offences Against the Person Act 1861 make no mention of the terms. S.24 renders it an offence to administer a poison 'with intent to injure aggrieve or annoy'. However, as previously mentioned, s.23 of the Act, which appears not to have been considered in *Clarence*, but which also deals with poisoning, does explicitly refer to poisoning resulting in the 'infliction of grievous bodily harm'. This tends to suggest that poisoning and therefore, arguably, the transmission of an infection can constitute 'infliction of harm'.

Thus, even if the transmission of a potentially fatal infection cannot be seen as an assault *per se* it is difficult to see how it cannot be construed as an infliction of grievous bodily harm, which would bring the knowing or reckless transmission of HIV within the terms of s.20 of the Offences against the Person Act 1861.

If this analysis is correct then further problems may arise as a result of the Court of Appeal's ruling in *R. v. Brown and Ors* ([1992] 94 CrAppR 302. The decision of the Court of Appeal was upheld in the House of Lords by a 3:2 majority on 11 March 1993 [1993] 2 WLR 556. The case is now the subject of an appeal to the European Court of Human Rights).

This case involved the conviction of a number of men for offences under s.47

and s.20 of the Offences Against the Person Act 1861. The men had engaged in consensual sado-masochistic activities which had resulted in minor injuries to some of the participants.

The Court of Appeal, upholding the ruling of the court below, stated:

> It is not in the public interest that people should try to cause, or should cause, each other actual bodily harm for no good reason . . . What may be 'good reason' it is not necessary for us to say.

It is inconceivable that a court would view the transmission of HIV as ever being in the public interest. It is possible therefore to envisage a situation in which a couple had engaged in sexual intercourse knowing that one of them was infected by HIV, with the result that the uninfected partner contracted the virus too, and as a result criminal liability arose despite the knowledge and consent of both parties.

There was, however, in *Clarence*, a general acknowledgement by the majority of the expediency of their ruling. For, if the transmission of a venereal disease in the circumstances of that case was an offence then why not the transmission of lesser infections through everyday social contacts? In short the Court was anxious not to open the floodgates to a series of speculative criminal prosecutions. The majority also acknowledged the difficulty in the s seeking to enquire into the exact details of the negotiations and courtship that occurs before two people embark upon a sexual encounter – and certainly such enquiries would be necessary if the s sought to intervene in such situations. In short *Clarence* afforded an illustration of 'the futility of trying to teach morals by the application of the criminal law to cases occupying the doubtful ground between immorality and crime' (per Wills, J. at 138). Those words and that analysis are surely just as relevant 130 years on. The current uncertainty of the law may either discourage a prosecution in the circumstances of the Roy Cornes case or may provoke a lengthy test case. (For an alternative analysis of the potential criminal liability arising from the transmission of HIV see *Spreading Disease and the Criminal Law* by Simon Bronitt ([1994] CrimLR 21).)

Transmission by 'violent' act

This may occur, for example, when the victim is stabbed with a syringe or, possibly, bitten. Understandably, the confirmed transmission of the virus is likely to be considered an aggravating factor in determining the sentence to be passed. This will be so even where transmission is threatened by an assailant but does not occur because of the certain distress caused to the victim having to wait at least three months for an HIV-antibody test.

Transmission of HIV by non-violent but unlawful sexual activity

This may occur, for example, during unprotected anal intercourse between two men at least one of whom is under 18. Again the failure to use a condom or otherwise engage in acknowledged safer sex practices is seen as an aggravating factor, even when the virus is not actually transmitted.

PROMOTING SAFER SEX INFORMATION LAWFULLY

A number of agencies, including The Terrence Higgins Trust, have been concerned to promote information about safer sex practices by using sexually explicit text and images. The rationale behind such a strategy is to ensure that the information is clear and does not rely upon ambiguous metaphors and also to make the information as attractive as possible to a target audience.

British law, however, places controls on the use and distribution of sexually explicit material. The principal piece of legislation is the Obscene Publications Act 1959 (amended 1964).

The Obscene Publications Act 1959

Section 2 of the Act makes it an offence to publish an obscene article or to have an obscene article for publication for gain. The latter prohibition may have limited relevance to the distributors of safer sex information as the vast majority of such information is distributed free rather than as a commercial exercise.

An 'article' is defined (s. 1(2)) as anything containing material to be read, looked at or listened to. 'Publishing' includes distributing, circulating, selling, hiring, showing, playing, giving, lending and offering for sale or hire (s. 1(3)).

The test of obscenity is contained in s.1 of the Act. The effect of the article taken as a whole must be to 'tend to deprave and corrupt [a significant proportion of] persons who are likely . . . to read, see or hear the matter contained' in the article.

There have been attempts to define the term 'deprave and corrupt', but such definitions have been largely tautological. In the *Lady Chatterley* case (*R.* v. *Penguin Books Ltd* [1961] CrimLR 176), 'deprave' was defined as 'to make morally bad, to pervert, to debase or corrupt morally'. 'Corrupt' was defined as 'to render morally unsound or rotten, to destroy the moral purity or chastity of, to pervert or ruin a good quality, to debase, to defile'.

These appear to be strong words – the suggestion is that what is being prohibited is something which might destroy the fabric of society. However, prosecution policy has rendered the phrase 'deprave and corrupt' largely devoid of any real meaning. In practice the legislation is applied by having, in effect, a list of forbidden images. Text is, since a number of unsuccessful prosecutions, left largely untouched. The blacklist is not static, however, but constantly changing as publishers seek to push the boundaries of permitted images forward and the prosecuting authorities seek to re-impose what they feel to be the appropriate limits.

For example, it was considered, until relatively recently, that an image of an erect penis was not permissible. The early 1990s, however, have seen an explosion of sexual guidance videos, which contain such images and yet have been certificated by the British Board of Film Classification, and have to date not been the subject of any prosecutions under the Obscene Publications Act.

These constant shifts in what is and is not permissible make it difficult to give certain advice to agencies which are preparing explicit safer sex material. Text is certainly less at risk from prosecution than images. There are also certain concepts within the Act which may be of assistance.

First, it is arguable that careful targeting of a specified audience (for example, only distributing safer sex material for gay men at gay venues) will lessen the risk of prosecution since the Act requires the corruption of persons who are 'likely to', as opposed to 'conceivably might', see the article. Consequently, it might be argued that if the target audience has regularly experienced such imagery then there is no risk of corruption. However, in *DPP* v. *Whyte* ([1972] 3 AER 12 HL), the House of Lords held that the Act was not merely concerned with the once and for all corruption of the wholly innocent, it equally protected the less innocent from further corruption and the addict from feeding or increasing their addiction.

Secondly, in the case of *R.* v. *Calder and Boyars* ([1969] 1 QB 151) (the prosecution of *The Last Exit to Brooklyn*), the of Appeal added the requirement that a 'significant proportion' of the likely readership would tend to be corrupted. This requirement was imposed to protect the publisher from speculation by a jury as to the possible adverse effect of an article on a young person who might just happen to see it. Targeting safer sex information is, again, therefore advisable. The 'significant proportion' test does not, however, require the prosecution to prove that a majority, or substantial number of readers or viewers, would be adversely affected.

Thirdly, the article in question must be viewed as a whole. Any isolated items of an apparently offensive nature must be viewed in their context. This may be of significance if safer sex material uses an explicit sexual image to attract the interest of its intended recipient, but otherwise contains text.

Finally, even if a prosecution is brought under s.1 of the Act there would, with safer sex material, be a chance of a 'public good' defence succeeding under s.4 of the Act. This states that the publication may be justified as being for the public good on the grounds that it is in the 'interest of science, literature, art or learning, or other objects of general concern'. It is possible to call expert evidence on the merits of a publication.

Some of the case law on this section appears to be unhelpful to the application of the 'public good' defence to sexually explicit material. In the case of Attorney-General's Reference (No. 3 of 1977) (following *DPP* v. *Jordan* [1977] 64 CrAppR 33) the of Appeal considered the relevance of calling expert evidence to establish that certain magazines contained material which had merit in the field of sex education or had value in teaching about sexual matters, with a view to founding the 'public good' defence. The ruled that expert evidence was not appropriate in such a case and that the provision of information about sexual matters did not fall within the scope of the 'public good' defence.

However, it is arguable that the ruling was largely expedient and sought principally to control pornography dressed up as sex education material. Safer sex information may still be regarded as possessing scientific interest if it extends an existing body of knowledge or presents known facts in a systematic way. It would certainly be arguable that safer sex information should be within the scope of the 'public good' defence.

The Act contains not only provisions to prosecute obscene material but also to seize it without prosecution (s.3). This power is frequently used because its use effectively places the onus upon the loser of the material to take action for its recovery. However, the power of seizure only applies to material which is kept for publication for gain and freely distributed safer sex information should, consequently, be exempt. Such material may still, unfortunately, be the subject of a speculative seizure.

Other relevant legislation

There are a number of other statutory provisions which may cause difficulties with the distribution and display of safer sex information. It should be noted that with respect to some of these provisions the test adopted is whether the material is 'indecent' rather than 'obscene'. Indecency is accepted to be a lower standard than obscenity and therefore more articles will be prohibited under legislation containing this test. Furthermore, such legislation does not contain provisions parallel to the 'public good' defence and the material would consequently be viewed in isolation rather than in the context of its overall purpose.

The Video Recordings Act 1984

This legislation makes it an offence to distribute a video which has not been certificated by the British Board of Film Classification. Any new video has, therefore, to be submitted to the Board before its release. In the early 1990s, the Board, under the leadership of James Ferman, has taken a liberal attitude to the certification of sex education videos containing explicit sexual imagery. This has extended to *The Gay Men's Guide to Safer Sex*, which was published in association with The Terrence Higgins Trust in 1992, and which received an 18 certificate from the Board.

Certification by the Board does not, however, preclude a prosecution under the Obscene Publications Act since the two pieces of legislation are not linked.

Importation of safer sex material

The Customs and Excise Management Act 1959 prohibits the importation of any obscene *or indecent* articles. One consequence of European Union (EU) legislation has been that Customs are prevented from using the broader indecency test for material imported from other EU countries – the obscenity test contained in the

Obscene Publications Act must still be applied. Again, Customs have the power to seize as well as to prosecute material.

Post Office Act 1953

This makes it an offence to send any indecent or obscene article through the post. Section 11 of the Act defines obscene as 'offending, shocking, lewd or indecent', which is a clearly different test from that contained in the Obscene Publications Act. The legislation does not apply to alternative distribution systems such as 'Red Star'.

Unsolicited Goods and Services Act 1971

It is an offence under s.4 of the Act for a person to send any book, magazine or leaflet which they know or ought reasonably to have known was unsolicited and which describes or illustrates human sexual technique.

Safer sex material should only, therefore, be sent when requested and not unsolicited.

Indecent Displays (Control) Act 1981

It is an offence under this legislation to display, in public, any indecent article. This may cause problems with, for example, a safer sex road show, which is displaying posters containing sexual imagery.

At the time of writing there have not been any prosecutions of safer sex material under any of the aforementioned statutory provisions, although the police and prosecution authorities have shown interest in a number of items including the video, *The Gay Men's Guide to Safer Sex*, and a German safer sex poster showing two men engaged in an act of oral sex.

Public Order Act 1986

Section 5 of the Public Order Act renders it an offence, punishable by fine only, to use threatening, insulting or abusive words or behaviour, or disorderly behaviour, or to display any writing, sign or visible representation which is threatening, insulting or abusive, in the presence of a person likely to be caused harassment, alarm or distress thereby.

The provision was used in 1993 to bring a prosecution against two of the managers of an AIDS information service based in Leamington Spa for displaying, in the window of the service's offices, a Terrence Higgins Trust safer sex poster which displayed a man kissing the inner thigh of another person. The prosecution was brought by the local police but was discontinued by the Crown Prosecution Service.

If the case had gone to trial the defendants would have made use of a defence stemming from s.6(4) of the Public Order Act, which specifies the mental element that the prosecution must establish to prove that an offence under s.5 has been committed. Section 6(4) provides that a person is guilty of a s.5 offence only if they intend their words, behaviour, sign or writing, etc., to be threatening, insulting or abusive or is aware that it may be so.

In *DPP* v. *Clarke* ([1992] CrimLR 60) the Divisional ruled that the 'awareness' limb of s.6(4) was a subjective awareness and that defendants who gave evidence that they lacked the requisite intention or awareness and were believed on such points, should be acquitted. The facts of *Clarke* neatly illustrate the stringency of the subjective awareness rule. The relevant events took place outside an abortion clinic. The respondents, who were opposed to abortions, demonstrated outside the clinic displaying pictures of an aborted foetus. The magistrates found that on an objective analysis the pictures were abusive and insulting, but accepted the respondents' evidence that they personally did not intend and were not aware that the pictures were threatening, abusive or insulting, and acquitted them.

PROMOTING SAFER SEX INFORMATION THROUGH COUNSELLING AND OUTREACH WORK

As with safer sex material there is a similar desire to explain safer sex practices in clear language, which avoids medical jargon. There is also a perceived need to target certain groups, for example men who make use of public lavatories for the purpose of sexual contacts or women engaged in prostitution, who may be most in need of the information.

It is an offence under s.43 of the Telecommunications Act 1984 to send by means of a public telecommunications service a message that is 'grossly offensive or of an indecent, obscene or menacing character'. 'Obscene' is not defined in the Act, but arguably, the definition will be the one contained in the Post Office Act 1953.

Presumably a prosecution under this provision might be possible if it was felt that advice, or counselling, relating to safer sex as given by counsellors to members of the public over the telephone was 'obscene', but it is very difficult, given the one-to-one nature of counselling, to envisage a complaint ever arising to provide grounds for a prosecution.

It is an offence under the Sexual Offences Act 1956 to aid, abet, counsel or procure an act of anal intercourse (buggery), between two men or a man and a woman, or an act of gross indecency (for example, oral sex) between two men. The Sexual Offences Act 1967 now amended only permits such acts between consenting males over the age of 18 in private.

If counselling or outreach work is confined to advising the likely participants in such acts how to perform them more safely it is very difficult to see how such counselling might be viewed as the promotion or encouragement of such behaviour. Again, from a practical point of view it is also difficult to envisage who the complainant to found a prosecution might be.

Understandably, outreach workers who liaise with male and female prostitutes may be involved in the provision of condoms to their clients. Whilst it is extremely difficult to envisage the distribution of condoms as placing the outreach worker at any practical risk of investigation or prosecution for a criminal offence, the carrying of condoms by male or female prostitutes can increase the risk of prosecution for them. This factor should be carefully considered by condom providers and it may be considered appropriate to advise the recipients about the risks.

The carrying of condoms by an individual is, by itself, clearly not sufficient to establish one of the several criminal offences associated with prostitution – for example, soliciting (s.1 of the Street Offences Act 1959 for women and s.32 Sexual Offences Act 1956 for men). However, the carrying of condoms has been used by the police as corroborative evidence to support an allegation before the courts that an individual is operating as a prostitute. Such strategies have been the subject of attacks by, amongst others, the English Collective of Prostitutes, as it discourages the carrying of condoms by prostitutes and consequently encourages the practice of unsafe penetrative sexual intercourse.

As a result of such lobbying the Metropolitan Police Service (London's police) indicated, at the end of 1993, that they would not seek, in the future, to rely on the carrying of condoms by women accused of prostitution as evidence in such cases.

In police prosecutions of brothels, gay saunas and the like the presence and availability of quantities of condoms and even safer sex literature on the premises (safer sex literature was seized by the West Midlands Police in their raid on the Greenhouse gay sauna near Birmingham in January 1994) has been used as evidence to indicate that unlawful sexual acts and/or prostitution are taking or are intended to take place. Again, using the presence of condoms and safer sex material as evidence in this manner is likely to lead to sauna and brothel managers restricting the availability of such items on their premises with the consequent increased risk of the spread of infection.

COUNSELLING INTRAVENOUS DRUG USERS AND ESTABLISHING NEEDLE EXCHANGES

Very similar analyses to those adopted in the preceding section regarding the 'risks' to safer sex counsellors in providing such information and condoms can be applied to the situation of those counselling intravenous drug users and providing clean needles through needle exchanges.

It is very difficult to envisage such counsellors or providers as being at risk from criminal prosecution. Even as a matter of academic argument it is hard to see how a possible charge of aiding and abetting an offence under the Misuse of Drugs Act 1971 of possession of prohibited drugs could be sustained since the connection between the counselling/needle provision and the possession is arguably impossible to establish.

Furthermore hypodermic needles are specifically excluded from the provisions of the Misuse of Drugs Act 1971 which make it an offence to supply drugs paraphernalia (s.9A Misuse of Drugs Act 1971).

It is an offence to incite another to commit an offence under s.19 of the Misuse of Drugs Act 1971, but arguably the provision of a clean needle to an existing drug user cannot be viewed as an additional incitement and, in any event, public policy criteria should operate to prevent a prosecution in such circumstances.

It is also an offence for the managers or occupiers of premises knowingly to permit the supply of drugs at the premises although it is not an offence to permit their intravenous consumption (s.8 MDA 1971). Managers of needle exchanges should, arguably, still have policies prohibiting drug possession, use and supply on their premises.

People attending needle exchanges may be placing themselves at risk of police investigation for drugs offences and those involved in establishing such exchanges may need to take steps to try and ensure security and anonymity.

Chapter 3

HIV and employment

Bernard Richmond

INTRODUCTION

Since the mid-1980s, the workplace has been, and still remains, somewhere where those living with HIV infection and disease have suffered discrimination from employers and, sadly, from fellow employees.

Despite a number of well thought-out information campaigns by trade unions, employers' groups, local authorities and government agencies, fears, some of them rational, some not (for example, the fear of transmission through toilet seats or sharing cups), remain unquelled.

Trade unions were quick to respond to the need for coherent and constructive HIV and AIDS strategies and by the mid-1980s, assisted by information and support provided by the Trades Union Congress, unions such as NALGO, NUPE and the TGWU had all implemented such 'AIDS policies'. Government agencies aimed their attention more at employers, at least at first. The Health and Safety Executive together with the Department of Employment issued a leaflet on AIDS which, to date, has been circulated to over 1.5 million employers; more recently, however, the Department of Employment has turned its attention to employees and has recently published a leaflet entitled 'AIDS and work'. The clear and simple message of this leaflet is that there is no risk of HIV transmission in a normal workplace.

It is also encouraging to note that employers' groups are involved in the campaign to combat fear through education. A good example of this is the leaflet recently published by the Confederation of British Industry which gives its members basic helpful information on AIDS.

The purpose of this chapter is to examine, first, the ways in which employers can promote constructive and supportive employment policies towards those living with HIV infection and disease and, secondly – regrettably of continuing importance – to make a succinct examination of the common issues and problems faced by those living with HIV but working in what is, or what they fear may be, an unsupportive or discriminatory environment.

AVOIDING PROBLEMS: FORMULATING A POSITIVE EMPLOYMENT POLICY

As well as evidencing an employer's commitment to preventing discriminatory or unfair treatment of those with HIV infection and disease, the process of formulating a policy on HIV/AIDS is of use in identifying potential areas of concern or areas of existing strength. A major area of concern is, usually, the attitude of fellow employees towards someone with HIV infection or disease.

Fear, of course, plays a large part in negative attitudes which may be displayed by fellow employees. The employees' response to their fears may vary from mere hostility towards the worker concerned, to more worrying aggression, discrimination or even industrial action. The fear is usually around the risk of being infected and so positive employment policies need to cater for the needs of those employees (by providing them with information, education and training) while also actively protecting those living with HIV infection or disease by making it clear that discrimination, harassment and the like will not be tolerated.

The Department of Employment guidelines provide concise and accurate information dealing with many of the above issues. They advise employers that workers are not normally at risk when carrying out their duties at work; the exception to this general rule is where employees come into contact with blood or other body fluids. The booklet suggests that employers ought to provide information to employees before problems arise. To that end, the Department of Employment encourages employers to photocopy and distribute their leaflet 'AIDS and work', in the hope that the basic message that normal working practices pose no problems will filter through to a large number of employees. An indication of the usefulness of this leaflet is that many employers who have formulated their own AIDS policies have done so with reference to the advice in 'AIDS and work'.

There are many important issues to be tackled by HIV/AIDS policies, including testing, confidentiality and discrimination. More and more employers are taking up the challenge by publicly declaring that they will not discriminate against people living with HIV disease; indeed, the most notable of these public declarations has been brought about with the help of the National AIDS Trust, which co-ordinated the drawing up of a charter entitled 'Companies Act', in which the signatories (who include Body Shop, London Weekend Television, Marks & Spencer, Midland Bank, National Westminster Bank and Sainsbury's) have declared their intention of implementing a supportive and progressive policy towards employees who have HIV infection or disease. Part of this policy is to treat those with HIV disease in the same manner as those with any other progressive or debilitating illness.

It is not just in the private sector that policies exist which give support to those with HIV infection or disease. Manchester City Council's policy provides that there will be no discrimination in recruitment practices and no employee will be under any obligation to submit to an HIV-antibody test. A specific strength of this policy is that the Council has given a great deal of thought to the question of implementation; for example, it has identified the need to appoint people within each department to take responsibility for implementing the policy and for them to allocate resources accordingly. It is even more encouraging to note that more councils seem to be adopting this approach.

POLICIES CONTRASTED WITH THE LAW

While such policies can never replace the law, they enhance it significantly and the increasing willingness of employers to formulate such policies reflects an awareness on their part of an informed response to the crisis of AIDS. Generally, however, these policies do not create any extra legal rights for an employee (unless they become part of a contract, e.g. by specifically including the policy within the terms of contract). It is now time to consider the legal rights of employees living with HIV infection or disease and how those rights may be protected.

HOW DOES EMPLOYMENT LAW OPERATE?

Employment law is based on the law of contract. Many people (even lawyers!) forget that contracts can be oral or written. A contract of employment can be a complicated affair and it is sometimes hard to isolate the contractual terms. As a starting point, the basic premise of a contract of employment is that it is an agreement between the employer and the employee that, in consideration for the employee being available for work and/or for providing such work, the employer will pay the employee an agreed sum of money.

While there is a general rule of 'freedom of contract', i.e. that the employer and employee can agree whatever terms and conditions of employment they wish, this freedom is restricted by a number of legal rules, some common law, some statutory, all aimed at ensuring that the employee is protected in a relationship where there is often inequality of bargaining power between employer and employee.

SOURCES OF EMPLOYMENT LAW

Employment law has a number of sources. It is, first and foremost, a creature of the common law and some areas (e.g. wrongful dismissal) still have little statutory regulation; however, much of employment law today is subject to (and in some cases born out of) statute. The major legislation in this area is as follows:

Employment Protection (Consolidation) Act 1978 (EPCA)
Equal Pay Act 1970
Sex Discrimination Act 1975
Race Relations Act 1976

European Community law

The topic of sources should not be concluded without some mention of EC law;

this is a vast area of study and it is impossible in this chapter to give it any degree of full consideration. However, much of the law, including case law, arises out of EC law, particularly in the areas of sex discrimination and equal pay. Where relevant, EC law and rights arising out of it are considered in the appropriate sections of the rest of this chapter.

Scottish and Northern Irish employment law

Employment law is also one of the areas where the law in England and Wales is similar to that of Scotland and Northern Ireland, so much so that decisions of the Industrial Tribunals and Employment Appeals Tribunals of those countries are often cited as persuasive authorities in all parts of the country.

WHO IS AN EMPLOYEE?

Employment rights, by and large, are only available to people who are employees and so it is important to be clear as to the basis upon which a person is employed. Some employers will try to use labels which suggest that someone is not an employee but, rather, an 'independent contractor' or someone who is self-employed. A self-employed person will not have any right to sick pay from an employer and many of the statutory rights available to employees (e.g. unfair dismissal) do not apply to them (although others, such as sex or race discrimination, still do). The tribunals and courts will assess each case to see whether the true relationship between the parties was that of employer/employee (a 'contract of service'), or whether the person working for the employer was, in truth, an independent contractor (working under a 'contract for services'). The labels which the parties ascribe to their relationship is only one of the factors considered. Also, it is possible to be employed by a 'non-person' such as a company or a local authority. Anyone who is told that they are being employed on the basis that they will work for the employer (and, possibly, only for that employer), but will be 'self-employed', should consider their position carefully and seek advice, if necessary.

TERMS AND CONDITIONS OF THE EMPLOYMENT CONTRACT

Every employee who has been employed for thirteen weeks is entitled to a written statement of the terms and conditions of employment. This written statement must provide particulars of the terms relating to the following matters: remuneration; holiday and holiday pay entitlement; sick pay; notice entitlement; pension provisions; disciplinary and grievance rules; and job title. An employee who does not receive a written statement of particulars on request may apply to an Industrial Tribunal for relief.

Classification of terms

Many terms of a contract are 'express terms'. This means that they are clearly defined somewhere within the contract. All the terms mentioned above will be express contractual terms. There are, however, unwritten (or 'non-express') terms of a contract, which will be implied into the contract for one of a number of reasons. These terms will be implied either by means of a statute or by the courts. The courts will imply terms into a contract, generally, for the following reasons:

1 to recognise custom and practice;
2 to give the contract 'business efficacy';
3 because the term is so obvious that it should be implied (obvious meaning 'obvious to any reasonable person').

Almost any term can be implied, but there are a number of terms which are regularly inferred into employment contracts. Of importance to those living with HIV infection or disease is the term of mutual trust and confidence. It is an implied term of most employment contracts and is important because, if there has been a breakdown in trust and confidence between the employer and employee, the employment contract may be considered to be at an end and the party who is not at fault entitled to damages. It is interesting to note that it has been held that this duty includes the obligation of an employer to provide support to the employee (and vice versa). An employer who is actively homophobic may well fail to provide the required degree of support to the employee.

It is also possible for terms to become incorporated into the contract, if that is the intention of the parties. An employment policy on HIV/AIDS could become part of a contract of employment in this way.

TERMINATING THE CONTRACT OF EMPLOYMENT

Essentially, there are two types of contract: those which end by notice and those fixed to expire at a certain date (fixed-term contracts). In the absence of an express term, the courts will imply that an employer will give reasonable notice to terminate the contract and the law provides minimum notice periods linked to length of employment (essentially, one week for every year of continuous employment up to a maximum of twelve weeks for twelve or more years).

No employee can be forced to work for an employer against his or her will, although in certain limited circumstances, it may be possible for an employer to prevent a (former) employee working for anyone else if there is an enforceable 'restraint' clause in the contract.

REMEDIES FOR THE EMPLOYEE IN CASES OF UNLAWFUL TERMINATION OF CONTRACT

Basically, for an employee whose contract is terminated in potentially unlawful circumstances, the two possible remedies are a claim for wrongful dismissal and a claim for unfair dismissal.

Wrongful dismissal

Wrongful dismissal (never to be confused with unfair dismissal) is compensation for the loss of contractual rights and is a common law remedy. The claim is usually a limited one in that at common law, however unfair it may be, an employer may terminate a contract on the giving of the appropriate amount of notice. If an employer fails to give adequate notice (or payment in lieu of notice), a claim for damages may be made; other items which may be recoverable by way of a claim for wrongful dismissal include holiday pay, lost contractual benefits during the notice period and loss of pension rights. There is no recovery, however, for distress or hurt feelings. An employer will also be entitled to dismiss, without notice, in cases of gross misconduct (see further under 'Unfair dismissal' below). Claims are brought in the County Court or (sometimes) the High Court, depending on the amount of claim. Normally, the claim will be for little more than the number of weeks' notice to which an employee was entitled but which he or she did not receive. Claims for wrongful dismissal must be brought within six years of the date of dismissal and wrongful dismissal claims will be considered first, if there are concurrent claims for wrongful dismissal and unfair dismissal in the Industrial Tribunal (as the Industrial Tribunal will stay any action for unfair dismissal until the resolution of the wrongful dismissal claim). In those circumstances, it is advisable to start an unfair dismissal claim first (doubly so as the time limit for applying for unfair dismissal is three months). Damages for wrongful dismissal are meant to put you in the position you would have been in had the contract not been broken, and therefore damages will normally amount to the loss of wages (net) for the period concerned.

Unfair dismissal

Unfair dismissal is a creation of statute and currently embodied in the EPCA 1978. An employee who fulfils the 'qualifying conditions' has a right not to be unfairly dismissed. A person is unfairly dismissed if dismissed for an unfair reason and/or in an unfair way. In any potential claim for unfair dismissal, therefore, the following four questions will be important.

1   Has the employee satisfied the 'qualifying conditions'?
2   Has there been a 'dismissal'?
3   Was the dismissal for a fair reason?
4   Was the manner in which the employee was dismissed fair (considering the circumstances and the procedures adopted)?

Each of these questions must now be considered in more detail.

1 Has the employee satisfied the 'qualifying conditions'?

Employees can only claim unfair dismissal if they have been continuously employed for two years by the same or an associated employer. It is not enough that they have been so employed, however, as it is also a condition that the employee must have worked a minimum of sixteen hours per week for that employer (unless they have been continuously employed for five years, in which case employment for a minimum of eight hours per week will suffice).

Great care must be taken to ensure that the employment is 'continuous'. In *Pearson* v. *Kent County Council* [1992] IRLR 110, the employee lost continuity when she retired from her job on medical grounds, had a week's break and then recommenced with the same employer in a lighter job. It was held that the week's absence broke the continuity of employment because it was not a week in which she was incapable of work.

The other qualifying conditions are generally less troublesome and will not be considered in detail here. Essentially, the employee must be an employee (and not self-employed) in the United Kingdom and must bring a claim within three months of the date of dismissal (N.B. *not* the date of suspension if there are internal hearings). The date of dismissal will usually be taken as the date when an employee finally exhausts any internal appeal procedures, if such exist.

2 Has there been a dismissal?

The EPCA recognises three types of dismissal. The first type is where the employer terminates the contract. The second is where a fixed-term contact reaches the end of its term, and the third is where an employee is 'constructively dismissed'.

Constructive dismissal is where the employee resigns because the employer's intolerable behaviour is such that it amounts to a breach of contract and gives a clear indication that the employee does not consider himself or herself any longer bound by the terms of the contract (usually of mutual trust and confidence and support). There are many examples of the sort of behaviour which can justify an employee resigning and claiming constructive dismissal. This is an important right because some employers, when faced with an employee they know or suspect to be HIV-antibody positive, will try to make life so difficult that the employee leaves.

Examples of behaviour which has amounted to constructive dismissal (1–3) or may well amount to such (4–6) include:

1   a reduction in status; particularly if the employee is singled out or there is no good reason;
2   the removal of an employee from his or her office into inferior accommodation;
3   being unsupportive, particularly when an employee is in a position of responsibility and should be able to expect support from an employer; similarly, where an employer embarrasses or deliberately undermines an employee in front of fellow employees (particularly if the embarrassed employee has supervisory or managerial responsibility for those employees);

4   it may well be that (of relevance to this text) an unwarranted or over-forceful request to take an HIV-antibody test may be sufficient (see below);
5   breaching an employee's confidentiality, e.g. by 'outing' him or her or disclosing his or her HIV-antibody status (the law on confidentiality is discussed elsewhere in this book – see pages 118–20);
6   being unsupportive to employees with HIV infection or disease.

In the hearing of a claim for unfair dismissal, the burden of proving that there has been a dismissal is on the employee (often this will be admitted by the employer, but probably not so in the case of constructive dismissal).

The HIV-antibody test in an employment law context

An employer cannot generally require an employee to take an HIV-antibody test and to do so may destroy the 'mutual trust and confidence' which must exist in all employer–employee relationships: a duty to maintain this relationship is implied in every contract of employment. Further, since there is an implied duty to maintain trust and confidence, an unwarranted request from an employer to an employee to take an HIV-antibody test may well destroy the trust and confidence essential to a tolerable working relationship, unless of course the employee is unfit for work.

Indeed, it has been held by the Court of Appeal in *Bliss* v. *South East Thames Regional Health Authority* [1985] that a request that an employee take a medical test (unless someone was absent through illness) would be sufficient to justify the employee resigning and claiming constructive dismissal. The Court said:

> It will be difficult, in this particular area of employment law, to think of anything more calculated or likely to destroy the relationship of confidence and trust which ought to exist between employer and employee than, WITHOUT REASONABLE CAUSE, to require a consultant surgeon to undergo a medical . . . and to suspend him from the hospital in his refusing to do so.

Of course, if there is a contractual term requiring an employee to submit to a medical examination when required, the position is different and not to attend would be a breach of contract, unless the term was being used oppressively. Few contracts will have such a clause, however; this term is only usually found in employment situations where employees must be at peak fitness (e. g. airline pilots), although an HIV-antibody test does nothing to indicate the current level of physical health of the employee or whether that level of health is liable to change in the future.

As a general rule, employees can and should refuse to take HIV-antibody tests, although they should seek advice from experienced advisers before making a final decision.

Should the employee agree to a test, it must be remembered that this is not a routine matter and it should not be administered by an occupational physician or without structured pre-test counselling. The test must be administered under the supervision of a doctor who should ensure that the person being tested fully understands the nature and possible ramifications of the test before proceeding on the basis of any consent given. If the doctor provided by the employer does not correspond to these high standards, an employee would probably be within his or her rights to ask to be tested by a suitably qualified doctor. Moreover, it is worth pointing out that an occupational doctor may well pass on the results of an HIV test to the employer.

Where the employee is a member or prospective member of an employee insurance scheme, testing may be required by the insurance company as part of the scheme. As the results of this test may be disclosed to employers, with the resulting problems that this may cause, it may be that some people will choose to exercise their right to refuse such a test, although this will probably mean that they forfeit the right to group insurance. A fuller consideration of the many problems involved in the area of insurance can be found elsewhere in this book.

3 Was the employee dismissed for a fair reason?

The EPCA makes it clear that the following are to be regarded as fair reasons:

1   capability;
2   conduct;
3   redundancy;
4   contravention of a regulation or law;
5   some other substantial reason.

These are only potentially fair reasons for dismissal, and it is for the employer to prove on a 'balance of probabilities' (i. e. that it is more likely than not) that the dismissal was genuinely for one of the above reasons and that the reason given by the employer for dismissal was actually believed by him at the time that he dismissed the employee. There cannot be justification after the event. An employer is obliged to provide a dismissed employee with written reasons for dismissal and it is always a sensible tactic to ask your (former) employer to give written reasons – if he or she refuses, you can seek redress in the Industrial Tribunal.

One of the most important mistakes made by employers is to think of AIDS as a disease in itself rather than the clinical definition it really is. No two people are affected in precisely the same way and many of the opportunistic diseases and infections can be controlled or treated. It would therefore be wrong and potentially unfair to dismiss someone because of a medical classification when he or she is perfectly fit for and able to work.

The test is always whether there exists one or more of the 'fair reasons' for dismissal; clearly, there may come a time when the employee's condition is such that he or she is incapable of work and it would be unreasonable to expect the employer to continue the employment.

It is, however, important to be clear since there are, unfortunately, many examples of cases where employers wish to dismiss an employee as a result of fear, prejudice, homophobia, etc., but are using other spurious reasons to justify the dismissal. Advisers must always be aware of this possibility.

Absence from work through illness as a fair reason for dismissal

It may be possible fairly to dismiss people because they have symptomatic HIV infection and are absent from work for an unacceptable period of time. What exactly constitutes an unacceptable period of time will depend on the circumstances of the case – in particular, the effect which the absence(s) has (have) on the employer's business. For this reason, it is not possible to stipulate an 'average' period of absence which will render a dismissal fair. The vital question which the Industrial Tribunal will ask is 'how long can the employer reasonably be expected to wait for the employee to return?' It should also be noted, however, that an employer may well be able to dismiss fairly where there have been shorter intermittent periods of absence: it is not always required that an employer should wait for one lengthy period of continuous absence.

In many cases, however, there will have been an absence which the employer is seeking to treat as 'long term'. The Industrial Tribunal will consider many things when deciding if the absence is a sufficiently 'long-term' absence to justify a dismissal. The expected length of absence will be significant as will the size and needs of the employer's business and whether a replacement will have to be employed to cover the work of the absent employee. Some factors may well weigh in favour of the employee; for example, the fact of being in receipt of Sickness Allowance will create an assumption that the contract exists for at least as long as the Sickness Allowance continues to be paid.

Note, however, the need for medical advice; if an employer makes assumptions about HIV-antibody status or its effects on a particular employee, the employer may well be held to have behaved unreasonably. If medical reports are obtained, however, the employer is permitted to rely on them and is not expected to assess the quality of the report or make decisions as to which parts to accept and which to reject.

Employment law does go some way to protect the interests of the sick employee and employers will be expected to have considered also the possibility of offering the employee alternative work, if such work is available. Further, an employer must discuss an employee's medical position and any prolonged absence with the employee before making a decision about dismissal; a failure to do this will render unfair any dismissal on the grounds of ill health (see *Wright* v. *Eclipse Blinds Ltd* [1990]).

It should be noted, however, that the conduct of the employee in medical cases is of great importance. If a request is made of an employee to consent to the release by his or her GP or hospital of medical information and this request is refused, while this will not justify dismissal in itself, it may well lay the foundation for a fair dismissal based on an assumption by the employer about the employee's capacity. Such an assumption is reasonable because the employer tried to obtain up-to-date medical information and was thwarted by the attitude of the employee. Employees who are worried about the release of medical information should seek urgent advice before so doing; employment lawyers at The Terrence Higgins Trust (as with any HIV/AIDS legal advisory service) have regular experience of this problem and can provide helpful advice.

It is also important that employees with HIV infection or disease do not give their employer the opportunity of dismissing them for a reason other than the real reason that they are away ill (and the employer does not like it!). In particular, reasons for even short periods of absence should be provided, although they should be general and not make any reference to the employee's HIV-antibody status.

Frustration as a fair reason

Sometimes employers try to argue that a contract has become frustrated, i.e. that the situation is such that the terms of the contract cannot possibly be fulfilled and that, therefore, the parties should be released from their obligations under the contract. This topic is not dealt with in detail in this chapter, but it should be noted that, in the view of the author, an employee would have to be away for a significant time, or be very ill indeed, before frustration would be considered, and the Industrial Tribunal and the courts are wary of allowing this as a fair reason for dismissal.

Capability

This is often a reason for dismissal and will be difficult to deal with, particularly if ill-health does, in reality, seriously affect the employee's ability to do the job. That aside, there are many examples of employers inventing spurious reasons for dismissal based on capability and it should not be forgotten that the burden of proving that the reason is a fair one rests fairly and squarely on the shoulders of the employer.

Conduct

Many of the unfair dismissals dealt with by legal advisers in this field concern dismissals where there has been an allegation of gross misconduct justifying dismissal. If proved, gross misconduct constitutes a valid reason for an employer to dismiss an employee summarily (i.e. without notice). These reasons have to be very serious and, consequently, the allegation against the employee is usually not HIV related and, more often than not, concerns dishonesty.

In these cases, the Tribunal will be concerned to ensure that the reason given was indeed the real reason for dismissal and that the employer has proved his good faith by investigating the allegation fairly and fully. In *Buck* v. *Letchworth Palace* [1987] a male employee was dismissed after being convicted by a court of having sex with another man in public. His fellow employees at the cinema where he worked heard that he had cut his hand at work and feared that, because of his homosexual lifestyle, he would infect them with HIV. One fellow employee was so concerned that he proceeded to disinfect the door handles. The Tribunal considered that the employer had overreacted to the situation and should have consulted the employee before dismissing him although they held that, as the employer would still have dismissed the employee, the dismissal was fair. Mr Buck appealed to the Employment Appeals Tribunal (on a point of law) but, before the case reached it, the employer conceded that, had proper consultation taken place, the dismissal would have been avoided; the case was then settled out of court.

Redundancy

Employers will often select an employee who is HIV-antibody positive for redundancy. It should always be remembered that an employer must select employees for redundancy fairly and an employee who has been made redundant when, in fact, he or she is not really redundant (redundancy being, essentially, where the employer is no longer doing the type of work that the employee was employed for, either generally or at the employee's place of work, or there is a reduced demand for that type of work) should claim unfair dismissal. Further, an employee can complain to an Industrial Tribunal if he or she has been unfairly selected for redundancy. It should also be noted that employers are under a general duty to consider the possibility of alternative employment before dismissal and to offer such work if it is available. Consultation with the workforce is also generally desirable before the final decision about redundancies is made.

Some other substantial reason

This is the remaining 'catch-all' category where employers who can prove that there was some other reason not falling in the above categories which is of substance will be held to have a fair reason for dismissal.

In the HIV/AIDS field, there have been a number of attempts to argue that the reaction of other employees, in particular the refusal by them to work with someone who has HIV infection, is a substantial reason justifying dismissal.

The general view of the Industrial Tribunal is that this is not a substantial or acceptable reason. The example of *Buck* v. *Letchworth Palace* has already been given. A further example is to be found in *Cormack* v. *TNT Sealion Ltd.* In this case, the employee was chef on board a ship and was transferred and then selected for redundancy after staff complained that he was an 'AIDS carrier'. In criticising the employer for accepting the complaints about AIDS without investigation, the Tribunal said: 'This is a problem which is likely to arise with increasing frequency and a good employer who is fair to his employees must be seen to act promptly to lay at rest all unfounded suspicions.'

Employers who are concerned about the attitude of fellow employees should heed the concise and sensible advice provided by the Department of Employment: 'There is a particular need to put to rest groundless fears by providing the facts about AIDS and to prevent discrimination against individuals. In most jobs there is little or no risk of becoming infected.'

A sensitive employer will approach the question of staff attitudes from a different angle, choosing to provide information and, if necessary, a chance to discuss these concerns with union officials or a health and safety representative; technically, employees could be dismissed for refusing to work alongside the employee with HIV infection or disease; this is, of course, undesirable as it will only serve to fuel resentment against the infected employee. In extreme cases, however, the only option may be to move the discriminator or give him or her a formal warning.

An employer should not be swayed by threatened walk-outs or strikes if he or she does not dismiss an employee with HIV infection. Section 63 of the EPCA 1978 provides that an employer cannot rely on a threatened strike or other industrial action as a fair reason for dismissal.

4 Has the employer behaved reasonably in dismissing the employee, even if there is a potentially fair reason for dismissal?

It is not enough for an employer to have a fair reason; the employer must behave reasonably in all the circumstances (s.57(3) EPCA). Failure to consult with the employee, to have a proper pre-dismissal investigation or to follow laid-down disciplinary procedures are all matters which could lead an Industrial Tribunal to decide that there has been an unfair dismissal. The employer has the burden of proving that he behaved reasonably; the Tribunal will bear in mind the size and administrative resources of the employer and anything laid down about procedures in the contract of employment. In HIV/AIDS-related dismissals, employers often behave unreasonably and it is well worth attacking a dismissal on this ground. About 95 per cent of all Industrial Tribunal cases hinge, at some point, on the reasonableness or otherwise of the dismissal.

An employer cannot argue that the result would have been the same whether or not consultation had taken place; this was decided by the House of Lords in *Polkey* v. *Dayton* [1987]. Consultation is, therefore, an important factor.

The importance of a proper and balanced investigation was stressed in *Bell* v. *Devon and Cornwall Police Authority*, in which a chef was dismissed from his job in a police canteen. The employers relied on statements by some staff that they would not eat food prepared by a homosexual. A major feature of the Industrial Tribunal's decision that the employer had unfairly dismissed Mr Bell was a criticism of the employer for relying on these complaints without further investigation, particularly without taking the views of other staff into consideration.

Remedies for unfair dismissal

In most cases, the remedy required will be monetary compensation, which is calculated on the basis of an award to compensate the employee for earnings or benefits, etc., lost as a result of the unfair dismissal and reasonable future loss that will be suffered. In addition, compensation may be payable to reflect the level of unfair treatment suffered by the employee. Most advisers have a checklist which they go through to assess the value of the award to an employee and it is well worth contacting an adviser for this purpose, even if one has not been contacted for other purposes.

It is also possible to ask for reinstatement or re-engagement, although most employees do not wish to return to the sort of working environment which has led them to the Industrial Tribunal.

There now follows a consideration of other specific topics within employment law of relevance to those living and working with HIV infection and disease.

DISCRIMINATION: THE LAW

People living with HIV infection and disease sometimes suffer terrible discrimination in this country because of their condition. This is never more true than in the workplace where people have been sacked or treated unacceptably because of their HIV-antibody status. It is regrettable that in this country the law recognises only sex and race discrimination. It is not specifically illegal to discriminate against someone on the basis of sexuality or HIV-antibody status. It may be possible, however, in certain circumstances, to use the current anti-discrimination law in an HIV-related situation.

In short, discrimination can be direct, i.e. treating a person differently because of their sex or race, or indirect which is more subtle; this is where the employer imposes a condition equally to men and women, for example, but the proportion of one sex who can comply is smaller than the proportion of the other sex who can. Indirect race discrimination operates along the same lines. The employer bears the burden of disproving race or sex discrimination.

In an HIV setting, it may be possible to apply these rules to allege sex or race discrimination; for example, a condition that all job applicants for a particular post must have tested HIV-antibody negative seems to have no sex bias in it, but, as there are currently more men in the UK with HIV/AIDS, this is indirect sex discrimination against men.

An employee who has suffered sex or race discrimination can make a claim to an Industrial Tribunal but must do so within three months of the act(s) complained of. The Equal Opportunities Commission (EOC) can also take action within six months of the discriminatory act and enforce changes in the general practice of employers.

An example of this occurred in 1987, when the (now defunct) airline Dan Air was investigated by the EOC because of its recruitment practice of employing only women for cabin crew posts. Although this was clearly direct discrimination, the airline sought to rely on a defence under the Health and Safety Act 1974. It said that, as over 30 per cent of men applying for the jobs in question were gay and as AIDS mainly affected homosexuals, there was a risk of infection if male staff had an accident aboard the plane, and therefore it was preferable and acceptable to employ women.

The EOC obtained evidence from two senior doctors, which suggested in clear terms that there was no risk to passengers. The EOC used its power to issue a notice declaring that Dan Air's practices were unlawful and requiring the company to change its recruitment practices and to produce evidence every year, for five years, to show that it had done this. Unfortunately, the airline did not survive long enough for any assessment to be made as to how successful this intervention proved, although certainly by 1988 there were male cabin crew working for Dan Air.

BENEFITS AND THE SICK EMPLOYEE

A detailed consideration of the various welfare benefits available to those living with HIV/AIDS is to be found elsewhere in this book, and also in the book on this subject written for The Terrence Higgins Trust and edited by Colin Nee. It may be a term of an employee's contract that he or she will receive sickness allowance when ill. The right may be implied or expressed, and the allowance is deemed to be available for a reasonable period or for the period agreed by the employer. It is not uncommon for large employers to give long-term sick employees their full pay for six months and half-pay for a further six months.

Statutory Sick Pay (SSP)

SSP is payable by the employer, not by the Department of Social Security, and is the minimum payment that an employer is obliged to pay an employee who is absent owing to sickness. An employee must notify the employer of his or her illness in order to qualify. For the first seven days' illness, the employee can certificate his or her own sickness; thereafter, a medical certificate is required. In cases of incapacity owing to HIV disease, it is undesirable for the medical certificate to refer to the illness as AIDS – another good reason for having a sensitive and helpful general practitioner – and it is usually acceptable and, in truth, accurate for the specific illness to be described in general terms (e.g. 'pneumonia' or better still 'chest infection' in a case of PCP [pneumocystis carinii pneumonia]). SSP is payable for 28 weeks, although it is not payable for the first three days off work. Where a number of separate periods off work have been taken, the 'waiting period' may be longer than three days. SSP is taxable and payable at three different rates depending on the level of the employee's usual wages. SSP rates are reviewed annually and employers can deduct SSP from National Insurance contributions otherwise payable to the state.

Permanent Health Insurance

This is an insurance scheme arranged between the employer and an insurance company, which provides that a payment shall be made in the event of an employee being incapable of work. It is an insurance which is particularly common among the self-employed, and the higher wage earner who can afford to pay the often high premiums. There are frequently specific rules relating to the entitlement to sums from the fund, e.g. that entitlements to Sickness Allowance and SSP must have been exhausted and that the person is incapable of work, although not necessarily permanently incapacitated. The company does have the power to require the employee to see the company doctor who will form a view as to ability to work which is independent of (and sometimes in conflict with) the employer's view of fitness to work. Advice should always be sought from an experienced insurance broker in these cases.

Retirement

Of course, any employee may retire from work, although this may not be a viable or attractive proposition in a case where the employee has not contributed to a pension scheme to which they can have early access. Each scheme will have its own rules, and close reference should be made to the policy book usually given to all participants in the scheme; again, advice should be sought from an experienced and sensitive pensions expert. The matters to be taken into account vary from case to case and advice about when and if to retire on the grounds of ill-health will vary accordingly; consequently, no attempt to summarise the rules relating to pension schemes is made here.

HEALTH AND SAFETY AT WORK

An employer must provide a safe working environment for employees. The basic duty is contained in Section 2(1) of the Health and Safety at Work Act 1974, which states that: 'It shall be the duty of every employer to ensure, so far as it is reasonably practicable, the health, safety and welfare of all [his employees].'

The Health and Safety Executive has published a useful booklet on AIDS and the workplace, which stresses the important point that 'normal social and work contact with an infected person is safe for both colleagues and the public' and reiterates that there has been no transmission of HIV in the workplace other than the rare instances where, for example, a health care worker has injected himself or herself with HIV. The Health and Safety Executive cites examples of occupations where there are risks which are largely medical in nature. They also make the reassuring and sensible point that established practices of hygiene and safety (e.g. re-sheathing needles after use) will preclude risks of exposure when dealing with infected body fluids. They also advise the use of plastic disposable gloves and bleach to deal with spillages.

An employer who is in charge of a working environment where HIV-infected materials, particularly blood, are or may be dealt with has a duty to ensure that employees are as safe as 'reasonably practicable'. This means that employers must do everything reasonably possible to ensure that employees are protected; in the

HIV/AIDS field this means that an employer must provide proper and adequate training in safety procedures, including the handling and disposal of waste, and that employees must be fully aware of the risks involved in the work they do. The new health and safety rules which have recently been published firm up the requirements on employers to introduce clearly established health and safety policies. Consequently, employers who fall below this high standard of provision may find themselves in real difficulty when defending a legal action.

The provision of adequate information about the reality of supposed risks is essential in the fight against the prejudice shown towards those living with HIV infection or disease, and employers are well advised to have regular information campaigns in the workplace.

If an employee is infected with HIV, allegedly in the course of their work, liability would be determined by examining whether the employer had breached a duty of care by insufficient warning, training or safe practices. The onus would be on the employee to show that it was more likely than not that infection took place at work and, further, the employee would have to prove that he or she did not agree to accept a risk of infection in working in his or her chosen occupation.

CONCLUSIONS

AIDS in the workplace is a serious problem, both socially and economically. In this country we have not yet reached the high levels of employee absenteeism experienced by employers in North American cities or in Central Africa. In this country, however, the social problems, particularly fear and prejudice, abound and strenuous efforts are still required to deal with them.

These levels of discrimination and prejudice in the workplace do not diminish as time goes by, and regular training and information remain as vital now as they ever were.

It is a lamentable fact that there is still no legislation which specifically affords protection to those experiencing discrimination because of HIV-antibody-positive status. Even if there were such protection, many would not avail themselves of their rights because of the publicity which a public hearing in an Industrial Tribunal might attract. This problem was considered by the parliamentary Social Services Standing Committee in 1986–7. It recommended that Industrial Tribunal hearings, where the applicant's HIV-antibody status was relevant, should be held in private and that different qualifying rules (e.g. shorter time limits) should apply.

In 1987, the then Liberal Chief Whip, David Alton MP, asked The Terrence Higgins Trust to make suggestions about legislation which would help in the area of AIDS. The Trust drafted a Bill to amend the EPCA 1978 so that, save where an employee is incapable of performing his job or where it would put the employer in breach of other enactments, it would automatically be an unfair reason for dismissal if someone were dismissed as a result of HIV-antibody-positive status. Unfortunately, the government's attitude was that this was an unnecessary provision and

David Alton did not proceed with the Bill. It is submitted that this Bill still represents the best way forward for people working and living with AIDS.

In 1989, Gavin Strang MP tabled an unadopted amendment to the 1989 Employment Bill. The British Medical Association and The Terrence Higgins Trust gave support to a draft which provided anti-discrimination protection for people with HIV infection or disease, outlawing discrimination in recruitment and employment as well as dismissal. (See Appendix 3.)

Any future proposals will only be successful if they enjoy the widest possible support, both politically and between employers' groups and trade unions. The present government seems unwilling to put forward any legislation and so the only hope seems to be a Private Member's Bill. It is to be earnestly hoped that sooner rather than later compassion and common decency will overtake political and economic interests and that this small but vital change in the law will occur.

Chapter 4

Housing law and people with HIV infection

Ginny O'Brien, Jane Carrier and David Ward
(revised and updated by Jackie Bates and the late Lauren Jackson, Housing Officers at The Terrence Higgins Trust)

INTRODUCTION

The following chapter looks at some of the main housing problems that people with HIV infection have encountered. Although the background information is given where appropriate, it does not attempt to provide a manual of housing law. It is rather a discussion of the ways in which advice workers may apply the knowledge they possess to the specific problems of people with HIV infection: we therefore hope that the chapter will be read in full rather than simply used as a reference text.

We begin by highlighting some of the information about local housing provision that advisers will need to have before the client comes to seek help. This preparatory work is important: mistakes can be difficult to rectify and potentially very stressful.

The chapter considers the major forms of tenures in the public and private sector and of owner-occupation. These sections are not wholly self-contained. Problems are considered in the text as they may be most commonly presented to advice workers.

By far the largest section considers the problems of applying to a local authority as homeless and in priority need. Not only has our experience been that these problems have led to the greatest number of enquiries, but it is also, perhaps, the area where there is more case law relating specifically to vulnerability and intentional homelessness.

Throughout the chapter the important role that advice agencies can play in influencing both housing policy and practice for people with HIV infection is emphasised.

INFORMATION

When advisers are working with a client with HIV infection who has poor housing, time is of the essence. There is a link between poor quality housing, stress, and the progression of the disease. It is therefore important to be aware of all relevant housing procedures and options to ensure that the swiftest route to housing is open to your client.

Clients themselves must always play a central role in the resolution of their housing difficulties. Advisers should therefore ensure that clients are always fully aware of all the available options, so they are in a position to reach a well-informed decision about their housing. Similarly, visits to the local authority housing department or to the building society are likely to be less daunting if the adviser takes the time to discuss with the client what is likely to happen to them.

Local housing resources to be considered include the following:

1 Emergency accommodation

Although most local authorities accept that they have a duty to house homeless people who have symptomatic HIV disease under the Housing Act 1985 Part III, there are some who do not take responsibility for homeless people who are HIV-infected but otherwise well (unless, of course, there are other priority need factors, for example, where the applicant is pregnant or has children). For people who are HIV-infected, asymptomatic, and literally homeless, advisers may have no alternative but to look at alternative housing resources such as special projects.

Bed and breakfast accommodation, which tends to be characterised by poor conditions and overcrowding, should be avoided if at all possible. If, however, there is no alternative, the Bed and Breakfast used should be warm and clean, with single rooms and with self-contained facilities. Access to cooking facilities is also important, as this increases control over diet and nutrition.

Similar physical standards should be applied to emergency hostels. In this case, it will be useful to find out whether local hostels have yet addressed existing policies or formulated new ones to incorporate HIV infection. If they have not done so, it may be appropriate to suggest that they should consider this.

It is essential to be aware of all the good quality temporary accommodation which exists in your area and also be familiar with all local provision for people with special needs: for example, whether there are any local emergency facilities which would be suitable for very young people or drug users who are HIV-positive.

2 Local authorities

Local authorities still have a major role to play in providing good quality housing for people with HIV infection. Advisers should be familiar with all local authority policies which are likely to have an impact on people with HIV disease. For example, what are the Homeless Persons Unit's policy guidelines on this issue, and who do they view as vulnerable under the Housing Act 1985? A number of local authorities, especially in the metropolitan areas, have now developed policies for use in their housing departments.

On a practical level, how does a homeless person make an application to the local authority? In some areas, applications are made at the Housing Aid Centre reception desk, in full hearing of queues of people. If this is the case, are confidential interviews available and is it possible to make an appointment in advance?

It is likely that the local authority's medical officer will have a strong influence over which applicants for rehousing are accepted on medical grounds (both through homelessness procedures and the housing waiting list). It is often helpful to have as detailed an understanding of the officer's role as possible.

Does your local authority have any allocation procedures which may affect people with HIV disease? For people with HIV disease who are already local authority tenants, how sympathetically is the housing department likely to view a request for an urgent transfer if their circumstances change, perhaps to accommodate a carer or to be closer to medical treatment?

3   Housing associations

Housing associations are well placed to respond quickly to changing local needs and they may be more flexible than local authorities. A number of housing associations have already formulated policies on HIV, while others are developing a range of schemes suitable for the needs of this group.

4   Other resources

Housing advisers need access to information on a wide range of resources available to people with HIV infection in the area such as counselling agencies, self-help groups, welfare rights agencies or advice centres and services provided by statutory bodies. Support services provided by social services departments, for example, include the home-help and meals-on-wheels services (see Appendix 2).

PUBLIC SECTOR HOUSING

The public sector has a major role to play in offering secure, low cost housing to all people with HIV infection. There are two access routes to public sector housing: the housing waiting list and the homelessness procedures.

The housing waiting list

In many districts and for many households, the waiting list is still a positive way to seek rehousing and people should be encouraged to register with their local authority.

For those people with HIV infection and in particular single households, the existing points scheme may not easily reflect the full extent of their inadequate housing and its related difficulties. Wider aspects of poor housing which may affect a damaged immune system, but which may not necessarily attract any points, include the following:

1   Shared facilities

Problems for people sharing accommodation are manifold. All attempts at control over one's own environment are affected by other residents. For somebody with

HIV infection who is suffering from extreme bouts of diarrhoea, a shared toilet may be a constant source of anxiety and embarrassment, quite apart from the obvious risk of contracting infections from other residents. In some Bed and Breakfasts, the standard of hygiene is very low and the individual has no control over it.

A nutritious balanced diet is important yet cooking facilities may not exist at all, resulting in people being forced to eat either in cafés or making do with unbalanced snack meals. Where cooking facilities do exist they are often shared and again it may be difficult to control hygiene standards.

2 Heating and hot water

For someone suffering from an illness or trying to maintain good health, lack of heat can lead to a range of problems from simply being permanently cold to dampness in beds and clothes which can aggravate (for example) chest infections. In many cases heating systems which do exist are inadequate and expensive, and may be controlled by landlords.

Many shared houses only have small hot water tanks or inadequate geyser systems in shared bathrooms. This lack of hot water is particularly distressing for somebody experiencing severe night sweats where sheets constantly have to be washed and changed. There is also no relief available from muscular aches and pains by hot baths.

3 Lack of privacy and space

Lack of privacy in shared housing can be a major contributor to stress. Neighbours may become suspicious about the person's health and begin forms of harassment.

For people with HIV infection or disease, wishing to have friends, lovers or carers to stay can cause additional problems. Often there is opposition from sharers or landlords, while resulting lack of space can lead to common infections being passed from one person to the other. Relationships can become strained due to over-close proximity.

Areas of conflict which previously did not exist can be opened up. People who had previously lived side by side with someone with AIDS may suddenly be overcome with fear, prejudice or feelings of helplessness and the care and support which had been given freely can become an area of resentment. Often this situation is resolved as soon as the person with HIV infection or disease acquires their own home.

4 Location

This factor is not reflected at all in the points system. For people who are in ill-health or vulnerable, the location of their homes takes on a whole new perspective. People with HIV disease will need to be within easy access of their specialist medical and social care, and be able to travel easily and cheaply between clinics and home to avoid any unnecessary hospitalisations. Being near to shops and community facilities is of major importance. Close proximity to friends, lovers and family is another factor in combating isolation.

5   General design

Accommodation that has many external or internal stairs will obviously be problematic for a person with HIV infection who has mobility problems. It may also be necessary to provide essential adaptations to bathrooms or kitchens to facilitate independent living. If this is not possible, because the rooms are too small, it could severely impede a person's ability to cook or wash. In many newly-built or rehabilitated properties, there is insufficient sound insulation. If someone is unwell and having to spend lengthy periods sleeping, the level of noise can cause extreme distress and hardship.

HOMELESSNESS

In many parts of the country, access to public sector housing will only be possible for people with HIV infection who are homeless if they follow the homelessness procedures that are laid down in the Housing Act 1985 Part III. It is therefore essential for advisers to be familiar with the legislation so that they will be able to present a strong and effective argument to the local authority in support of their clients' applications for rehousing. It is also useful for advisers to have knowledge of the Code of Guidance which local authorities must have regard to when discharging their duties under Part III.

The Housing Act 1985 Part III, as amended by the Housing and Planning Act 1986, gives a local authority the duty to secure permanent accommodation for anyone who is (a) homeless, (b) in priority need, and (c) not intentionally homeless. Where they rehouse will depend upon the local connection; and what kind of accommodation is offered depends upon a number of factors including both the particular needs of the person and general housing circumstances. Both of these will be considered later in more detail.

It is important to note, however, that following the Asylum and Immigration Appeals Act 1993, Councils no longer have a duty to secure accommodation for people seeking asylum if they have reasonable accommodation available to them, however temporary. If the asylum seeker has no accommodation whatsoever the Council is only obliged to provide temporary accommodation until the person's immigration status has been decided. If he or she is granted leave to remain, the provisions of the 1993 Act will cease to apply. At this stage he or she will be treated as a newcomer to the homelessness provisions and the case may be reconsidered by the housing authority.

Councils may, if they so wish, give equal treatment to homeless asylum seekers, however, and advisers should find out local approaches to this issue to advise applicants fully.

These provisions do not apply to people who have refugee status or who have exceptional leave to remain.

Advisers should also be aware of the effect of the decision in *R.* v. *Secretary of State for the Environment ex parte the London Borough of Tower Hamlets* [1993] and the subsequent amendment to the Code of Guidance issued in February 1994. This means that for an applicant entering the country illegally or who has remained in the country unlawfully the housing authority owes no duty. In addition it places a duty on the housing authority to inform the Home Office Immigration and Nationality Department (IND) where it is satisfied that a person is in the country illegally.

Who is homeless?

Obviously people are homeless if there is nowhere that they are entitled to live – that is, if they do not have any legal right to occupy any accommodation. Included amongst the homeless, therefore, will be not only those who have literally no roof over their heads, but also those who have no legal right to remain where they are staying, for example squatters or people living in temporary refuges.

If your client has a restricted contract or a licence to occupy some accommodation, although the legal right to remain may be weak, it may exist and a local authority may insist that any right to occupy is formally brought to an end by a court order before considering the person as homeless. The new Code of Guidance suggests though that in the case of some licences, local authorities should not ask applicants to get a court order, but accept proof of termination of licence as evidence of homelessness. This would apply where people who have been staying with friends are then asked to leave. People who are threatened with homelessness within 28 days come within the terms of the Act.

A person may also be deemed homeless if it is likely that continued occupation of a property will lead to violence, or threats of violence from another person residing there. The Code of Guidance suggests that local authorities look sympathetically at applications from men or women who are in fear of violence.

There were a number of amendments introduced to the Housing Act 1985 which may extend the definition of homelessness to the benefit of people with HIV infection and disease. These bring within the scope of the Act those who may have accommodation, and who may have a legal right to remain there, but where it would not be 'reasonable for him (or her) to continue to occupy' such accommodation. The test is not whether it would be reasonable to leave the accommodation, but rather whether it would be reasonable to stay.

The factors which may make it not reasonable to remain include the following:

The physical conditions of the accommodation

If the accommodation is unfit for human habitation, overcrowded, or lacking in basic amenities, as defined by housing law, then a strong case could be made for your client being homeless. But you should be quite clear how low these standards are. A dozen or more people could live in a three-bedroomed flat, if they were of the right age and gender, but the property may not be statutorily overcrowded. In one case of intentional homelessness, it was held that a rat-infested hut, 10 feet by 20 feet, without mains service, except from a nearby caravan site, was 'reasonable' to be occupied by two adults and two children. It only became 'unreasonable' upon the birth of the third child.

However, housing standards set by law will not provide the only test. The local authorities may have regard to the general housing circumstances in their area This 'one ray of hope for the authorities', according to Lord Denning, permits the local authority to take account of whether there are many people in the area living in worse conditions than the applicants – although the local authority should not restrict itself to considering only this issue, and would have to provide evidence to merit its decision.

The personal circumstances of the individual

For people with HIV disease their health should be a major factor in determining whether it is reasonable to remain in occupation of the premises. Thus, in the case of someone with PCP (pneumonia) who has to climb three flights of stairs to poor standard accommodation, it may be argued that it would not be reasonable for them to stay in that property, even though they had a legal right to occupy and that such accommodation may be satisfactory for others.

The new Code of Guidance states that it may be unreasonable for someone to continue to live in premises which they can no longer afford (for example rent arrears because of illness leading to a drop in income) or conditions which cause severe emotional stress. It also suggests that violence or threats of violence from outside the home should be taken into account. Examples given include racial harassment, violence against a person and sexual abuse.

Harassment

In the present climate of fear this is sadly a far from unusual situation. One area that may be difficult is where your client has a strong legal interest in premises suited to their needs, but feel they cannot remain because of harassment. Advisers should note that the response of many local authorities to this problem may be to insist that the applicant pursue every legal remedy that may exist before being accepted as homeless.

This approach rests on several test cases around intentional homelessness which have found in the local authorities' favour; but it should be very strongly resisted in the case of people with HIV infection. Harassment which takes place because the tenant is black, or a woman, or gay, or indeed if the tenant is HIV-positive, is not illegal; although in the case of ethnic minorities some harassment may be an offence under sections 30/31 of the Race Relations Act. The housing law around the issue of harassment tends to deal mainly with landlords and only with a narrow set of circumstances and behaviour which can be reasonably said to interfere with an occupant's peace and comfort, or is likely to cause an occupier not to exercise any legal rights.

The major legal remedy open to a person with HIV infection who is being harassed by, for example, a flatmate, because of their HIV status, is civil action. There have been cases where a local authority has advised a person with HIV disease to take out an injunction against a flatmate who was harassing them. Apart from the intolerable stress this would cause a person with HIV disease, it should be argued that if there had been violence or threats of violence within the home the person with HIV disease should be deemed as homeless under the 1985 Housing Act Part III. The Code of Guidance also states that using injunctions is not necessarily effective. However, in cases of this kind, where a client has been advised by the local authority to seek civil redress for harassment, it is important that the client does not give up the accommodation, even if he or she has had to find temporary respite in another property as the client could be deemed to be intentionally homeless if he or she then makes an application for housing under Part III of the 1985 Act.

If the harassment comes from outside the home, local authorities can be referred to the Code of Guidance which specifically mentions harassment and threats of violence as possible grounds for homelessness on the basis that it is unreasonable to remain.

Local authorities may also seek to rely on the Protection from Eviction Act 1977, as amended by the Housing Act 1988, in cases where the client is being harassed or evicted by the landlord. Advisers may well find themselves having to resist this argument too. It is important that advisers understand the law in this area fully. To consider first the civil wrong of harassment, introduced in the 1988 Housing Act – while court action may result in the payment of compensation, some legal authorities argue that this may make it more difficult to obtain an injunction to reinstate the occupier – in civil law an injunction is usually only obtained if financial damages alone would not compensate a person for his or her loss; and no damages are likely to be awarded if the occupier is reinstated by a court order or by the landlord. Secondly, many people will be excluded from the Protection from Eviction Act 1977, as amended, if, for example, they began occupancy after 15 January 1989 and share part of their accommodation with their landlord or landlord's family – exactly the situation in which many clients will find themselves. In such circumstances occupiers can be evicted without the landlord having to obtain a court order.

It can be argued that to rely on such legal protection is not sufficient if landlords would in the longer term gain possession anyway – as they would, for example, if they were resident landlords, or if the client had the limited protection of an assured shorthold tenancy. Furthermore advisers should be prepared to argue the 'reasonable to occupy' test in such cases.

Who is involved in the application?

Not only the applicant but also anyone who can reasonably be expected to live with them should be considered. In case law this will typically be a member of the family who normally resides with them and does so in circumstances in which it is reasonable for them to live together.

Same-sex partners may seek accommodation under this latter provision. Given the civil case law around lesbian and gay relationships it may often be the case that such a relationship may not be treated sympathetically by some local authorities. It may be argued that the health needs of the person with HIV disease, including the emotional health needs, form the grounds on which it is reasonable for the couple to live together. Accommodation may be offered to the couple, but often the tenancy is only granted to the person with HIV disease, leaving his or her partner with few legal rights, including possibly no right of succession. If the couple wish to have a joint tenancy, it is important that advisers argue the case. The partner may themselves be HIV-infected and this or other medical factors should be considered. In the public sector, the granting of joint tenancies can be a question of housing policy and gay partners are particularly discriminated against in this area. Sometimes a local authority is willing to offer a heterosexual couple a joint tenancy but does not offer one to a lesbian or gay couple because the validity of the partnership is questioned. An adviser could possibly use the local authority's own Equal Opportunities and Equal Access policies to try to prevent this happening.

Many advisers have also experienced difficulty with clients who wish to live with someone who is their 'carer' rather than their partner or lover. This carer may be a close friend of long standing who was already living with the person with HIV disease prior to his or her becoming homeless. Some local authorities seem reluctant to accept such a relationship, however, unless it is with a member of the family, only agreeing to consider the application as a couple. The significance, of course, lies eventually with the offer that may be made – as a couple it will probably be a one-bedroomed flat, as applicant and carer it should be two-bedroomed accommodation.

Priority need

Only those who fall within the priority-need categories will be rehoused under the Housing Act. Section 59 of the Act defines the priority-need categories as pregnant women, households with dependent children, anyone who has lost his or her accommodation as a result of an emergency such as a fire or flood, and people who are vulnerable because of old age, mental illness or handicap, physical disability and other special reasons.

The starting point is that medical vulnerability makes it such that the applicant is 'less able to fend for himself so that injury or detriment will result where a more able man [*sic*] will be able to cope without harmful effects', and several cases have held that such vulnerability must be assessed in housing terms, rather than in any other context.

On the question of vulnerability on medical grounds, there is likely to be a fairly restricted interpretation given by the local authority, usually allowing only those people with symptoms of HIV infection to be considered in priority need. Many of those local authorities that originally defined all people who were HIV-infected as being in priority need have since backed away from their decision. Advisers always need to emphasise the link between health and housing and should be prepared to argue each case. Even if a person is infected with HIV but well, when confronted by the physical problems associated with homelessness and the emotional trauma, their health may well deteriorate.

Local authorities must not 'fetter their discretion' by following a blanket or predetermined policy; they have to consider each application on its own merits. Any evidence of vulnerability presented to local authorities must be taken into account: they cannot simply ignore it, but rather, if necessary, seek additional information for themselves. Nor would it be reasonable for an authority to rely solely on the opinion of its medical advisers; it has to take into account all other relevant factors. Medical opinion in itself may not be conclusive: for example, in cases where the vulnerability may also lie in the more general factor of 'other specific reason', the expertise of a counsellor or social welfare worker has to be taken into account. This was reiterated in a recent case, when in assessing the suitability of accommodation for the needs of a homeless person, the local authority's decision was quashed as there had been a separation between medical and non-medical factors at the moment of decision-making (*R.* v. *Lewisham LBC ex parte Dolan*, Times Rep 9/92).

It is not sufficient for a local authority to conclude that someone is not vulnerable simply on the evidence of a medical assessment form without the medical officer consulting with a practitioner who has examined him or her. One could also argue that the discrimination suffered by, for example, a gay man or a drug user who has contracted the virus could be a factor in determining priority need.

If a person with HIV infection is young, it may be possible also to look at their vulnerability in terms of the Children Act 1989. Section 20 places a duty on local authorities to provide accommodation for any child in need within their area if they satisfy certain criteria and, for those over 16, a further provision states that accommodation should be provided if the child's welfare is likely to be prejudiced if they do not provide accommodation. Although there is little case law as yet on how these provisions will be implemented in relation to housing, the Children Act will be an essential tool in the assessment of young homeless people with HIV infection. Even though the definition of vulnerability under the 1988 Housing Act and 'serious prejudice' in s.20 of the Children Act are not interchangeable there should clearly be liaison between the Housing Department and Social Services.

It is in the case of borderline medical vulnerability that some of the problems of advising clients become most apparent. It is important that your client should be aware of both the purpose and the content of any negotiations you undertake on their behalf, and is allowed to remain in control. Thus, for example, it is unfortunately the case that you may not be able to guarantee the confidentiality of any information you disclose to the authority, and you should discuss this with your client. Advisers should bear in mind when considering this point the large numbers of people within the local authority who will inevitably know about the applicant's HIV status.

Further, you should be aware of the emotional problems your clients may face in having to come to terms with their diagnosis. At the same time as they are trying to cope with being positive about their well-being, you may be arguing the seriousness of their case to the authority: that in itself may require some sensitivity on your part.

Intentional homelessness

The area of 'intentionality' has caused the most controversy in the law relating to homelessness.

It is not possible here to deal fully with the jungle of law around intentionality, but we will consider some of the general principles as they might apply to people with HIV infection.

Let's consider the definition of intentionality: the relevant section is fairly clear, namely that people are considered to be intentionally homeless if as a direct result of any deliberate act or omission they cease to occupy or are forced to leave accommodation that had been available to them and in which it was reasonable for them to remain. Several points should be noted. First, whether or not an act or omission is deliberate is judged from the point of view of a reasonable and fair-minded observer, not simply by the perception of the homeless themselves; but, secondly, an act or omission carried out in good faith and by someone unaware of a relevant fact will not be regarded as deliberate.

The provision regarding the ignorance of a relevant fact may not include your client's ignorance of their legal rights, and will certainly not if they simply ignored any advice from the local authority.

The 'reasonableness' test is important. It is the same test that was imported, by the 1986 amendment, into the definition of homelessness; much of the case law around intentionality is now very relevant to the definition of homelessness itself. We need not repeat that discussion again, but you should note that in considering what is reasonable the local authority can and will take into account the local housing conditions; also note what other steps your client can take to prevent him or her becoming homeless. The authority may expect a tenant to seek police protection from harassment or seek a civil injunction rather than leave the accommodation; it may argue that your client should have sought a legal remedy to force the landlord to undertake repairs to poor accommodation; or it may argue that the housing debt could have been renegotiated rather than simply ignored.

Finally, we should note that local authorities will look back to the initial, rather than only the immediate, cause of homelessness. This may involve considering your client's housing record over many years, and looking to the last secure accommodation your client had and examining the reasons why he or she did not continue to occupy it.

Some common reasons why people with HIV infection lose their home include: illness which leads to them not being able to pay mortgage payments; giving up accommodation because it was physically unsuitable due to illness; or leaving secure accommodation because of harassment.

If properly handled these sorts of cases should not lead to a finding of intentionality. The Code of Guidance now covers many of these examples suggesting that local authorities may not necessarily make an intentionality finding. Advisers should not anticipate that a local authority will apply any different standards to people with HIV infection than those they would apply to other groups. In most cases, if your client has accommodation that would have excluded them from the definition of being homeless under the law before the 1986 amendment, we suggest that you advise the client to apply to the local authority as soon as they are threatened with homelessness, before leaving the accommodation, and argue the case at that stage.

Local connection

At law this is established by:

- normal residence by choice (not Crown Service or prison);
- employment (not casual);
- family connection (of at least five years' standing);
- other special circumstances (health care?).

It is also the case that if a person is unintentionally homeless and in priority need but does not have a local connection with any local authority in England, Wales or Scotland, the local authority applied to has a duty to ensure that permanent accommodation is made available.

People with HIV disease have faced the problem of being offered accommodation close to family, who do not necessarily support them, rather than to friends who do. An applicant who objects to being referred to an area on account of family associations should not be so referred.

The 'other special circumstances' is an important area for this client group. Some local authorities have accepted the importance of health care facilities as establishing a local connection, and it is important that if it is your client's wish, this argument is pursued.

Offers of accommodation should reflect the availability of counselling and hospital services, friends and such factors as the location of public transport systems. It should not be considered suitable to make an offer based on a 'local connection' to one's parents, for example, if that is not where the support lies. It will be more beneficial for a person with HIV disease to be near to one good friend who supports him or her than to live close to an entire extended family who have cut them off. Under the Housing Act 1985, if a person has a connection with a district because of 'special circumstances' then this must be considered.

Even if you and your client manage to get over all the hurdles outlined in the above paragraphs, the question of what kind of accommodation they are offered remains, and it is to this which we now turn.

Housing services should recognise that people with HIV disease must be rehoused into suitable, permanent accommodation as soon as possible and with the minimum of trauma. The accommodation should satisfy certain housing needs which are essential for people with HIV disease. For example, the property needs to be warm so it should have central heating, it needs to be on a lower floor in case the person has mobility problems, the offer of a bedsit would not be suitable in the case of single people as there would not be sufficient space for a carer to stay. If the accommodation offered is 'unsuitable' it may be necessary to get expert advice to support this.

Temporary forms of accommodation

People often have to wait a long time to be permanently rehoused. In areas where there is a severe shortage of public housing, such as London, the wait could be as long as a year. It is therefore important that the standard of temporary accommodation provided is suitable to the needs of homeless people. For people with HIV disease this is an essential requirement as spending six months to a year in substandard accommodation will have a detrimental effect on their health.

Advisers should bear in mind that Part III of the Housing Act 1985 places no duty on the local authority that any temporary accommodation it provides be suitable, only that it be available. The Code of Guidance does advise authorities that they should have regard to a number of factors when placing people in temporary accommodation and that it should meet acceptable standards. It suggests that there should be no disruption to a person's access to other services (e.g., school, hospital, social worker) and should if possible be within the borough's boundaries.

The adviser should be prepared to make these points to the housing authority bearing in mind, however, that the code is only an advisory instrument and that authorities do have discretion to interpret their duties.

While case law has made it clear that the standard of temporary accommodation need not be as high as that of permanent accommodation, it must be appropriate to the needs of the applicant and their family (*R. v. Ryedale DC ex parte Smith* [1993]).

There follows a brief summary of the types of temporary accommodation most commonly used by housing authorities.

Bed and Breakfast

Before 1989, the most commonly-used form of temporary accommodation was Bed and Breakfast hotels. After a brief respite from this for a couple of years, many local authorities are unfortunately widely using Bed and Breakfasts again. Wherever possible, as we have already argued, people with HIV disease should not have to stay in Bed and Breakfast hotels. The rooms do not have sufficient space for a carer, bathrooms and toilets are shared and often there are completely inadequate cooking facilities. People with HIV disease are also more susceptible to harassment in hotels. If there are no other alternatives, it would be best for advisers to be aware of local B&B options and standards in order that a stay will be as comfortable as possible.

Private sector leasing (PSL)

Since 1989, many local authorities have begun to use private sector leasing schemes. These are generally properties rented from private landlords and managed by housing associations. The properties are leased on, for example, three-year contracts and offered to local authorities as temporary accommodation for homeless people. The accommodation is self-contained flats or houses which have basic furnishings and generally offer a much higher standard of housing than B&B. If PSL schemes are offered in your area, it is always advisable to ask housing departments to place people with HIV infection in them and so avoid many of the problems encountered in Bed and Breakfast accommodation. Unfortunately, because of a government decision to withdraw certain subsidies, there are now capital finance implications for local authorities using these schemes, forcing some of them to return to hotel provision.

Homeless at Home

Some local authorities operate a 'Homeless at Home' scheme which involves a partner or friends offering extended stays once a local authority has agreed to rehouse someone. If this facility exists then it should be allowed without extending the waiting period for a permanent offer of rehousing. Advisers should be aware of the local authority's policy on this matter. Being able to go 'Homeless at Home' allows people with HIV disease to stay with friends and relatives who can provide essential support, rather than moving somewhere just on a temporary basis. It is also a lot less stressful, especially if the only other alternative is a hotel.

Other schemes

Some boroughs have developed short-life schemes, managed by housing associations, for use as temporary accommodation. There are also a few HIV-specific projects which offer temporary shared housing for those who would prefer to stay in low support housing until they are allocated permanent accommodation. The only satisfactory long-term answer though is for existing permanent stock to be made more readily available despite heavy demand.

Permanent accommodation

As far as permanent accommodation is concerned, the authority has a duty to ensure that it is suitable. This can be by a variety of ways (housing association, council accommodation, privately-rented assured tenancy, for example), but whatever means the authority uses to discharge its duty the clear obligation is that it be suitable. The Code of Guidance advises that the authority must 'take into consideration the circumstances of the particular household'. This would include health and social needs.

Recent case law has helped develop the definition of suitability and the adviser should be prepared to challenge offers of accommodation they believe to be unsuitable. However, the only legal challenge to the local authority decisions on suitability of accommodation is by way of judicial review. The costs will not interfere with an authority's discretion merely because the outcome is harsh or unreasonable, except where the decision is so perverse or absurd that no reasonable authority could possibly have made it. They will examine the way the authority reached its decision.

The most important aspect of the entire rehousing procedure is that it should be as swift and clear as possible in order to minimise the period of uncertainty for the person with HIV infection. If there has to be a period in temporary accommodation, then the client should be made fully aware of any implications surrounding this, such as periods of possible additional expense and disruption in the future. In any circumstance where a less than ideal situation can be found, discussions must include the person with HIV disease.

Succession of tenancy

For Housing Act 1985 secure tenancies, certain people have automatic right to succession of tenancy, for example, a legal spouse or a common-law partner, providing that they can prove residence at the property over a reasonable time; direct members of the tenant's family may also have rights to succession. However, no such automatic right extends to unrelated friends and/or carers. Under s.113 of the 1985 Housing Act members of the family are defined as 'spouses, parents, grandparents, children, grandchildren, siblings, uncles, aunts, nephews and nieces'. It also includes step-relations, half-relations and illegitimate children. Same-sex partners are not defined as members of the family as they cannot be 'considered to be living together as husband and wife' (*Harrogate BC* v. *Simpson* [1986]). Housing legislation completely ignores the rights of same-sex partners and the validity of their relationships. They have no statutory right to succeed to a tenancy and, at present, advisers will have to depend on the discretion of local authorities when advising same-sex partners in this area. We would argue that local authorities should be urged to adopt policies which would address these issues and result in security for people in these circumstances.

One further general comment is perhaps appropriate. The clear intention of the

Housing Act 1988 is to reduce the importance of local authority housing. No mention is made in the Act of 'homelessness', and at present councils still retain the responsibility to rehouse those people who are unintentionally homeless and in priority need. At the same time there are government restrictions which affect a local authority's ability to build more property and they have lost some of their housing through the 'Right to Buy' scheme. A local authority is in the position of having continued responsibility while its actual housing stock decreases. Although local authorities have access to housing association stock, this is unable to fill the gap in provision. The issue of what kind of accommodation, where it is located, and on what terms of occupation, becomes all the more important.

The problems for people with HIV infection are not restricted to gaining public sector accommodation. Problems exist for those who are already in, or who are about to move into, local authority stock.

Estates management

For those people who have HIV infection or disease, and who are living in public sector accommodation, there may be a need to contact the Estates Management office to request modifications to existing accommodation or to request a transfer to somewhere more suitable. Good working practices in these offices, with particular regard to sensitivity and confidentiality, will be of major importance. The office will often be located directly within the community where the person with HIV disease is living, and for information to be leaked here would be disastrous, resulting in forms of harassment and persecution which could be extremely difficult to handle.

People working in Estates Management offices must at all times be sensitive of how situations might arise that could place the person with HIV disease in confrontational circumstances. Gossip may surround a tenant who is having central heating installed whilst other people on the estate might have been waiting longer; questions about the person's illness, why meals-on-wheels are delivering, or why a person is being collected by ambulance, may be asked. It is absolutely paramount that swift action be taken against other tenants or workers at the offices who give out confidential information and that there are disciplinary structures to deal with such breaches of confidentiality.

Transfers

The impact of HIV on each individual is unique and it therefore follows that each housing resource should ideally be tailored as much as possible to that person's needs. Circumstances may also change during the person's life and as far as possible it will be necessary to address these issues by means of transfers and adaptations to existing properties. Whilst recognising that some people who are terminally ill will choose to die in hospital or a hospice, services and facilities should be available to enable the choice to extend to being cared for and dying at home.

Accommodation originally offered might become too small for somebody needing 24-hour care; accommodation might not facilitate wheelchairs or special AIDS; a tenant might need a transfer nearer the hospital or away from a noisy estate.

As in the waiting list points procedure, transfers are generally judged fairly widely, with emphasis on such factors as mobility and harassment. If a tenant is experiencing severe harassment they should contact the local authority for a management transfer, whereas if a tenant wishes to move because their accommodation has become unsuitable for health reasons, they can apply for a transfer on medical grounds.

All the above discussion has focused on local authorities, but much of the comment would also apply to housing associations. The main distinction is that since the implementation of the 1988 Housing Act, housing associations are now classified as private landlords. They offer assured tenancies, instead of secure ones and are not 'fair rented'. Many though still have a charitable basis and aim to provide low cost suitable housing. While potentially they are more flexible than council housing, the corollary is that associations' practices vary enormously. Some, particularly in areas where the initial impact of HIV infection was greatest, have responded positively; but it would be wrong to assume this is always the case. Many of the concerns expressed above apply equally to this sector, and advisers would do well to consider in advance their approach to these agencies.

THE PRIVATE SECTOR

This century has seen a sharp decline in the importance of the private rented sector. Some of the sector is characterised by poor conditions, lack of security, and high rents. It therefore represents a standard of accommodation which may not be suitable for people with HIV infection.

However, the private rented sector has traditionally housed large numbers of single people, the group which represents a significant percentage of those severely affected by AIDS in the UK (although this situation is changing).

Many of the problems faced by advisers will be those of clients trying to leave privately-rented sector accommodation. Issues of poor conditions, high rents, and harassment have therefore been considered in the previous discussion. But not all clients will wish to leave their accommodation, or are likely to be offered public sector housing were they to do so.

Detailed knowledge of welfare and housing benefits will be invaluable. In cases of harassment not only will the adviser be called upon to assist in the more usual provision of legal advice, but he or she should also recognise that the person may need considerable support either from the housing adviser or from a more appropriate agency. The responsibility of finding both temporary and permanent accommodation will, from time to time, inevitably fall to the advice worker, and it will have been necessary to have planned well in advance. In particular, advice agencies have a crucial role to play in encouraging good working practices within hostels and special projects; and being aware of the services offered and the policies on health and safety and confidentiality clearly make for a more confident referral for your client.

Rented accommodation in poor conditions

It would not be appropriate or possible here for us to work through the detailed legislation affecting the private rented sector, but one area at least may be worth further discussion. Local authority Environmental Health Officers (EHOs) have wide-ranging powers regarding privately-rented property which is in poor condition. The relevant legislation is contained in the Environmental Protection Act 1990. The primary aims of the legislation are to prevent the fabric of the housing stock from deteriorating and to protect the health and well-being of occupiers.

For people who have HIV infection and are living in private rented accommodation, the intervention of an EHO can substantially improve the quality of their housing, although this may be a lengthy process. Where accommodation is in a poor state of repair, the EHO has the power to serve a notice on the owner of the property, requiring him or her to carry out the necessary repairs within a certain period. Depending on the nature of the repairs, the work may be grant-aided by the local authority. If the landlord fails to carry out the repairs within the specified period, the local authority has the power to intervene and carry out the works in default. The Housing Act 1988 strengthened the powers a local authority has to issue and enforce repairs notices, including the fact that non-compliance may be a criminal offence.

However, the greatest of care must be taken with these procedures given the changes introduced under the Housing Act 1988. Since the implementation of the Act, private landlords often give tenants assured shorthold tenancies, which offer only a minimum of security. They are often for fixed terms (six months' minimum) and provided the landlord gives proper notification usually on a prescribed form the tenancy can be terminated. Advisers need to be careful with these tenancies as if threatened with the intervention of an EHO, a landlord could just end the tenancy at the end of the fixed period. The Act also introduced a wholly new ground for possession for assured tenancies, namely that the landlord intends to demolish, reconstruct, or carry out substantial works to the property and the work cannot reasonably be carried out without gaining possession. There is no requirement that the landlord must provide suitable alternative accommodation, only 'reasonable removal expenses'. If the landlord offers a reduced part of the premises for your client to occupy there would appear to be a requirement that he or she give back the original accommodation once the work is completed. Advisers should note that this is a mandatory ground of possession, rather than discretionary – that is, the courts will have no choice but to grant possession if the circumstances apply.

In housing stock of very poor condition the result may be that the serving of a notice by an EHO results in the landlord instituting proceedings for possession.

Ironically, however, in the case of a person with HIV infection, the intervention of an EHO may be required most frequently in support of an application for rehousing under the homelessness legislation, rather than in improving the housing in which they are currently living. This may particularly be so in local authorities that do not have specialist workers in housing or social services departments who are dealing with issues around HIV infection. This can pose some problems, as EHOs may not necessarily be alert to the factors which may make accommodation unsuitable for a person affected by HIV. Thus, for example, an EHO who is requested to report on accommodation occupied by a person with HIV infection may note that the fire exits are inadequate while failing to identify a shared kitchen or constant traffic noise from a busy main road as environmental problems.

The person with HIV disease may take the decision to inform the EHO of his or her HIV status before the inspection visit in order to resolve this difficulty, but this will clearly raise issues of confidentiality. A clear environmental health report is a useful tool when assembling evidence in support of an application under the Housing Act 1985. However, it is important that the person with HIV disease is aware of the implications of following this course of action.

Legislative change in the private rented sector

Deregulation of the private rented sector forms one of the central pillars of the government's housing policy. These changes are likely to have a direct impact on people affected by HIV, and those advising such clients should note some of the more important ones.

The 1988 Housing Act has now been in force for several years. Most new lettings are either assured tenancies or assured shorthold tenancies. Assured tenants are paying market rents, negotiated with the landlord. Mandatory grounds for possession are extended to include rent arrears of more than three months or thirteen weeks if the rent is payable weekly or fortnightly; and persistent delay in rent payments is a further discretionary ground, as is 'arrears of rent'. The minimum period for a shorthold tenancy is reduced to six months, after which a landlord is able to recover possession.

The most common form of letting is the assured shorthold tenancy, which offers the tenant a minimum of six months' security. This low degree of security and resulting increase in stress can have a detrimental effect on people with HIV infection.

People with HIV disease are likely to be wholly or partially dependent on benefits during periods of sickness. They are therefore unlikely to be in a strong position when it comes to negotiating a rent with landlords. The importance of this point should not be underestimated. The intention of the Act is to allow landlords to be as free as possible to charge market rents, and new lettings are at whatever rent is agreed between landlord and tenant. Further, the power of the rent assessment committees to monitor the level of rents fixed is considerably undermined by the limited circumstances in which tenants may approach the committee without threatening their security, and by the fact that even if a market rent is set by the committee, a higher rent can be charged if both the landlord and tenant agree to a higher rent. It is not difficult to imagine circumstances in which clients with HIV infection will be persuaded to 'agree' to higher rent levels.

Most private landlords ask for both a deposit and rent in advance, yet over the past few years changes in social security legislation have made it practically impossible for people on benefits to obtain that sort of money. Crisis loans are discretionary, cash-limited and repayable which just intensifies the financial difficulties of people with HIV infection. Similarly, people living in assured tenancies may find that they could potentially lose their accommodation as a result of persistent housing benefit delays.

The 1988 Housing Act has also affected rights of succession and has a major impact on the carers and partners of people with HIV disease living in the private rented sector. Even existing fully-protected tenants are affected by the changes: only a surviving spouse retains full rights of succession to a regulated tenancy. There are no rights of succession attached to assured tenancies or assured shorthold tenancies, except for a surviving heterosexual spouse or partner.

OWNER-OCCUPATION

A higher proportion of people than ever before now own their homes in this country and it is the government's stated intention to increase this percentage still further. In the last four years though, as the economic recession has deepened, there has been a corresponding slump in the housing market. The numbers of homes repossessed in 1991 leapt to a massive 75,400 while 784,000 households were in mortgage arrears (*Roof*, July 1991). Many people who bought property during the housing boom years find they now have a 'negative equity', i.e., the mortgage is higher than the value of the property. The government responded to the crisis by setting up mortgage rescue schemes with building societies and suspending the stamp duty for a fixed period. The rescue schemes have so far been able to help only a fraction of the households in difficulty and the stamp duty returned in August 1991. Agencies are seeing an increasing number of people affected by HIV who are in severe financial difficulties or facing repossession and their needs have to be addressed by advisers.

Obtaining a mortgage

The problems experienced by people who are HIV-antibody-positive, or considered by an insurance company to belong to a 'high risk group', in obtaining life insurance in connection with a mortgage application are discussed in the chapter on Life Assurance. It is important to note that not all mortgages require any form of life insurance.

Difficulties with repayments

People with HIV infection may find themselves in difficulty with their mortgage repayments as a result of a reduction in their income. It is vital to inform the mortgage company of any difficulties with repayments at an early stage, before arrears are allowed to accrue. At one time, if there were substantial arrears, most mortgage companies would have had no hesitation in foreclosing the mortgage and obtaining a court order and this is still the case with some of the smaller mortgage lenders. Now, though, many of the larger lenders are more reluctant to go for repossession so quickly because properties are not selling and it would further damage the housing market. Such a stance could change though if the housing market stabilises. If a person with HIV infection wishes to stay in the accommodation all options need to be looked at including maximising benefits and renegotiating mortgage payments with the lender.

If it is not possible to remain or the increasing financial difficulties are causing severe stress, a person with HIV disease could approach their local authority and attempt to make a homeless application on the grounds that it is unreasonable to remain in a property which they cannot afford. The Code of Guidance suggests that local authorities should not just consider people who are repossessed as unintentionally homeless but also those who are obliged to sell because of arrears or financial difficulties. Specific mention is made when these situations are caused by illness. Local authorities will need proof of the applicant's financial situation. It is not advisable just to give in the keys: always investigate the possibility of a homeless application with a local authority first.

Grant assistance

If someone affected by HIV wishes to stay in their accommodation but is having difficulties because certain adaptations are needed, they can try to apply for a grant. Under the Chronically Sick and Disabled Persons Act 1970, a local authority should make arrangements for the 'provision of assistance for that person in arranging for the carrying out of any works of adaptation – designed to secure his greater safety, security, comfort or convenience'. This could potentially cover small additions such as nursing equipment, appliances and wheelchairs or for major additions there may be grants that can be applied for (Department of the Environment – House Renovation Grants). There are renovation grants used to make properties suitable for human habitation, but the grant particularly relevant to the needs of people with HIV infection is the Disabled Facilities Grant. To obtain this grant a person needs to be registered disabled and they can be an owner-occupier, a private sector, housing association or council tenant. The grant is means tested and obtained for major adaptations such as chair lifts, changes to bathrooms and kitchens, even central heating. The main problem with this grant is the length of time involved to actually get the works agreed and paid for.

There are also minor works grants which are available for owner-occupiers and private sector tenants. These grants are discretionary and the maximum grant payable is just over £1,000, although repeat applications are possible. They only cover particular works though such as thermal insulation, or 'staying put' for those over 60.

THE WAY FORWARD

All too frequently, HIV disease is viewed in isolation purely as a health problem. The Department of the Environment is beginning to acknowledge its role in initiating resources for people with HIV disease. The Department of Health, meanwhile, recognises the importance of good quality housing for people affected by HIV, but has no housing responsibilities.

People with HIV infection who are ill cannot be cared for outside hospitals unless they have somewhere suitable to live. People with HIV disease who are suffering from specific infections such as PCP or have high care needs such as those related to HIV brain disease and are being assisted by hospitalisation or schemes such as London Lighthouse, should also have the choice to be nursed at home if it is at all possible.

Similarly, for people infected with HIV but are currently well, and wish to maintain good health, housing will be an important part of their care package. The type and location of the accommodation offered to a person who is affected by HIV is of paramount importance. Housing is the linchpin from which all other caring services can run effectively.

This chapter has concentrated largely on gaining access for people with HIV infection to public sector housing via the Housing Act 1985. In London, where to date the highest concentration of people affected by HIV is located, following this route to housing is, in effect, the only way in which access to secure, affordable housing can be guaranteed. Several of the London boroughs have responded sensitively and swiftly to the challenge of housing people with HIV infection, in spite of the financial restrictions placed upon them. In these areas, a close partnership between the statutory and voluntary sectors, working together with the frontline organisations representing people with HIV infection themselves, has ensured that the development of policy and practice has been, at least in some measure, appropriate to the needs of this group.

Through their close contact with people with HIV disease and awareness of the changing needs of the group, agencies which provide advice are well placed to promote good policy and practice and to make known the housing requirements. Advice agencies therefore have a central role to play in ensuring that local authorities work sensitively within the framework of existing legislation when dealing with people who are affected by HIV.

CAMPAIGNING

Agencies have first hand knowledge of the housing problems facing people with HIV disease, and this knowledge should be used to help argue their case. Thus, for example, most agencies have on record large numbers of statistics which illustrate the extent to which people with HIV disease are affected by housing problems. These can form the basis of a powerful argument for increasing housing resources, on both a local and national level. Locally, statistics can be used in support of materials such as reports on the problems faced by people with HIV disease like the Tenants Survey (AIDS and Housing Project) or the report on Housing and HIV in South London (AHP/Landmark). These reports are evidence of the levels of need which exist.

On a national level, locally-based information has an important role to play in resourcing and feeding the wider campaign for housing people with HIV infection and disease. Agencies such as The Terrence Higgins Trust are in a position to respond quickly to any changes in national legislation that may have an effect on some of their client group.

CO-ORDINATED ACTIVITY

Agencies which work together to promote good policy and practice will inevitably have greater success than those which work alone. However, the difficulty of providing a co-ordinated response to the needs of people with HIV disease cannot be underestimated. A coherent local housing strategy for people with HIV disease must involve representatives from the statutory and voluntary sectors, including the housing department, social services, housing associations, special projects, advice agencies and, most importantly, people with HIV disease themselves. Co-ordination at a local level is essential in order to avoid duplication of some services, while other important services remain unprovided.

ACCESS TO LOCAL AUTHORITY AND HOUSING ASSOCIATION TENANCIES – A CONSULTATION PAPER (DOE, JANUARY 1994)

The government has published a consultation paper which proposes radically to change the rights of, and corresponding duties and obligations that local authorities owe to, people who are homeless.

The proposals as they stand could shift the priority for housing away from those who are homeless, and to those people on the council's waiting list for housing. The consultation document promotes the use of the private rented sector, probably in short-term assured shorthold tenancies, for accommodating those people who find themselves homeless.

These proposals, if implemented, could have a devastating effect on people living with HIV infection and it is important for specific HIV agencies to register their protest, and respond to the consultation document.

Chapter 5

AIDS and immigration

Wesley Gryk

INTRODUCTION

The United Kingdom can take some pride in its record with respect to how HIV and AIDS have been dealt with in the context of its immigration policy.

The World Health Organization (WHO) has consistently called upon all countries to avoid the imposition of entry restrictions on those affected by HIV and AIDS, as has the Council of Europe. Yet dozens of countries – including some such as the United States and other countries whose own populations are themselves widely affected by HIV – have none the less imposed various forms of border restrictions on HIV-antibody-positive foreigners.

The United Kingdom, to its credit, has avoided this approach. At the same time, British immigration law includes a minefield of technical complexities and its implementation can be extremely discriminatory in a variety of ways. Crucial rights can be lost if an individual does not make an application or file a notice of appeal within a strict deadline.

Those affected by these issues, therefore, and persons advising them, should seek competent professional advice. Several agencies are listed in Appendix 1 which should be able to help. Either they themselves will be able to advise or else refer the problem on to a sympathetic solicitor with expertise in this field. Such a solicitor should be able to advise without charge in cases where the client meets the savings and income criteria of the legal aid 'green form' scheme.

The purpose of this chapter, therefore, is not to provide a substitute for such professional advice which must be tailored to the particular situation of an individual. Instead, it seeks to outline some of the main immigration-related issues likely to be relevant to people affected by HIV and AIDS.

It discusses how AIDS may become an issue when an individual seeks entry to the United Kingdom at a port. With respect to those already in the country, it suggests approaches which may be taken with respect to applications to prolong one's stay. In particular, it describes how – even where there would appear to be no category into which an individual fits in immigration law – it may be possible to make a successful application to remain in the United Kingdom on compassionate grounds, either because of one's own HIV-related medical condition or that of a loved one. Finally, it discusses briefly the problems of HIV-positive persons who are contemplating travel to other countries.

ENTERING THE UNITED KINGDOM

The immigration system controlling the entry of individuals into the United Kingdom is an extremely complicated one. It is set out in the Immigration Act 1971 (as amended by the Immigration Act 1988 and the Asylum and Immigration Appeals Act 1993) and in the Immigration Rules laid down by the Home Secretary as provided for in the Immigration Act. The most recent compendium of these Immigration Rules was laid before Parliament on 23 May 1994 (House of Commons Paper (HC)395).

British citizens

'British citizens', as defined by the British Nationality Act 1981, are not subject to control on entry. This is more complicated than it seems, however, since the category of 'British citizen' is only one of six categories of British nationality. The other five categories are subject to immigration control: British Dependent Territories citizenship, British Overseas citizenship, British subject status, British Protected Person status and British National (Overseas) status.

Commonwealth citizens with 'right of abode'

Some citizens of countries in the British Commonwealth also have the right to enter without being subject to immigration control but this is a very narrow category of individuals said to have the 'right of abode'. This right is available only to Commonwealth citizens born before 1 January 1983 one of whose parents was born in the United Kingdom and to women Commonwealth citizens who were married prior to that date to a man who either had British citizenship or the right of abode in the United Kingdom. (Another category of Commonwealth citizens separated out for favourable treatment are those who have at least one grandparent born in the United Kingdom. Under paragraphs 186–93 of the Immigration Rules, such Commonwealth citizens can come to the United Kingdom to seek or take employment without a work permit although they are subject to immigration control.)

Irish citizens

A special exemption from immigration control is also generally applicable to Irish citizens travelling to the United Kingdom directly from the Republic of Ireland. Under the Immigration Act 1971 both the United Kingdom and the Republic of Ireland constitute part of a 'Common Travel Area' within which citizens of the two states can travel without immigration control.

Citizens of other European Economic Area states

The right of entry to the United Kingdom by citizens of other European Economic Area states is governed by European law rather than British immigration law. As of mid-1994, European Economic Area nationals ('EEA nationals') include European Community nationals and, under the agreement establishing the European Economic Area, nationals of Austria, Finland, Iceland, Norway and Sweden. Such EEA nationals have the right under such law to enter the United Kingdom to work or seek work and to provide or seek services. Members of their families also have the right of entry even if these family members are not themselves EEA nationals. Students, pensioners and other categories also have specifically-defined rights of entry. The Home Office has, however, developed procedures for challenging the continued presence of EEA nationals it does not believe are meeting the criteria for remaining in the United Kingdom.

Restrictions on the right of entry by EEA nationals can be imposed upon grounds of public health. Neither AIDS nor any HIV-related illness, however, is listed in the annexe to Directive 64/221, which under Article 4 of that Directive comprises the only list of diseases or disabilities justifying refusal of entry. Happily it would appear that no change in this policy is contemplated.

'Visa' and 'non-visa nationals'

Other categories of individuals will be subject to the full application of British immigration law when they seek to enter the United Kingdom. Under the provisions of the Immigration Rules, these can be grouped under two main headings – 'visa nationals' and 'non-visa nationals'.

The so-called 'visa nationals' are citizens from certain countries. These countries are mostly in the developing world and/or are countries from which the United Kingdom Government is particularly concerned about the possibility of large numbers of persons arriving to claim political asylum. Countries are added to this list from time to time when such fears arise. 'Visa nationals' must always obtain a visa (also called an 'entry clearance') from the British Consulate in their country of residence before seeking to enter the United Kingdom. This applies whether the individual is coming for a short-term visit, for studies, for work or for any other purpose. Obtaining such a visa will not be an absolute guarantee that an individual will be admitted by an immigration officer on arrival (if, for example, circumstances have changed or the individual is found to be lying in some respect). Failure to obtain such a visa will, however, make it impossible for such a 'visa national' to be admitted to the United Kingdom upon arriving here. One frequent exception to this rule is an individual applying for political asylum. Getting to the United Kingdom would, however, be very difficult for such a would-be asylum applicant because of the stiff financial penalties imposed by law on airlines and other carriers found to have brought 'visa nationals' to the United Kingdom without the requisite visa under the Immigration (Carriers' Liability) Act 1987, as amended in 1991.

'Non-visa nationals' are those who under the Immigration Rules do not require a visa when they are coming to the United Kingdom as visitors or for certain other temporary purposes such as studies. These individuals as well, however, must obtain a visa beforehand at the British Consulate in their country of residence when they are coming for various other purposes defined in the Immigration Rules, such as permanently to join a spouse, fiancé/e, or other family member, to set up a business or to take employment.

Government policy relating to admission under the Immigration Rules of those affected by HIV and AIDS

With respect to those individuals who are subject to the Immigration Rules, both 'visa' and 'non-visa nationals', the position of the United Kingdom Government is that 'HIV infection (including AIDS) should not in itself be considered justification for a recommendation on public health grounds to refuse leave to enter the United Kingdom'. In a response to a Parliamentary Question on 13 January 1992 (c526, Commons, Oral), Secretary of State for Health Virginia Bottomley, indicated that this position had been reiterated when her Department had reissued guidance to port medical inspectors of health in the form of an executive letter (PL/CM0(91)15) in October 1991.

The major constraint in this policy – a constraint which applies similarly to all medical conditions – is that immigration officers considering whether to admit an individual can under certain circumstances consider whether that individual will be in a position to pay for medical treatment which may be required because of HIV-related illness during the course of a stay in the United Kingdom. This would clearly apply to individuals who are coming for a visit of less than six months. It should not apply, however, with respect to someone allowed to stay or legally intending to stay permanently or someone who has 'ordinary residence' in the United Kingdom. 'Ordinary residence' includes not only those intending to stay permanently but individuals who have lived in the United Kingdom for a period of not less than one year, work permit holders and various other categories. A full explanation of the definition of 'ordinary residence' is included in the National Health Service (Charges to Overseas Visitors) Regulations 1989 (1989 No. 306).

Those coming from countries with reciprocal health care agreements with the United Kingdom, including EEA nationals, could not, of course, be excluded on the grounds of potential inability to pay for necessary medical treatment.

Some indication of how the government has sought to implement this policy was given by the publication, in the *New Scientist* of 6 July 1991, of excerpts from a letter from the Chief Medical Officer to port medical inspectors. The letter stated the government's position that 'the diagnosis of AIDS or HIV (infection) should not in itself be considered justification for a recommendation on public health grounds to withhold leave to enter the UK'. It continued:

However, if the Medical Inspector considers that an entrant who is subject to

Immigration Control is likely during his stay . . . to require medical treatment for AIDS or for illness associated with HIV infection . . . he/she should provide an estimate of the cost of such treatment in order to enable the Immigration Service to decide whether the passenger has the means to meet these costs.

At the time, the letter was headlined by the *New Scientist* as 'Britain's back door ban on HIV immigration', and fears were expressed that the policy would be widely applied to prevent the admission of HIV-antibody-positive individuals. While isolated cases have been reported of the application of this approach to justify the refusal of admission to HIV-positive individuals, they would appear to be rare. One factor, of course, may be the simple fact that in most cases an immigration officer is not likely by visual inspection to determine that an individual is HIV-positive and then refer the case to the Medical Inspector.

STAYING IN THE UNITED KINGDOM

Once a person has managed to arrive in the United Kingdom, the nature of the immigration problems encountered will vary according to that individual's particular status and situation.

'Temporary admission'

Some such individuals will be in the anachronistic position of having physically entered the United Kingdom, with full knowledge of the immigration authorities, but without yet having been recognised as having legally entered the country. These will have been issued a form by the immigration authorities indicating that they have 'temporary admission' and setting out the address where they must continue to reside and other conditions which must be met. This is a status which can be given to people who have been refused entry to the United Kingdom but have been temporarily admitted for a short period of time for compassionate or practical reasons. It also applies, however, to individuals with respect to whom no final decision as to legal admission has been taken.

Included in this group are the large numbers of individuals who arrive at United Kingdom ports of entry each year and apply immediately for political asylum. In order to qualify for such asylum, they will need to demonstrate that they fall within the definition of 'refugee' set out in the United Nations Convention and Protocol Relating to the Status of Refugees. They need to show that they are seeking to escape persecution for reasons of race, religion, nationality, membership of a social group, or political opinion. The Home Office may take months and often years to decide such a case and, in the meantime, individuals who lodged their applications immediately upon arrival will continue to have 'temporary admission'.

Individuals with 'leave to enter' or 'leave to remain'

Other individuals will already have been granted a legal right to stay in the United Kingdom, at least for the time being. They may have a current 'leave to enter' the United Kingdom which will have been granted to them by immigration authorities at the time that a decision was taken to admit them legally into the United Kingdom. Alternatively, some will have sought an extension of their 'leave to enter' and been granted a further 'leave to remain' in the country.

Such individuals may be concerned about extending their stay further in the United Kingdom. The Immigration Rules relating to such extensions can be particularly labyrinthine. To take a simple example, someone coming for a visit to the United Kingdom will be given a maximum of six months' leave to enter the country. It is impossible to extend ordinary visitor's status beyond six months. It is in certain circumstances, however, possible to switch from one status to another while within the United Kingdom. A 'non-visa national', for example, could make a successful application to change to student status provided that it can be demonstrated that the individual will be self-supporting without need of resorting to employment or public funds (defined for these purposes as including income support, housing benefit, family credit, housing under Part III of the Housing Act 1985 or council tax rebate), is enrolled in a full-time course of studies and intends to leave at the end of the course of studies. On the other hand, under the Immigration Rules, a 'visa national' cannot make this particular change in status within the country. He or she is required under the rules to return home and apply for a new visa to enter as a student and will need to demonstrate the same things. There are other categories, however, under the rules into which a 'visa national' can switch from within the country.

This brief chapter is not the appropriate place to attempt to describe these sometimes unpredictable variations. Affected individuals and their advisers, however, must be aware that the rules are complex and professional guidance is essential.

It is also crucial to bear in mind that any application made to extend a person's legal stay in the United Kingdom must reach the Home Office immigration headquarters (Immigration and Nationality Department, Home Office, Lunar House, 40 Wellesley Road, Croydon CR9 2BY) no later than the last day of that person's current leave to enter or remain in the country. This is to protect the right of appeal to the independent immigration appellate authorities which may be available if the application is unsuccessful. Such appeal rights are lost if the application is received even one day 'out of time'. Applications, which should be accompanied by the individual's passport, should be sent recorded delivery or can be delivered by hand during office hours.

'Overstayers' and 'illegal entrants'

An individual who does fail to extend leave to enter or remain in the United

Kingdom becomes an 'overstayer' and ultimately will become liable to 'deportation'. This is the technical term for the formal procedure whereby the Home Secretary signs an order requiring the person to leave the country and prohibiting re-entry. While an 'overstayer' can make an application to the Home Office for 'leave to remain' in the United Kingdom, the usual appeal rights will not be available in the case of an unsuccessful application. An appeal against any eventual decision by the Home Secretary to make a deportation order will be available, but this is for the most part a technical right of appeal unless the person has already been in the United Kingdom for seven years at the time of the decision. (A positive development under the Asylum and Immigration Appeals Act 1993, however, has been the provision of a substantive right of appeal in every case to those who have been refused political asylum.)

The term 'illegal entrant' refers to an individual who never obtained an effective 'leave to enter' the United Kingdom, either because of evading immigration control altogether or because of using deception about identity or grounds of entry to the United Kingdom. The 'illegal entrant' is subject to immediate 'removal' from the United Kingdom without the procedural safeguards, such as they are, which attach to 'deportation'. An individual found to be an 'illegal entrant' can try to challenge the decision by lodging an application for judicial review of the decision with the High Court but there are no appeal rights within the immigration law system (with the exception, again, of those seeking political asylum). Any application by an 'illegal entrant' for leave to remain is likely to be unsuccessful except in the most compassionate circumstances.

Applications to stay in the United Kingdom by persons affected by HIV and AIDS – a general approach

The individual seeking to remain in the United Kingdom would certainly be best advised to consider all of the potential options available under the Immigration Rules. Even if one of the concerns about remaining is the individual's own HIV-related health problem or that of a loved one, the most sensible initial approach would be to consider the applicability of the existing Immigration Rules. The commendable stated policy of the United Kingdom Government is that HIV status in and of itself ought not to be a factor in immigration decision-making and, therefore, it need not and ought not to be referred to if not directly relevant to an application made within the categories set out in the Immigration Rules. The only category where it is clearly likely to be relevant would seem to be an application (under paragraphs 51–6 of the Immigration Rules) to enter the United Kingdom or to extend a stay to undergo private medical treatment at the applicant's own expense.

One primary rationale for making an application within the Immigration Rules whenever possible is the existence of appeal rights which attach to most such applications. Under such appeal rights, the unsuccessful applicant will probably have a right of appeal to an adjudicator and, if unsuccessful there, may have subsequent rights of appeal to the Immigration Appeal Tribunal and perhaps even to the Court of Appeal. These appeal procedures are likely to take many months and sometimes years and the individual will continue to have the right to remain in the United Kingdom while the appeal is pending.

Applications for exceptional leave to remain on compassionate grounds

An individual need not give up all hope, however, just because no relevant category can be found within the Immigration Rules or because an application has been pursued to the end under those Rules without success. The Home Office can and often does grant individuals leave to enter or remain in the United Kingdom on an exceptional basis where there are strongly compassionate circumstances. Again to the credit of the Home Office, this approach has been taken relatively frequently with respect to people who themselves are in poor health because of an HIV-related condition or who have a loved one in this country who is ill and who would benefit from the continued presence, care and support of the applicant.

An application made on the basis of HIV-related illness should be accompanied by as much information as possible regarding the compassionate nature of the particular case. A doctor's report setting out as fully as possible the individual's condition should be included, and this report should provide a frank prognosis of the applicant's long-term prospects. Experience seems to show that applications coming from those who have already suffered serious HIV-related illnesses and whose immune systems are most severely compromised are most likely to be successful. The Home Office has shown increasing sophistication in dealing with such applications and may respond initially by asking further medical questions about factors such as the individual's T-cell count. The Home Office may also seek permission to have access to the individual's medical records and to have an examination carried out by a Home Office-designated doctor.

Other compassionate factors should be cited in such applications. If there is very little prospect of effective treatment in the individual's home country, this should be explained. Again, the Home Office can show some sophistication in its knowledge of conditions in other countries. Decision-making officials are unlikely to be impressed where good health care may exist in the applicant's home country but the inability to pay for it is cited as the reason for the compassionate application. The individual's ties in the United Kingdom and the emotional support available from friends, relatives or other support networks here should be cited. Letters of support from social workers, friends, relatives and help agencies might be appropriate to include. It may sometimes be relevant to provide some history regarding the onset of the HIV-related illness. Obviously, cases where the applicant has been caught unawares in the United Kingdom by a medical crisis are more likely to be treated sympathetically than those cases where an individual appears to have come into the country specifically to seek medical assistance without being able to pay for it privately.

If the application is being made to remain exceptionally in the United Kingdom to stay with and assist another person affected by HIV-related illness, the same sorts of compassionate factors should be cited. The nature of the relationship should be described. If it is the case, an important factor to outline is how the applicant's presence in the United Kingdom will in fact represent a savings to government expenditure on health care and social services support because of the care which will be provided by the applicant. This is an important argument to make and one which not surprisingly is viewed sympathetically by the Home Office. It should be noted, however, that quite often the proposed carer who is given exceptional leave to remain in the United Kingdom on this basis will be specifically prohibited from working during the period of that stay, on the basis that holding down employment would be inconsistent with providing the level of care and support expected. The Home Office generally appears initially to give one year's exceptional leave to remain when such applications are successful but this is renewable if the same factors are relevant at the end of that period.

It is worth noting that the Home Office's otherwise toughly negative attitude regarding the immigration situation of the foreign partner in same-sex relationships is softened in this context. A statement of the Government's attitude in this regard was provided in a letter dated 8 March 1993 to Wilson & Co., solicitors, and quoted in *United Kingdom Immigration Law and Rules As They Affect Same-Sex Couples* (Stonewall 1994):

> The Home Office policy concerning such matters is clear. There is no provision in the immigration rules for a person to be granted leave to remain in the United Kingdom on the basis of a homosexual relationship. Applications for leave to remain on the basis of such a relationship accordingly fall to be considered as a matter of discretion outside the Immigration Rules. Ministers have indicated that such applications are unlikely to be approved unless there are genuinely exceptional circumstances. . . . I would not hold out much hope that a person would be admitted solely on the basis of such a relationship unless the circumstances were wholly exceptional such as the grave illness of the British partner.

In fact there have been a number of successful applications made where the British partner has been seriously affected by HIV-related illness.

If an application for exceptional leave to remain in the United Kingdom is made while the individual concerned still has existing leave to remain in the country, that individual should be afforded a right of appeal to an adjudicator (judge) in the immigration appeal system should the application be unsuccessful. Time limits are again crucial and the notice of appeal will need to be with the Croydon office of the Home Office within fourteen days of the negative decision. When the appeal case is finally heard, generally many months later, the adjudicator will not have the right to overturn the Home Office's negative decision since the application by its very nature falls outside the Immigration Rules. At the same time, the adjudicator, if convinced that the case was a compassionate one, could make a recommendation to the Home Office to reconsider the application and such recommendations carry some authority although they need not be followed. In any event, the appeal process itself generally takes many months and the individual continues to have the right to remain in the United Kingdom while the appeal is pending.

If the Home Office continues to maintain its negative decision, ultimately it may be a useful idea to get a Member of Parliament involved to raise the case directly with the relevant minister. The appropriate Member of Parliament should be the one representing the area where the applicant lives. The MP should be provided with as much background information as possible and any available supporting information from doctors and other relevant sources.

It is probably also worth noting that one approach occasionally taken by the Home Office – inadvertently or not – on such applications for exceptional leave outside the Immigration Rules is to leave them pending for a very long time without any decision. The effect of course is to permit the individual concerned to remain while awaiting resolution of the case. It is probably a good strategy not to push for a quick decision in such cases.

Finally, a couple of cautionary notes should be sounded with respect to such applications. First of all, while an application is pending, the individual concerned cannot leave the United Kingdom or the application will be considered withdrawn. Such an individual is not likely to be readmitted to the United Kingdom since he or she will not fall within one of the Immigration Rules permitting the granting of leave to enter. Once an application has been successful, the individual concerned should be able to travel and to return to the United Kingdom within the period of exceptional leave granted.

Another problem frequently faced by those applying for or obtaining such exceptional leave is that they are separated from close family members in their home country, such as children, parents and spouses. If the country concerned is a country whose citizens are 'visa nationals' it is likely to be very difficult for these family members to obtain a visa to visit. The entry clearance officer in the British Consulate is likely to maintain that such family members, given the situation, would not leave the United Kingdom at the end of their prescribed visit and therefore refuse the application.

Nor is there any category in the Immigration Rules to permit such family members to join the individual in the United Kingdom for the duration of the exceptional leave which has been granted. This is a serious problem faced by many individuals who find themselves separated from their closest family members at a time when their presence would be most important. If a close relative wishes to obtain a visa to visit, as much information as possible must be submitted to the British Consulate indicating that the ties of the individual to the country of origin are so strong that return is likely. Professional and family obligation in particular can be cited.

TRAVELLING ABROAD

The main purpose of this chapter has been to outline the position in United Kingdom immigration law with respect to individuals affected by HIV and AIDS. It is perhaps worth saying a few additional words about the problems which may be faced elsewhere in the world by individuals from the United Kingdom who wish to travel abroad.

Dozens of countries currently have some form of border restrictions relating to the entry of HIV-positive people. The nature and applicability of these restrictions vary enormously. Policies are also subject to change. A small number of countries require proof of a recent negative HIV test simply to come for a visit. Others impose a similar requirement with respect to people who wish to immigrate permanently. Probably the largest category of restrictive countries, however, have theoretical limitations on the entry of HIV-positive persons which are only applied if the immigration officer happens upon the information that the would-be entrant is HIV-positive.

Information on countries imposing HIV-related restrictions on travellers can be obtained from the National AIDS Manual or The Terrence Higgins Trust, but it would be a sensible step to contact the relevant embassy to check any information about the country's policy in this regard before making any travel arrangements. Obviously such enquiries should be made without providing details which would identify the person proposing to travel.

In those cases where there are theoretical limitations on the entry of HIV-positive individuals – but where no documentary 'proof' of HIV-negative status is required – the individual concerned is going to have to weigh up the potential risks of travelling. While an HIV-positive individual is likely to look perfectly healthy to an immigration officer, problems can arise if, for example, AZT or other drugs perceived as HIV-linked are to be carried. A trip intended to be a relaxed and pleasant sojourn could become an expensive and traumatic débâcle if entry is refused after a long journey and the traveller is bounced back to the United Kingdom, perhaps after a period of detention. Much thought and planning needs to go into any such travels and the risks involved need to be realistically assessed.

The simple solution of course would be for the world community to accept the view of the World Health Organization that the screening of international travellers is ineffective, impractical and wasteful. Governments, however, are all too often like the people they govern. When faced with a problem involving a complexity which makes them feel impotent, they find themselves incapable of addressing the underlying issues involved. Instead they reach out for the grand gesture which, while perhaps totally ineffective, makes them feel momentarily safe. The attempt by governments to erect immigration barriers against HIV and AIDS represents just such a grand but empty gesture.

Chapter 6

AIDS and insurance

Peter Roth and Wesley Gryk

INTRODUCTION

The emergence of AIDS created difficult problems for the insurance industry. There were a number of factors related to the initial incidence of the disease in the United Kingdom which in particular led the insurance industry to take rapid measures in response. Those factors alerted insurers to their potentially great financial vulnerability if they did not make provision for the possible long-term effects of the spread of AIDS and HIV disease.

One such important factor is that the disease has so far largely affected the younger segment of the population. This includes many individuals who under ordinary circumstances might be considered good insurance risks as they would be likely to lead long and healthy lives. Indeed, during the two decades prior to the emergence of HIV and AIDS, actuaries had predicted falling mortality rates for the general population. Such predictions had been taken very much into account in setting the level of premiums offered by life assurance companies keen to undercut their competitors.

In this seemingly improving environment of sophisticated medical treatment and declining death rates, the phenomenon of AIDS came as a rude shock. Before 1982 AIDS was unknown in the United Kingdom. But by the mid-1980s, as the significance of AIDS became appreciated as a new disease for which there was no cure, there were forecasts of a rapid spread of an AIDS epidemic. That had two particular consequences for the insurance industry. First, insurers were concerned that they might face a large number of AIDS-related claims from existing policyholders, to whom the insurers were bound under continuing contracts in which the premiums, and therefore the level of insurers' capital reserves, did not reflect the prospect of such claims. Secondly, as regards new policies, insurers were anxious to screen out those whom they thought might be most at risk of developing AIDS and HIV disease in the future,

The difficulties of forecasting and detection were complicated by the fact that the virus HIV leads an elusive existence and can lie dormant for many years in those whom it infects, often giving no indication of its presence. Moreover, many of those affected by HIV and AIDS in the United Kingdom have come from social groupings whose members – because of the discrimination and disapproval that they face in society – often seek to hide their membership of such groups.

Given this background, it is not surprising that the insurance industry has been unable to develop sound projections about the long-term incidence of AIDS in the United Kingdom. Insurers have the clear obligation to make adequate financial provision now, so as to be able to meet all future claims of those whom they insure. Yet they find this necessarily difficult in the face of such uncertainty with respect to the HIV epidemic.

The insurance industry has been struggling to resolve this dilemma and has found no easy solutions. Furthermore, the lack of an insurance regulatory structure in the United Kingdom has meant that the important public policy issues arising in this area have not been adequately addressed. Consequently, many of the approaches taken so far by the industry have been unduly self-serving and discriminatory, often based on surmise rather than fact, and having little regard to their implications for public health issues. Many of those practices arose from panic at the initial projections in the mid-1980s of the rapid spread of HIV and AIDS. The industry has been slow to adjust those practices as the actual spread of the disease has fortunately proved to be limited.

This chapter attempts to outline the state of affairs as of July 1994. It therefore takes account of the announcement by the Association of British Insurers (ABI) of an important new Statement of Practice which finally determined that insurers should not ask anyone applying for insurance whether he or she had previously had a negative HIV antibody test or counselling about AIDS. This significant change followed a sustained campaign by The Terrence Higgins Trust culminating in the threat of Parliamentary legislation. There will doubtless be further developments and this must be borne in mind when considering the information included below.

The two areas of insurance cover which have been most directly affected by the emergence of HIV as a threat to health and life in the United Kingdom are – not surprisingly – health insurance and life assurance. These areas are considered separately in the next sections of this chapter.

HEALTH INSURANCE

In the area of health insurance (i.e., medical expenses cover), the existence of the National Health Service (NHS) has meant that insurers have in effect been able to avoid or postpone their exposure to potential liabilities arising from HIV infection. The trend has been that newly-written private health insurance policies in the United Kingdom specifically exclude coverage for HIV-related illnesses, either altogether or for a significant period.

For example, the British United Provident Association (BUPA), a leading provider of private health insurance, provides that any claimant who joined a United Kingdom BUPA scheme after 1 July 1987 will not be entitled to 'Treatment arising from AIDS or Human Immunodeficiency Infection present at any time within five years after the Date of Enrolment'.

Such exclusion clauses – absolving the insurer of liability for AIDS-related claims either for a set period or throughout the period of coverage – are now the norm with respect to ordinary private health insurance in the United Kingdom. The individual applying for a new health insurance policy should therefore examine the terms of a proposed policy closely in this regard and compare the terms of exclusion provided by different companies before signing an agreement with any company. Even with respect to those insurers who will cover the AIDS risk after a set number of years, variations exist as to the nature of that cover. Initial diagnosis and treatment of AIDS-related illness may be covered, for example, but not long-term treatment.

Those who already have private health cover may have taken out insurance prior to the introduction of such exclusion clauses and their coverage may, therefore, include AIDS-related illness. In such cases, however, it is important that the cover be maintained continuously by prompt renewal. If the insured individual allows the old policy to cease for whatever reason and then seeks to renew coverage, it is likely that this renewal will be on a new set of terms incorporating an AIDS exclusion clause. Again, it is important to read the proposed terms carefully before signing anything.

The existence of such exclusion clauses for HIV-related illness is obviously less problematic in the United Kingdom than it would be in other countries, such as the United States, where health insurance coverage is mainly provided in the private sector. Private cover remains something of a luxury here, taken out by some 10 per cent of the population and thus supplementing rather than supplanting the National Health Service. The privately-insured individual contracting an HIV-related illness during the effective period of an AIDS exclusion clause would simply turn to the NHS for treatment. Under present circumstances, this would occasion no particular hardship for the insured, given that most expertise relating to the treatment of HIV-related illness in the United Kingdom is currently to be found within the NHS – as are compassionate staff and well-equipped facilities, at least in those urban areas where such illness is most prevalent.

At the same time, however, the response by private medical insurers to AIDS indicates the problems involved in any shift of general health care provision to the private sector effectuated at least in part through private health insurance, without at the same time creating the regulatory power necessary to ensure that insurers would perform this function adequately. The argument is made that the insurance industry can be counted upon to take over to some extent the function of assessing the future medical needs of the population and then responsibly spreading the financial burdens connected with the meeting of those needs through private insurance policies. If this is so, it seems crucial that the industry should not be permitted to opt out of the process when particularly difficult problems arise, such as the emergence of AIDS and the attendant uncertainties relating to its long-term effect on the medical needs of the British population. There is otherwise the danger that the NHS will find itself uniquely burdened with only the most onerous and unpredictable of caseloads.

Two special categories of health insurance should also be mentioned – so-called 'permanent health' insurance and travel health insurance.

Permanent health insurance

Permanent health insurance (PHI) does not cover medical expenses but is intended to provide regular income payments to insured parties who are incapacitated by sickness, disability or accident. For this reason it is sometimes referred to as 'income protection' insurance. The majority of PHI policies in the United Kingdom are group policies provided by an employer to cover the eventuality of employees becoming incapacitated. While group PHI policies continue to be available without AIDS exclusion clauses, most individual policies now incorporate such an exemption.

Notwithstanding that liability to pay in the event of HIV-related illness has been excluded, insurers may still apply with regard to PHI cover the sort of procedures described below with respect to life assurance applications before accepting an application or in setting the premium. In 1988, for example, some PHI insurers were requiring HIV-antibody tests with respect to applicants requiring cover over certain limits (£15,000 and £25,000 maximum annual benefits were the limits cited by two companies). Failure to agree to such testing or a positive result would mean the rejection of an application for PHI cover. An applicant for such a policy should examine the application form and the policy conditions carefully before proceeding.

Travel health insurance

Travel health insurance policies are taken out by United Kingdom residents travelling abroad who want protection against the potentially very high cost of medical care should they need treatment for personal injury or illness in another country. Again, the prevailing approach of insurers is to exclude HIV-related illness altogether. In some cases this may be done by explicit language (the policy referring by name to AIDS), while in others the approach taken may be more indirect. Insurers may, for example, challenge HIV-related claims on the basis of clauses excluding expenses 'arising from chronic medical conditions existing at the commencement of the insured period and not disclosed to the insurer'.

Understandably, insurers have been sensitive to allegations that in the initial period after the emergence of AIDS some affected individuals travelled to other countries specifically to seek newer and more sophisticated treatments and sought to claim on such policies when doing so.

An interesting footnote regarding the effect of AIDS on the travel insurance industry is that insurers doing business in this area maintain that the level of claims against them has risen appreciably because of another HIV-related reason. They cite the growing number of claimants who are demanding repatriation when afflicted with illness in countries where they fear infection with HIV attributable to contaminated blood transfusions, recycled hypodermic needles or other treatments.

LIFE ASSURANCE

Because of the existence of the NHS and its ability to assume responsibility for the treatment of the vast majority of HIV-related cases in the United Kingdom, there has been little public comment or controversy with respect to the policy of private health insurers in excluding HIV-related illness from their coverage. Criticism of the approach taken by the insurance industry with respect to HIV and AIDS has been directed largely towards life assurance companies. So far, the life assurance industry has for the most part not followed the health insurers in specifically excluding from their policies coverage related to deaths from HIV-related illness. Industry representatives generally cite two main reasons for this.

First, life assurance policies are frequently taken out to provide a form of security in a financial transaction. Any individual or organisation whose interests are meant to be secured by such a life assurance policy is likely to be seriously dissatisfied with a policy containing an AIDS exclusion clause.

Endowment mortgages provide a good example. A person takes out a life assurance policy which is to mature in a specified number of years, providing on maturity a lump sum sufficient to pay off the principal amount of a mortgage loan made by a bank or a building society. In the meantime, the insured individual pays only interest on the mortgage loan and premiums on the life assurance policy, with no repayment of the principal amount outstanding on the mortgage loan. If, however, the individual dies before the end of the designated term, the life assurance company will pay off the principal amount of the mortgage loan, leaving an unencumbered property in the individual's estate.

If such a policy contained an AIDS exclusion clause and the insured individual died of an HIV-related illness, nothing would be paid out by the insurer. This would be an unsatisfactory result from the viewpoint of both the bank or building society and of the insured's estate. The bank or building society, rather than receiving the automatic lump sum repayment it had expected, would need to go to considerable additional trouble and expense, seeking repayment of the mortgage from the deceased's estate or taking possession of the mortgaged property and arranging for its sale to obtain repayment. It would then face the risk, of which banks and building societies are acutely conscious since the decline in property values, that the resale price might prove insufficient to discharge the mortgage debt. At the same time, from the viewpoint of the deceased's estate, life assurance premiums would have been paid pointlessly over a period of perhaps many years.

Of course, not all life assurance policies arise in the context of such financial transactions. Individuals seeking such coverage may simply want to make provision for relations or other dependants in the event of death. They may further feel confident that they have not been exposed to HIV and do not face the risk of such an exposure. Even with respect to such cases, the insurance industry has been reluctant to institute policies with AIDS exclusion clauses. An explanation given by the industry is the difficulty which would arise in policing the application of such an exclusion clause.

In particular, industry spokespersons refer to the problems inherent in ascertaining whether or not a given death was HIV-related. The immediate cause of death stated on the death certificate may give no indication that a death was HIV-related. Given the prejudice and misunderstanding surrounding the disease, both the family and medical professionals involved may seek to minimise the chance for the AIDS connection to become public knowledge. In such an atmosphere, a life assurance investigator would need to call on considerable resources and would provoke much resentment in sorting out each doubtful case.

This sort of problem is much less likely to arise for insurers in the context of exclusion clauses in health insurance and PHI policies, because there the insured individuals are likely to be alive and available. They may find that, as a condition of collecting under the insurance policy, it may be necessary to answer questions, submit to medical examinations and perhaps even to HIV-antibody testing if disputes arise relating to the applicability of an AIDS exclusion clause.

For these two reasons – the unacceptability of policies with exclusion clauses as security and the reluctance of insurers themselves to police claims made under such policies – there has been no significant movement towards the writing of such policies by life assurance companies. Policies which exclude coverage for HIV-related death would not in any event be likely to be appreciably cheaper.

Instead, insurance companies used the threat of their potentially great financial vulnerability occasioned by HIV and AIDS to justify very significant overall increases in premium levels for life assurance. In 1988 there was a spate of such premium increases and options for policy-holders to increase or extend the level of cover were removed from new policies. On policies for males, premiums in some cases were raised by 150 per cent. In light of the very unclear actuarial projections available to assess the insurers' eventual vulnerability in this area, it seems uncertain how these increases were calculated and whether they were justified. Some accused the life assurance industry of using the AIDS threat as an excuse to move premiums higher. In any event, the Institute of Actuaries AIDS Working Party, which had produced in 1987 predictions of the number of AIDS-related deaths that had so alarmed the assurance industry, very substantially revised its forecasts in 1991 to reflect the much more limited spread of the disease. Announcing their new Statement of Practice on *Underwriting Life Insurance for HIV/AIDS* in July 1994, the ABI referred to the fact that payouts made by insurance companies for AIDS-related deaths had been 'considerably lower than first envisaged'. The logical result is that premiums should now be reduced. At the time of writing it is too early to say whether this will happen.

Far more controversial has been the life assurance industry's two-pronged 'exclusionary' strategy which it developed in the hope that this would minimise future vulnerability to claims deriving from HIV-related deaths. Under this strategy, insurers have sought means (1) to identify individuals with HIV, for the purpose of excluding all such individuals from coverage, and (2) to identify all those individuals whom the insurers believe to be *at risk* of contracting HIV, for the purpose of either excluding them from coverage or offering coverage only at yet further increased premiums.

This strategy has necessarily involved the life assurance industry in seeking detailed, highly confidential information not only about the medical history of some applicants but about their private lives, sexual mores, etc. On the basis of such information as has been collected, insurers have also attempted to draw presumptions about the future behaviour of applicants, in particular whether those who have not been exposed to the HIV virus are likely to face eventual exposure in the future. In their attempts to balance their own commercial interests with the right to privacy of their applicants, life assurance companies have been walking through a minefield of personal sensitivities.

The first limb of this strategy has involved insurers asking applicants to take an HIV-antibody test. The ABI issued guidelines to the industry in 1987 that in essence advised requesting an HIV-antibody test from all male applicants seeking cover in excess of £150,000, and from single male applicants seeking more than £75,000 sum assured. Since then individual companies have developed their own practices and some now routinely request applicants to take an HIV-antibody test at considerably lower levels.

The second limb of the strategy, also developed under ABI guidance, led to virtually all applicants being asked whether they had received any counselling about AIDS or had taken an HIV test. People who answered 'yes' to either of these questions, along with many single male applicants, faced not only further investigation of their medical history but also questions of a highly confidential nature about their private lives and sexual conduct. From such information insurers drew conclusions about an applicant's future behaviour and the apparent risk of that applicant becoming infected with HIV.

It is not surprising that considerable criticism was directed at the latter approach. The decision by the ABI in 1994 to advise its member companies that they should no longer ask whether an applicant has had an HIV test but only whether the applicant has tested antibody positive, was a belated response and marks a significant change. The insurance companies should introduce new proposal forms accordingly by the end of 1994 and it is expected that all companies will follow the ABI's new code of practice. However, the use of supplementary questionnaires asking whether an applicant is homosexual, and sometimes intrusive questions about his or her personal life, will continue. The imposition of substantial extra premiums on homosexual applicants remains a cause of concern. The future trend is unclear and many people are understandably confused about insurance practice.

The vast majority of cases in which individuals are now likely to seek advice about HIV and insurance therefore arise when these individuals either contemplate taking an HIV-antibody test and are concerned about the implications for a subsequent insurance application, or are considering (or are in the process of) making an application for life assurance. The next section of this chapter considers the procedures followed by the life assurance industry in this area and some potential pitfalls which may be encountered by the individual applying for life assurance.

Applying for life assurance cover: a checklist of steps

The following subsections are intended to give some guidance in this area to individuals applying for or concerned about life assurance cover, and to those advising such individuals. The most important features of the application process are set out, with an outline of the considerations which an individual should bear in mind when deciding whether to pursue an application for life assurance. It must be emphasised, however, not only that variations in practice exist as between different life assurance companies, but also that the pattern of the industry generally is subject to change, as recent developments illustrate.

1 Is the life assurance necessary?

This question should be asked by anyone who considers taking out a life assurance policy. The question is all the more important where HIV-related issues are likely to arise, since in those cases individuals may have to disclose details of their private lives and to undergo medical testing which they would not otherwise desire. Furthermore, an unsuccessful application for life assurance cover may affect the chance of obtaining such cover in the future from another insurer, since the names of applicants who for 'medical reasons' have been rejected, or are offered cover only at a higher premium, are recorded on a computer database by the insurance industry.

The question of whether to take out life assurance can arise for various reasons. An individual may be considering a house purchase, and the financial institution approached for a mortgage may require life assurance with respect to loans over a certain limit, or may be promoting the idea of an endowment mortgage. An employee may be offered a life assurance scheme at work. An individual may be considering appropriate plans for the financial security of a dependant in the event of death.

In each case, it is important to weigh up the necessity of seeking life assurance cover. It may be that the expense and potential difficulties which may be encountered in applying for such cover may not be worthwhile unless the proposed beneficiary under the policy is someone whose security cannot be provided for in any other way. As regards mortgages, in particular, it may well be that there is no particularly strong need for life assurance cover. A straight repayment mortgage – that involves no insurance cover but where the house purchaser gradually pays off the principal as well as making interest payments – may be a suitable alternative to an endowment mortgage, and may even work out cheaper. This may especially be so where there is no particular need for the mortgage to be paid off in its entirety in the event of the purchaser's death.

Financial institutions are often keen to promote an endowment policy because the sale of such policies earns them a commission. In other cases, a particular bank or building society may have a requirement for insurance cover with respect to mortgage loans over a certain amount. Sometimes, this may not be in the form of an endowment policy, but a 'mortgage protection policy', which is a form of life assurance attached to a straight repayment mortgage and which will pay off as much of the mortgage as remains outstanding upon the death of the insured. In any event, if individuals decide that they do not wish to seek life assurance with respect to an intended mortgage, it is essential to shop around. Some financial institutions may be willing to provide a mortgage without such insurance cover.

2   The applicant's duty of full disclosure

Once an individual has decided to proceed with an application for life assurance (called a 'proposal') it is important to understand the duty of full disclosure which applies. Under English law, contract of insurance falls into the exceptional category of 'contracts of utmost good faith'. This means that the proposer (i.e., the applicant) and the insurance company are under the obligation to disclose to each other all 'material facts' which the other party should take into account before entering into the agreement. For these purposes 'material facts' means any information which a 'prudent insurer' would want to know in order to decide whether or not to accept the proposal in question and undertake the insurance risk.

Many proposal forms ask, at the end of a whole series of specific questions, whether there are any other particular facts that affect the proposer's health and which should be drawn to the insurer's attention. As a matter of strict law, any failure to reveal 'material facts' is a breach of the duty of utmost good faith, and therefore constitutes material non-disclosure. In practice, however, as regards insurance purchased by individuals resident in the United Kingdom, the British insurance companies have adopted a code of practice whereby they will take into account a failure to disclose only matters within the knowledge of the proposer and which the proposer could reasonably be expected to disclose. Where specific questions are asked, however, it does not matter if the proposer feels that the questions are irrelevant or unfair. It is a safe assumption that a failure to answer honestly will be regarded as 'material non-disclosure'.

The ultimate penalty against a proposer who fails to reveal or is otherwise dishonest relating to material facts is a severe one. In such a case, the insurance company may at any time void the contract of insurance if this was a matter which influenced the company in its decision to grant insurance cover. This means that it can refuse to pay out any benefits under the policy and can indeed seek a refund of any benefits already paid out. In cases where it can show that material facts have been wilfully or fraudulently withheld, the insurance company is also entitled to keep the insurance premiums which have been paid to date.

A proposer who responds dishonestly to questions arising during any of the stages of the application process described below, therefore, risks obtaining, and paying substantial premiums towards, a life assurance policy which will ultimately prove worthless.

3   The initial proposal form

The initial proposal form is used as an extremely important screening device by the insurance company. Many proposals are accepted on the basis of the answers given to the questions on that form alone. Many of the important questions relate to the proposer's previous medical history. There is no standard format, but questions may be asked, for example, about all contacts with a doctor over the previous five years, or about any history of sexually-transmitted diseases. In the HIV-related context, the basic information given regarding age and marital status may affect the insurer's decision on whether to seek a medical report from the proposer's general practitioner (see section 5 below).

Until now virtually all proposal forms asked whether the proposer has had an 'AIDS test' (i.e., an HIV-antibody test) or counselling about AIDS. The reference to counselling was probably intended to cover the proposer who had considered taking an HIV test and therefore received pre-test counselling before taking a decision not to proceed with a test.

In April 1991 the ABI issued a Statement of Practice declaring that the fact of having had an HIV test would not 'of itself' lead to the rejection of a proposal or the imposition of special terms. That decision depended on the explanation given for taking the test and the response to further enquiries. For example, if the test had been taken in the context of giving blood or routine ante-natal screening, it was disregarded. But if it had been sought at the proposer's own initiative, the insurer's reaction was unpredictable. The proposer was almost certain to be sent a supplementary questionnaire, as described in the next section, and a report might be sought from the proposer's general practitioner (section 5 below).

However, the problem over previous 'negative' HIV-antibody tests should be largely resolved. In July 1994 the ABI issued a new Statement of Practice that replaces its earlier code and states:

Insurance companies will no longer ask about negative results to HIV tests or counselling. They will continue to assess risks and must ask clear questions on matters material to the risk. Proposers should answer all questions on the form to the best of their knowledge.

The accompanying guidance suggested the following as a revised question for proposal forms:

Have you tested positive for HIV/AIDS or Hepatitis B or C, or have you been tested/treated for other sexually transmitted diseases or are you awaiting the results of such a test?

The suggested formulation seems cumbersome and it may be that individual life assurance companies will instead choose to ask several shorter questions. But no one should now have to disclose the fact that they have previously had a negative HIV-antibody test. However, it is important to note that the insurers will continue to use the fact of previous testing for *other* sexually-transmitted diseases as an indication of a 'high risk' lifestyle. This should be borne in mind if one is offered such tests in conjunction with an HIV-antibody test.

If the proposer had tested HIV-antibody-positive, the insurance company will certainly reject the proposal. Although the French government has arranged with French assurance companies a scheme whereby life assurance companies provide short-term insurance cover to people who are HIV-antibody-positive, there is no similar arrangement in the United Kingdom.

Another question that is almost standard on proposal forms is whether any previous application of life assurance from the proposer was rejected or accepted only on special terms. The implications of that are discussed in section 7 below.

4   Supplementary questionnaires

Since 1987 the British life assurance companies have been using a supplementary AIDS-related questionnaire. The decision as to which proposers should be sent this questionnaire is a matter for individual companies. Most companies have guidelines whereby the questionnaire is sent to proposers applying for cover above a certain threshold, varying according to the proposer's sex and marital status. In addition, a supplementary questionnaire is likely to be sent to anyone whose answers on the initial proposal form aroused the insurer's concerns. This may well include, for example, cases where a proposer had previously had a test for sexually-transmitted diseases other than HIV.

The standard form of supplementary questionnaire asks whether the proposer belongs to one of the following 'AIDS high risk groups':

(a) homosexual men
(b) bisexual men
(c) intravenous (i.v.) drug users
(d) haemophiliacs
(e) sexual partners of any of the above

In 1992/3, again at the suggestion of the ABI, many insurance companies introduced expanded questionnaires that also ask whether the proposer has been resident abroad (and where), and whether the proposer has received blood products outside the United Kingdom.

A proposer may be rejected at this stage if the insurer believes that there has been a lack of frankness in the responses given, or considers that the questions are unsatisfactory in some other way. The insurer has complete discretion to draw its own conclusions regarding the information gathered and is unlikely to give an explicit explanation for rejection of the proposal. If instead the insurer imposes an extra premium, this fact should be drawn to the attention of the proposer, but the insurer is not obliged to state the reason for the surcharge.

Although in the late 1980s some companies rejected outright life assurance proposals from individuals identified as homosexual males, such automatic rejection is now less likely to occur. However, a proposer who states that he is homosexual will almost invariably be required to submit to HIV-antibody testing. He is also likely to be charged a considerably higher premium if eventually successful in his application.

To determine that premium, some companies have been using a further supplementary questionnaire that asks personal questions regarding the proposer's sexual conduct and lifestyle. These questions are likely to include: whether the proposer is currently in a steady relationship with one partner, and for how long that has lasted; and how many sexual partners the proposer has had over the last x years. Some forms also ask whether the proposer always engages in 'safe sex'. Opinions differ in the insurance industry regarding these 'second' supplementary questionnaires. Some life underwriters regard them as valueless because the accuracy of the answers is impossible to verify. It is not at all clear how, or whether, the responses given are in fact generally used as a factor in determining premiums. It may be that such questionnaires are used by some companies more to deter those whom they do not wish to insure from proceeding further with the insurance application.

Curiously, disclosure by a male proposer that he is bisexual is still likely to lead to automatic rejection, at least by some life assurance companies. Perhaps this is on the basis that by definition there is a greater likelihood of a bisexual male having multiple partners. Disclosure of intravenous drug use is similarly likely to lead to automatic rejection. Haemophiliacs are not likely to be rejected outright but will certainly be required to submit to the medical examination and HIV-antibody testing procedures referred to below.

5 General practitioner's report

The main proposal form generally asks for the name of the proposer's general practitioner (GP), and for consent to the provision of information by the GP to the insurance company. If the proposer has had particular treatment by other doctors, request for consent to a report from them may also be sought.

If they are contacted by the insurance company, GPs will be asked to provide what is called a Private Medical Attendant's Report (PMA Report). This is usually in the form of a questionnaire to the doctor but it is important to note that the questions asked are not necessarily restricted to medical questions. GPs may be asked to express an opinion as to the proposer's lifestyle, sexual orientation, etc. Many GPs refuse to answer such questions and it is the policy of the British Medical Association that doctors should not be put in the position of providing such information about their patients. Much, however, depends on the attitude of the particular GP. An individual cannot be sure that a doctor will not tell a life assurance company that he is gay or in another 'high risk group'. It may therefore be sensible not to volunteer information about such areas of one's life to one's GP unless directly relevant to medical diagnosis or treatment.

Under the Access to Medical Reports Act 1988, an individual has the right to see his or her own doctor's medical report prepared for an insurance company before it is sent. Generally this is accomplished by the insurer asking if the proposer wants such access to the report. If the proposer requests this, the insurer must notify the doctor accordingly *and the proposer must then contact the doctor within twenty-one days to make arrangements to review the report.* Alternatively the proposer may apply directly to the doctor for access to the report without first notifying the insurance company, but such application must be in writing and it is, again, necessary to make arrangements within twenty-one days to review the report. It is always a good idea to notify the doctor straight away in writing when access to any report is desired, even when the insurer itself has been notified and is under an obligation to tell the doctor.

This legislation gives patients various additional rights with respect to such reports. They can make a written request to their doctor to alter the report if it is incorrect or misleading. If the doctor refuses, they can then demand that their own statement be attached to the report. Finally, they can refuse to consent to the report being sent at all, in which case the doctor is prohibited from supplying it to the insurer. In such a case, however, insurance cover is likely to be refused unless the proposer immediately withdraws that proposal before the refusal can be made. The serious effects of receiving such a refusal with respect to future attempts to obtain life assurance are described in section 7 below.

Finally, the proposer has a continuing right to request a copy of the PMA Report from the doctor. Although it is obviously preferable to see a copy of the report in advance, that right can still be useful where an insurer has imposed a higher premium or rejected the proposal altogether and the individual wants to see if there is a medical explanation for this.

6   Medical examinations and HIV-antibody testing

A further form of medical scrutiny used by insurers is to ask the proposer to undergo a medical examination. That is routinely done when a proposer seeks a high level of insurance cover or has revealed particular health problems. It will probably also be done even at much lower levels of cover if the insurer suspects or knows (e.g., as a result of the answers to the supplementary questionnaire) that the proposer will almost certainly be asked to take an HIV-antibody test. Some insurance companies ask proposers to attend their GPs for such examination and testing or have arrangements with hospital genito-urinary clinics for the conduct of HIV tests on their behalf. The more common practice, however, is to ask proposers to attend the insurance company's own nominated doctor.

Four points should be borne in mind about such insurance-related examinations and tests:

(a) The protection afforded by the Access to Medical Reports Act 1988 only applies to reports prepared by the proposer's own doctor. Therefore there is no right to see the report of the insurance company's nominated doctor.
(b) An insurance company's doctor is likely to ask explicit questions about the proposer's lifestyle.
(c) If any specific HIV-antibody test is required, the proposer is specifically asked to consent to this in writing. If he or she refuses to agree to a test, the insurance proposal will automatically be rejected.
(d) Even if they consent to an HIV-antibody test and the result is negative, some proposers will none the less be offered cover only at an increased premium as described in the following section.

7 Rejection of the proposal or the imposition of 'special terms'

The above description of the life assurance application process should make clear that, in cases where the proposer may be considered by the insurer to be in a 'high risk group', he or she faces numerous points during the procedure when the proposal may be rejected. For example, a proposal will almost certainly be rejected in cases where:

- The proposer has had a positive HIV-antibody test result prior to, or during the course of, the application procedure.
- The proposer has a history of frequent sexually-transmitted disease in recent times.
- The proposer is an i.v. drug user.
- The insurer suspects that the proposer is not responding frankly to questions posed.
- Information obtained from supplementary questionnaires, a GP or elsewhere leads the insurer to believe that the proposer is 'promiscuous'.
- The proposer refuses to fill out a supplementary questionnaire or to be examined by a doctor or to submit to an HIV-antibody test.

The insurer is under no obligation to explain the reasons for rejecting a life assurance proposal and is unlikely to do so. *Rejection by one company makes it much harder to obtain life cover elsewhere.* The individual will be obliged to disclose on all future life assurance proposal forms that he or she has been previously refused cover by another insurer. Furthermore, the British insurance industry maintains a centralised computer record listing of all individuals who have been refused life cover for 'health reasons'. This record is called the 'Impaired Lives Registry'.

It is, therefore, most important that an application which is going to be refused either should not be made in the first instance or, once made, should be formally withdrawn as soon as it becomes apparent that a refusal is likely. This should be done, for example, if a request for an HIV-antibody test is made and the proposer does not wish to have such a test. Any such formal withdrawal should be in writing and should state that the proposer wishes to withdraw the application and that the insurer should proceed no further with it. No explanation or reason for withdrawal need be given.

Where the insurance company has decided that the proposer belongs to a 'high risk group' it may reject the proposal outright. In cases where such a proposer has tested negative in the HIV-antibody test, the insurance company may decide to offer cover but probably only at a higher than ordinary premium. This is referred to as 'acceptance on special terms'. In the case of term assurance, the premiums charged can be as much as three times the normal rate.

In such a case the insurer, agent or financial intermediary will write to the proposer setting out the terms and the proposer must decide whether or not to accept them. It should be noted that, if any proposal is then made to another company, the proposer will be obliged to say that there has previously been an offer of coverage 'on special terms' and this will lead to extra scrutiny of the proposal.

Furthermore, acceptance on special terms is also something that may be entered on the Impaired Lives Registry (even if the proposer does not go ahead with the insurance). As with rejection, such an entry should only be made where this was 'on medical grounds'. In a number of instances, however, entries have erroneously been made on the Registry for individuals who were charged higher premiums only because they were homosexual.

If the proposer decides to accept the terms of cover, he or she should write back to say so. Under insurance law, the contract is completed when the first premium has been paid to the insurers and accepted by them. A policy acceptance letter or policy document will then be issued and sent to the proposer.

Selling or surrendering a life policy

A life assurance policy is a valuable asset, at least after the first few years during which the premiums largely go to the administration costs of setting up the policy. Unlike, for example, household or motor insurance, an individual life assurance policy is usually not a one-year contract which the insurer can refuse to renew or renew only on different terms. However much the health of the policy-holder changes, he or she can continue the policy by paying regular premiums, the rate of which is generally fixed once and for all at the time when the policy is taken out. Therefore, although a person with AIDS or who is found to be HIV-antibody-positive at the time of applying will be unable to obtain life assurance, if a policy-holder contracts HIV and develops HIV disease after the policy is taken out, the insurance remains fully effective (unless, of course, the policy can be avoided on some other grounds such as material non-disclosure – see section 2 above).

This means that it is very important to keep up payment of the regular premiums. If the policy-holder ceases payment, the insurer may have the right, sometimes after a short period (this will depend on the exact policy terms), to terminate the continuing insurance contract. In any event, if the policy-holder interrupts payment and later wants to recommence, the insurer will ask for a 'declaration of continued good health', usually by the completion of a short form. If by then the individual cannot confirm continued good health, the insurer will not continue the policy. If the policy does not lapse altogether, it will be treated, in the jargon of the insurance world, as 'paid up'. This means that the monies paid in will remain in the policy (building up through interest and possibly bonuses) but the amount of life cover will be reduced to reflect only the premiums paid to that date.

But what if the policy-holder can no longer afford the premium payments? For example, ill health may have led to the loss of employment or increasing debts. If the need is only for an immediate capital payment, it may be possible to borrow against the policy from the insurance company on better terms than could be obtained from a bank. That option, however, involves continuing to pay regular premiums, the very thing that may have become difficult or impossible. Another option is to cash in the policy with the insurer. This is known as a 'surrender' of the policy, for which the insurance company will pay the 'surrender value'. The insurer can be asked to quote the surrender value of an existing policy at any stage (although in the first few years of a policy it may be negligible because of the start-up costs). Depending on the terms of the contract, if the policy-holder stops paying the premiums that may be treated by the insurer as an automatic surrender of the policy.

In recent years some alternatives to surrender have developed as ways in which the policy-holder may be able to realise a capital sum from a fully paid up policy. Auctioning the policy may be one possibility. Foster and Cranfield are a well-established auction house that specialise in the sale of life policies and are much used by banks and building societies that have taken an assignment of a life assurance policy as security for a mortgage loan that is in default. There are significant limitations on the forms of policy that will be accepted for such a sale. It must be a 'with profits endowment' or 'whole of life' policy. It usually has to be over ten years old or have run more than a quarter of the term. In general it must be with one of the leading companies. If the policy meets such requirements, however, the amount raised may be 25–30 per cent more than the surrender value.

On an auction sale, the purchaser takes over the obligations to pay the premiums and will receive payment from the insurance company on the policy's maturity. Over the last few years a number of dealers in life assurance policies have been established who will themselves purchase a policy for resale or act as agent for the policy-holder in finding a buyer. They act as market-makers, since such 'second-hand' policies are now being purchased as investments. These dealers are regulated under the Financial Services Act 1986 and in 1992 set up their own Association of Policy Market Makers. The requirements for a policy that such dealers will accept are similar to those of the auctioneers. As of late 1993, only one dealer, Life Benefit Resources Ltd, had entered this market specialising in 'impaired lives', dealing with people having a fatal illness who can produce medical evidence that their life expectancy is limited (less than two years is the current requirement). On that basis, the sum received for the policy may be higher and, contrary to ordinary practice, a 'term policy' (i.e., a policy that pays out only in the event of death within a specified period) may also be sold.

This market is sophisticated and developing. The available options vary and the requirements may change. If the holder of a life assurance policy wants or needs to stop paying premiums and wishes to obtain access to the capital, it is important to consult an independent financial adviser with experience in this field. One should ensure that the adviser is regulated by the Personal Investment Authority, the professional regulatory body, although even among PIA members this is a specialised area.

THE INSURANCE OMBUDSMAN

The Insurance Ombudsman Bureau was set up in 1981 as part of the effort by the British insurance industry to resist statutory control of the terms and conduct of insurance companies. Although it is financed by the insurance companies, their representatives are only a minority on the Bureau's controlling council and the Ombudsman has established a firm tradition of independence.

The Ombudsman only handles complaints regarding insurance by or for the benefit of individuals but this would probably extend, for example, to a company's health insurance scheme for its employees. Within those terms, the Ombudsman has a broad jurisdiction to investigate, request information and make recommendations and awards that are binding on the insurance company involved. That includes an award of compensation, binding up to a ceiling of £100,000 (or £20,000 p.a. in respect of a PHI policy). The Bureau is currently resolving over 4,000 complaints a year.

The Ombudsman's terms of reference also exclude matters of actuarial policy. That certainly covers the calculation of paid up and surrender values and, in the context of HIV and AIDS, may also prevent the Ombudsman considering the level of special terms imposed on homosexual men. But any adverse decision on a proposal or any maladministration, including the handling of an HIV-antibody test requested by an insurance company or a case where unreasonable assumptions have been drawn from the answers to a supplementary questionnaire, can be assessed by the Ombudsman according to a broad concept of 'general principles of good insurance or marketing practice'. If a life assurance company departed from the ABI Statement of Practice (referred to in section 3 of the checklist above [p.99]) and, for example, continued to ask about previous negative HIV tests there seems little doubt that the Ombudsman could intervene. As well as resolving the individual complaint, the Ombudsman publishes details of the case – but not the names of the individual concerned – in his annual report, which brings the benefit of publicity as a sanction exposing bad practice.

Any person wishing to make a complaint must first bring the matter to the attention of senior management within the insurance company, usually by writing to the chief executive. A complaint must then be made to the Insurance Ombudsman within six months of receiving the company's response.

SUMMARY OF PRACTICAL ADVICE

This chapter has reviewed some of the main effects which the emergence of AIDS has had on the approach taken by the insurance industry in the United Kingdom. The following is a summary of the practical advice that might be given to an individual who has or is seeking insurance:

Individuals who obtained health or life insurance cover prior to the introduction of the insurance industry practices outlined above would do well to maintain such cover. They should renew it promptly and avoid doing anything – such as increasing cover or otherwise seeking a change of terms – which would make them susceptible to accepting new terms imposed by the insurers, such as an AIDS exclusion clause, intrusive re-application procedures, etc. The insured should examine the terms of renewal carefully and, if in doubt, consult an independent financial adviser who is regulated by the Personal Investment Authority. Following upon this advice, an old endowment policy ought not to be surrendered when a mortgage is paid off, since it can be applied towards the security of any subsequent mortgage loan.

If the premium payments on an existing life assurance policy cannot be kept up, the policy-holder can, with the consent of the insurer, make the policy 'paid up'. It will then still pay out a sum based on the accrued premiums in the event of death. If, however, the policy-holder wants to raise immediate capital from the policy, an independent financial adviser should be consulted to explore the possibility of a sale of the policy by auction or on the 'second-hand' market, which may raise considerably more than is offered by the insurance company for surrender of the policy.

The terms of proposed new health or life policies should be examined carefully. If the terms are not included with the proposal form, but are sent out only when the proposal is accepted, there will be a period in which the insured can cancel at no cost. If the terms seem to exclude HIV-related sickness, incapacity or death, a decision needs to be taken whether this is acceptable given the particular needs of the proposer seeking the insurance. Such an AIDS exclusion clause is unlikely in a British life assurance policy, but if it is one of the terms then that policy may not prove to be acceptable security for a mortgage loan.

An individual who may for some reason face difficulties in obtaining life assurance should consider, before applying, whether it is necessary at all. In particular, in the context of seeking a mortgage, a straight repayment mortgage may be obtainable without any insurance cover whatsoever. It is best to shop around for favourable life assurance and/or mortgage terms and an independent financial adviser should be able to help. The adviser should be a member of FIMBRA, the professional regulatory body.

An individual who has been tested HIV-antibody-positive will not get life assurance and should not apply for it.

An individual who has had a test for another sexually-transmitted disease (STD) such as syphilis or gonorrhoea (but not an HIV-antibody test or a test for Hepatitis B or C), will probably be asked to disclose this on the proposal form. Even if the result was negative, he or she will be treated with some suspicion by the life assurance company unless this can be explained as taken in 'routine' circumstances (e.g., as part of antenatal screening or on making a blood donation). That may well apply in the case of syphilis, although people are often unaware that a blood test includes screening for syphilis and so obviously cannot be expected to disclose this to an insurance company (see section 2 above). But if the individual had specifically requested a test for such other STDs, he or she is likely to be regarded as a potential member of a 'high risk group'. This will lead to additional enquiries and will almost certainly delay the processing of the life assurance proposal.

An individual whom the life assurance company believes to be homosexual or a member of another 'high risk group' will be required to take an HIV-antibody test as part of the application process, if the company is prepared to offer life cover at all. Such individuals should always seek counselling before agreeing to undergo this test. In the event that such individuals do agree to be tested and obtain a negative result, they should get life assurance, but in the case of homosexual proposers it is virtually certain that any policies offered will be at significantly inflated premiums.

While an individual applying for insurance is under a duty to answer any questions put by the insurance company truthfully and completely, there is no need to volunteer information which might be interpreted to indicate that the individual is in a 'high risk group'.

An individual should also not volunteer facts about lifestyle to his or her GP unless they are directly relevant to diagnosis or treatment. In the event that an individual's doctor is asked to prepare a report to an insurance company, the individual has the legal right to see that report before it is sent and should take appropriate steps to exercise that right if there is any cause for concern.

It is important to avoid getting into the position of having a proposal for life assurance refused, as that will prejudice future applications for life cover. If an individual does not wish to proceed with the proposal, he or she should withdraw it in writing and instruct the insurer not to take it any further. This should be done, for example, if the insurer requests that the proposer submit to a medical examination or HIV-antibody testing and the proposer does not wish to do so.

If applying for life assurance in connection with a mortgage, an individual should be conscious of possible delays and should never exchange contracts until the life assurance application has been accepted.

Where an individual feels that an insurance company has behaved unreasonably on a matter that does not concern actuarial calculations, a complaint to the Insurance Ombudsman can be considered. Before such a complaint can be lodged, the matter must be raised in writing with the chief executive of the insurance company.

SOME CONSIDERATIONS OF POLICY

This chapter, like this book as a whole, has attempted to provide a straightforward guide to the effects which the emergence of HIV and AIDS has had on a particular area related to the law. The tone therefore has been descriptive rather than critical. It would, however, be inappropriate to conclude without some comment on the policies and attitudes of insurers in the United Kingdom which have led to the procedures described above.

Prior HIV test

It is understandable that an insurance company receiving a proposal for health or life assurance wishes to know if the proposer has tested HIV-antibody-positive. Being infected with HIV is a medical condition and, as with other medical conditions about which the insurer may enquire, it has an obvious effect on the likely need for future medical care (in the case of health insurance) or on life expectancy in actuarial terms (relevant for life assurance).

This same reasoning cannot, however, apply to a previous test result that was negative. There was never any statistical or other evidence that indicates that people who have sought an HIV-antibody test and tested negative are more likely to contract HIV in the future. That the British life assurance industry should none the less have persisted in including this question in proposal forms for seven years was a disturbing feature of its approach to HIV and AIDS. The barely-concealed assumptions behind this question were that those who asked for a test must have been worried about AIDS/HIV, that they therefore probably have a 'risky' or promiscuous lifestyle and, accordingly, that although they tested negative they are more at risk in the future. Not only was that reasoning mistaken, as it overlooked the myriad reasons that led individuals to seek a test and the educational process that the attendant counselling involves, but it also had the effect of putting people off having an HIV antibody test. A national survey published by the Department of Health in 1991 concluded that thousands if not tens of thousands of people are deterred from coming forward for testing by the life assurance questions. Although this is a very small proportion of the total population, the survey concluded that it constituted a much higher proportion of those who might otherwise seek a test.

As efforts at persuasion by Health Ministers and influential outsiders proved unsuccessful, The Terrence Higgins Trust finally drafted legislation that would have prohibited this practice. Faced with a Private Member's Bill, that would have been introduced at the start of the 1994/5 session of Parliament and was attracting increasing support, the ABI prudently backed down and announced the change of practice described above. The insurance industry explained the change on the basis that HIV testing had become more commonplace whereas payouts by insurers for AIDS-related deaths had been less than anticipated.

The use of HIV tests by insurance companies

That an insurance company can itself request a proposer to take an HIV-antibody test has been less controversial but it is not without problems. Tests are likely to be required if the amount of coverage sought is above a certain limit or if the applicant is believed for whatever reason to be a member of a 'high risk group'. The result may well be that an individual who needs life assurance is compelled to take a test which he or she does not desire, which may create much anxiety and which, at worst, may profoundly traumatise and stigmatise. There is at least one documented case of an American soldier committing suicide after a positive result from a compulsory test.

At the same time, insurers have traditionally asked proposers seeking a high level of cover or whose medical history suggests any particular risk to attend for a medical examination. They point out that they are treating infection with HIV like any other serious medical condition that they need to investigate.

Whether insurers ought to have complete discretion to impose a requirement of an HIV-antibody test as a condition for granting life assurance is a complex question. So long as such tests are required, there should be clear criteria for deciding when the test may be administered, the standards for testing, the provision of adequate counselling both before and after the test and strict confidentiality. After a few unfortunate lapses, the attitude of the industry to the provision of results and the protection of confidentiality has improved in recent years. Concern remains, however, that the standard of counselling given to a proposer who has to decide whether or not to take a test is often woefully inadequate. The British Medical Association has played a useful role in attempting to enforce a requirement that adequate counselling must be provided in connection with such testing by the insurance industry.

Reinforcement of stereotypes and discrimination against gay men

Public health education about HIV and AIDS in Britain, although criticised in some respects, appears to have been relatively successful. Certainly the initial predictions regarding the rapidly multiplying spread of HIV across the population have fortunately not been fulfilled. The essential message of the health education campaigns has been that HIV spreads through 'unsafe' or 'high risk' behaviour and is not restricted to any particular group in society.

The approach of life insurers has undermined that message. The whole thrust of their approach to AIDS has been expressly in terms of 'high risk groups' focusing specially on sexual orientation. The initial proposal form, the supplementary questionnaire and doctors' reports are all used to determine whether the proposer is a gay male and, if so, either to deprive him of insurance cover altogether or to offer it at substantially inflated rates, regardless of whether there is any indication that he is at real risk of contracting HIV.

Indeed gay males today are more likely than any other group to recognise the risk of exposure to HIV and to take steps to avoid it, precisely because their community has been so seriously affected. Fortunately, a very large majority of the gay males in the United Kingdom have not contracted HIV, and studies have indicated that the spread of the virus within the gay population has been significantly curtailed through the adoption of safer sex practices.

The AIDS Working Party of the Institute of Actuaries, in its Bulletin No. 5 (1991), called for a change in emphasis of life underwriting from sexual orientation to sexual behaviour. The introduction by some insurance companies of a second supplementary questionnaire that asks true lifestyle questions may be an attempt to make an individual assessment although so far these questionnaires are used only for gay proposers.

Moreover, the very substantial additional premiums imposed on gay males do not appear to be based on any actuarial calculations of risk. In some cases, indeed, it seems that the premium is pegged at such a high level to deter the proposer from taking out a policy at all.

It is now opportune for the Institute of Actuaries' AIDS Working Party to look at this issue, with a view to consideration of the relative risk of spread of HIV among uninfected homosexual men compared to heterosexual men.

As with its previous approach to negative HIV-antibody tests, the practice of the British insurers contrasts with that in a number of other countries where similar initiatives by insurance companies have been closely monitored and controlled by independent regulatory authorities. In the United States, the umbrella organisation bringing together all state insurance regulators has produced guidelines calling for the complete elimination of discrimination on the ground of sexual orientation and this has been implemented in the laws of the majority of states. Such discrimination is also forbidden in Canada and Australia.

This chapter began by sketching the very real problems faced by the insurance industry upon the emergence and spread of HIV. These difficulties must be acknowledged as substantial and challenging.

The approach which the British insurance industry has adopted in response to those difficulties has been described above. Unfortunately, this approach has been for the most part misconceived, arbitrary and discriminatory. The various methods were developed at a time when forecasts predicting a very rapid spread of HIV in the United Kingdom caused much alarm to British insurers. They have been very reluctant to reconsider how far those methods are proportionate, effective or fair in the light of the experience with the epidemic in the past few years. Moreover, the British insurance industry has been unwilling to compare its approach with the procedures adopted by the insurance industry in other western countries or to have regard to the effect of its approach on public attitudes and education concerning HIV and AIDS. Against this history, it would be unduly optimistic to regard the ABI's 1994 Statement of Practice as a turning point. That may prove to have been no more than a defensive response by the insurance industry to a specific legislative threat, but it may, perhaps, help to encourage a more sensitive and sophisticated approach to the other insurance issues presented by HIV.

In the past, when it was argued that the insurance industry in the United Kingdom should be subjected to greater independent regulation – as is the case in many other countries – the industry replied that it can be counted on to regulate itself responsibly and for the common good. So far, at least, in confronting the problems posed by HIV, the record of the British insurance industry has been distinctly unimpressive.

FURTHER READING

Association of British Insurers, *Statement of Long-Term Insurance Practice* (2nd edn, January 1986).

Association of British Insurers, *Statement of Practice – Underwriting Life Insurance for HIV/AIDS* (July 1994).

Barton, S. and Roth, P., 'Life insurance and HIV antibody testing', *British Medical Journal*, Vol. 305: 902 (1992).

Department of Health, *AIDS and Life Insurance* (HMSO, 1991).

Slade, L., 'AIDS – insurance practice in the making', *Journal of Society of Fellows of the Chartered Insurance Institute*, Vol. 6: 2 (1992).

The Terrence Higgins Trust, *Mortgages and Life Assurance* (4th edn, 1993).

USEFUL ADDRESSES

The Personal Investment Authority, Hertsmere House, Hertsmere Road, LONDON E14 4AB

The Insurance Ombudsman Bureau, City Gate One, 135 Park Street, LONDON SE1 9EA

Chapter 7

Medico-legal aspects of HIV infection and disease

The late Colin A. M. E. d'Eça
(revised and updated by Timothy Costello)

ASPECTS OF TREATMENT AND CONSENT

Requirement for consent

The courts have recognised the fundamental right of all adults to have control over their bodily integrity and protect that right through the civil and criminal law.

The threat of unlawful physical force against the person (assault) or the application of that force (battery) can give rise to a legal action in the courts for damages unless the touching is negligible. All medical treatment, including examination and diagnostic procedures, is a potential battery in the absence of consent, necessity or statutory sanction. Doctors also owe a duty of care to their patients and will be liable for negligence if they do not properly obtain their patients' consent to medical treatment. A doctor who treats a patient without consent may also be subject to professional disciplinary proceedings before the General Medical Council, the body which has statutory responsibility for regulating the practice of medicine.

The law recognises, however, that some patients are incapable of giving consent to medical treatment. The position concerning the treatment of people aged under 18 is complex and is dealt with in more detail in Chapter 1. No one can give consent to medical treatment on behalf of a person who is 18 or more years old and is incapable of making such a decision. For the medical treatment of such a person to be lawful there must either be statutory sanction (for example, under the mental health legislation) or the treatment must be justified under the principle of necessity discussed next.

Necessity

If the patient is incapable of giving consent and there is no one else able to consent on the patient's behalf, a doctor is permitted to carry out such treatment as

- is in the patient's best interest and
- cannot be delayed until the patient is able to consent.

It is sometimes thought that when a patient is temporarily unconscious and unable to consent, a doctor can give treatment without consent. This would only be lawful if the proposed treatment is in the patient's best interest and any delay, in order to await consent, would be harmful to the patient. The application of this exception to the requirement for consent is very limited. In most cases HIV-anti-body testing is not necessary for immediate medical treatment and therefore any delay does not harm the patient.

Implied consent

In English law consent may be either expressed or implied. However, the limits are not closed. Implied consent may arise from the nature of the conduct of the parties; where a patient requests treatment from a doctor and does not question the doctor's actions, it will be implied that the patient has consented to all the subsequent procedures even if unaware of the extent of those procedures. However, it is clear that the patient must be aware not only of the physical aspects of the treatment but also of its nature and quality.

What amounts to consent

There is much discussion amongst the medical profession and the general public to the effect that informed consent is the only valid consent. English law rejects the concept of informed consent. The doctrine requires that the patient shall have been informed of all material factors which might influence the patient's decision to consent to the treatment. It is subject to a therapeutic privilege, namely, the exercise of clinical judgment that revelation of certain facts might be prejudicial to the patient. Only if the consent is obtained by fraud or misrepresentation as to the nature of what is to be done, can it be said that an apparent consent is not a true consent. Failure to inform the patient of substantial factors which may influence the giving of consent may also vitiate consent.

HIV-antibody testing

HIV-antibody testing usually relies on the touching of the subject to remove a sample of blood. It is the act of taking the blood without consent, not the actual testing, which will normally give rise to the action for battery. This is an important distinction as will be seen below.

A person's remedy in law for any testing, where the person actually, or by implication, consented to the taking of the blood, lies in an action for negligence and not battery. There remains the possibility of arguing that there is no consent where the nature and quality of the physical withdrawal of blood, namely its purpose, was not understood by the patient. The requirement for pre-test counsel-ling makes it more likely that such an argument would succeed.

In an action for trespass to the person, once the unlawful touching is proved, damages may be recoverable without establishing anything else. However, in an action for negligence, damages will only be awarded if harm is suffered which was foreseeable and not too remote.

How can an action in negligence be brought against a doctor for testing without consent? Part of a doctor's duty of care to the patient is to inform the patient of the nature and purpose of any proposed treatment and of the risks and implications of the treatment. The extent to which information should be given to any individual patient depends upon the circumstances and is essentially a matter of clinical judgment. A doctor is not obliged to explain the proposed treatment in detail, for example, every test which might be performed on a blood sample, nor to advise upon every risk involved in a particular treatment. If a patient asks specific questions, the extent of the explanation given is a matter of clinical judgment. The yardstick used is based upon what a responsible body of medical opinion practising in the area concerned believes should have been done in the same circumstances.

The medical profession has accepted that there should be adequate pre-test counselling. This means that an action will lie in negligence if this counselling is not performed, because although the patient may have consented to the physical action of withdrawing blood, the patient will not have appreciated the nature and quality of the action and further that the doctor will not have satisfied the duty of care owed to the patient by not giving the appropriate counselling.

The General Medical Council in 1988 issued guidelines relating to the ethical considerations of HIV infection and AIDS. These guidelines were reissued without amendment in 1991 and revised in June 1993. Doctors are expected to obtain patients' consents to investigative procedures or invasive techniques. It is stated that:

> Only in the most exceptional circumstances, where a test is imperative in order to secure the safety of persons other than the patient, and where it is not possible for the prior consent of the patient to be obtained, can testing without explicit consent be justified.

The British Medical Association at its 1988 conference adopted the following resolution:

> HIV testing should be performed only on clinical grounds and with the specific consent of the patient. There may be individual circumstances where a doctor believes that in the best interests of a particular patient it is necessary to depart from this general rule, but if the doctor does so he or she must be prepared to justify this action before the courts and the General Medical Council.

Finally, the official view of the government as expressed by the then DHSS is that:

> As a positive HIV test has serious implications, counselling of patients prior to carrying out the test is essential, and further counselling must be offered if the test proves positive. . . . Routine screening of all patients for HIV infection is not desirable.

That view is incompatible with testing without explicit consent.

In December 1990 The Royal College of Surgeons of England issued a statement on AIDS and HIV infection incorporating the following recommendation:

> If the surgeon or another member of the operating team is injured during treatment of . . . a high risk patient in whom the serological statement is not known, it is the view of the Council that the surgeon has the right to test the patient . . . whether or not the patient has previously given consent for testing.

The recommendation then goes on to state that the passage from the General Medical Council (GMC) Guidelines quoted above will apply.

It is hard to see how testing a patient without consent after an injury to a doctor can be compatible with the GMC Guidelines. Testing the patient cannot secure the safety of the person injured in the course of an operation; the most it can achieve is some measure of reassurance if the test proves negative. For it to be lawful to test without consent, the test must be in the best interests of the patient and it must be essential to perform the test before the patient is capable of consenting. Neither of these requirements will be satisfied. Given the accepted need for pre-test counselling as well, surgeons testing without consent will not be complying with the ethical requirements of practice and will expose themselves, any others concerned in the testing and any person vicariously responsible for their actions, such as the Health Authority or NHS Trust, to a legal action for damages.

In view of the general opinion of the health authorities and the medical profession, testing without explicit consent will, except in the most rare circumstances, be a breach of a duty of care and actionable in negligence. The difficulty in such an action will be proving loss which the law recognises as giving rise to a claim for damages. It is for this reason that the sanction of professional discipline is important. While proceedings in the courts may not be seen to be financially justifiable, the Guidelines issued by the General Medical Council give an indication that the Council will be prepared to discipline doctors who do not comply with them. Recent experience of the GMC has demonstrated a reluctance to apply sanctions even in the case of blatant breach.

Terminal care

Another aspect of the requirement for consent to treatment, which particularly affects those in the last stages of AIDS, is the desire of some people living with HIV disease not to undergo treatment which simply postpones their dying rather than contributing to their quality of life. So long as they remain capable of making the decision whether or not to accept a particular form of treatment, they are free to withhold consent if they wish. The problem arises when they are no longer capable of deciding for themselves. This can occur not only as a result of neurological damage caused by HIV itself but also through general infirmity.

In those circumstances normally there is no one who can give consent to medical treatment and no consent is required for treatment which falls within the necessity criteria. Furthermore, a doctor will be professionally obliged to give appropriate treatment and may be exposed to a legal claim in negligence from the patient (if the patient survives) or the patient's personal representatives after death, if treatment is withheld.

This has given rise in other jurisdictions, notably in North America, for legislation providing a regime for what are called 'living wills'. A living will is an advance direction made to a doctor describing how a patient wishes to be treated after becoming too ill to make decisions. It may be combined with a proxy, which appoints another person, perhaps a friend or relative, to be consulted or involved in medical decisions made by the patient's doctor. In the United Kingdom although the status of a living will has been clarified by a number of recent cases, it remains uncertain. A proxy has no legal effect but can help a doctor decide what is in the best interests of the patient.

Medical practitioners wish to comply with the wishes of their patients. However, if they are unaware of these wishes or if the wishes have not been clearly expressed, doctors will naturally be concerned for their own professional and legal responsibilities. For obvious reasons a doctor is unlikely to initiate a discussion of these issues but there is every reason why a patient should be advised to talk the matter over with the doctor; in this way the wishes of the patient will be clarified and communicated directly to the doctor.

If a doctor persists with treatment of a mentally incapable patient, which is otherwise completely appropriate but contrary to the wishes of the patient expressed in a living will, the doctor will not necessarily be exposed to any sanction. There seems to be no reason why an appropriately executed living will should not protect the doctor from legal action by the patient's personal representatives. It seems very unlikely that a doctor could be subject to disciplinary proceedings as a result of observing the terms of such a living will.

It is assumed in discussing this topic that the living will deals only with restriction of available treatment and not the administration of any means of hastening the death of the patient. This would amount to homicide and is a criminal offence.

Another approach which can be combined with a living will is for the patient, while still capable of making a decision to do so, to appoint an agent to take decisions about medical treatment on the patient's behalf. There seems to be nothing which prevents a person from appointing someone else as their agent to give consent to medical treatment. However, the agent's authority terminates when the principal becomes mentally incapable. This problem was solved, at least for agents appointed to deal with the principal's property by the Enduring Powers of Attorney Act 1985. However, an enduring power made under the Act cannot authorise an attorney to take decisions regarding medical treatment.

If, as seems most likely to be the case, the doctor is keen to co-operate, a living will is likely to be effective both in achieving what the patient wants and protecting the doctor from legal claims and disciplinary proceedings. It will, however, be very desirable to discuss with a doctor (preferably the doctor who is likely to attend the patient during the final illness) the terms of the living will so that the patient's wishes can be expressed as specifically as possible. A working party of The Terrence Higgins Trust Legal Services Group carried out a project on living wills with the Centre for Medical Law and Ethics of King's College, London. This culminated in the publication of a form of living will which is available from The Terrence Higgins Trust.

The doctor's obligation to treat

A doctor is not obliged to accept anyone as a patient. It is proper for a doctor who does not have the requisite expertise or has a conscientious objection to undertaking a particular course of treatment to refer someone who has been accepted as a patient to a professional colleague. It is otherwise unethical to refuse treatment or investigation of a patient, on the grounds that the patient has a condition which might expose the doctor to personal risk or to withhold treatment on the basis of a moral judgment about the patient's lifestyle. Any such refusal would constitute grounds for a charge of serious professional misconduct.

The fact that a patient is willing to undergo particular treatment does not oblige the doctor to give the treatment if the doctor exercising professional judgment considers that it is inappropriate.

MEDICAL RECORDS

Confidentiality

There is no law of privacy in the United Kingdom. Protection of a person's 'right' not to have information disclosed or published lies in the law of libel and slander or in the law of confidence. In some circumstances information is protected by statutory provision.

In the main, medical information about a person is protected by the codes of professional conduct for health care professionals including doctors and nurses. The General Medical Council rules provide:

Patients are entitled to expect that the information about themselves or others which a doctor learns during the course of a medical consultation, investigation or treatment, will remain confidential. Doctors therefore have a duty not to disclose to any third party information about an individual that they have learned in their professional capacity, directly from the patient or indirectly, except in the case discussed [later in the rules].

The exceptions concern disclosure with the consent, or in the best interests, of the patient, in compliance with a court order or other legally enforceable duty and, in very limited circumstances, where the public interest so requires. Examples of circumstances where the public interest overrides the duty of confidence include the investigation and prosecution of serious crime or where there is a current or future (but not a past and non-current) health risk to others.

The General Medical Council in its guidance on HIV infection and AIDS provides that when diagnosis has been made by a specialist and the patient, after appropriate counselling, still refuses permission for the general practitioner to be informed of the result, that request for privacy should be respected. The only exception would be when failure to disclose would put the health of the health care team at serious risk. In this case disclosure is justified on a 'need to know' basis. All people receiving such information must consider themselves to be under the same obligation of confidentiality as the doctor principally responsible for the patient's care. Occasionally the doctor may wish to disclose a diagnosis to a third party other than a health care professional. The Council think that the only grounds for this are when there is a serious and identifiable risk to a specific person, who if not so informed would be exposed to infection. A doctor may consider it a duty to ensure that any sexual partner is informed regardless of the patient's own wishes.

The provisions governing nurses, midwives and health visitors are in similar terms.

These ethical codes do not have statutory force and can be changed at any time. Breach of the codes is not something which entitles the patient to recover damages from the doctor, although it could found the basis for proceedings for serious professional misconduct.

The legal duty of confidence

The duty of confidence arises whenever information is imparted from one person to another either expressly in confidence or in circumstances where such confidence is implicit. In the case where the information passes from a patient to a health care professional, in part because of the professional rules referred to above, there will be found an implied understanding that the information will be kept in confidence. Although the duty of confidence between a health care worker and a patient arises out of the special nature of that relationship, there does not have to be a special relationship between the parties: communications between friends can be covered by the law, if circumstances so warrant.

The duty of confidence, however, is not absolute. The courts recognise a number of exceptions, namely, where the law requires disclosure, to assist in the investigation or prosecution of a serious crime, to prevent a continuing and serious threat to health of either specific identifiable persons or the public at large, where disclosure is necessary in the performance of a public or statutory duty and where it is necessary in the public interest. Upon death, the legal duty of confidence may come to an end but a doctor is generally obliged by professional rules to continue to respect the confidentiality of a deceased patient. A doctor is required to state the cause of death when certifying death, although it is unnecessary to state 'AIDS' on the part of the certificate which is reproduced in the death certificate issued by the registrar of deaths.

The public interest or health risk argument may be raised as a defence by a doctor for disclosure to third parties of a patient's HIV antibody status. This is particularly likely to succeed where the sexual partner of the patient is also a patient of the doctor and the patient is unwilling to inform the uninfected partner of a positive HIV-anti-body test result or allow the doctor to do so. If the doctor did not ensure that the sexual partner was informed, the sexual partner might have a cause of action against the doctor, especially if the sexual partner was also the doctor's patient. The General Medical Council considers that breach of confidentiality in these circumstances could be justified.

Where breach of confidence is anticipated, an injunction can be sought. In the vast majority of cases, the first thing the subject knows about the breach of confidence is that the disclosure has been made and the only remedy is damages. The courts have shown themselves very willing to preserve the confidentiality of medical records and, in particular, information relating to AIDS. In the case of X v. Y [1988] 2 AER 479, a health authority sought to restrain a national newspaper from publishing information relating to the fact that two doctors employed by the health authority were still practising although they had both been diagnosed with AIDS. The information had been obtained as a consequence of the breach of confidentiality by an employee of the health authority. The Judge said:

> Preservation of confidentiality is the only way of securing public health; otherwise doctors will be discredited as a source of education . . . I keep in the forefront of my mind the very important public interest in the freedom of the press. And I accept that there is some public interest in knowing what the defendants seek to publish . . . But in my judgment those public interests are substantially outweighed when measured against the public interest in relation to loyalty and confidentiality both generally and in relation to AIDS patients' hospital records. The records of hospital patients, particularly those suffering from this appalling condition, should, in my judgment, be as confidential as the courts can properly keep them.

The National Health Service (Venereal Diseases) Regulations 1974 (as amended)

In the area of HIV there is also some statutory protection of confidential information through the operation of the above Venereal Diseases regulations. They only apply to health authorities and to NHS Trusts, not to general practitioners or private hospitals or clinics. Health authorities are required to take all necessary steps to secure that any information capable of identifying an individual obtained by officers of the authority (or Trust) with respect to persons examined or treated for any sexually-transmitted disease shall not be disclosed except:

- for the purpose of communicating the information to a medical practitioner, or to a person employed under the direction of a medical practitioner in connection with the treatment of persons suffering from such disease or the prevention thereof; and

• for the purpose of such treatment or prevention.

Those provisions would allow disclosure to the health authority's contact tracers or a general practitioner's practice nurse. The Regulations apply to all sexually-transmitted disease; although HIV infection is not transmitted exclusively sexually, the general view is that the Regulations apply to all cases of HIV infection. The Regulations do not prevent disclosure with the consent of the patient or where the law requires disclosure.

MEDICAL RECORDS AND REPORTS

Medical records of patients under the National Health Service are not the property either of the doctor or the patient. Hospital records are under the control of the local health authority (or the hospital trust) and general practitioners' records are under the control of the relevant Family Health Services Authority. Medical records of private patients belong to the doctor concerned.

Access to medical records

Under the Data Protection Act 1984, individuals are permitted to have copies of most data about them which are maintained on computers. If the data are incorrect, the individuals may have it corrected. Medical records are included within the kinds of information covered by the Act. It has thus been possible for some time to have access to medical records held on computer and to correct inaccurate information.

The Access to Health Records Act 1990 effectively extends to medical records maintained in written form the same protection that is provided by the Data Protection Act 1984 to records held on computer.

The Act permits a patient to have access to a health record made after 31 October 1991. The doctor does not have to give access to the health record if it is considered that it might be seriously detrimental to the patient's health or to any part of a record which might give information about any other person or reveal the identity of any other person who has supplied the doctor with information about the patient. If the patient considers that any record is inaccurate, the holder of the record must either correct it or keep with it a note of the respects in which the patient considers it inaccurate. Except for the Access to Health Records Act (and the Data Protection Act) patients have no right to see or correct their records.

Medical reports

The most usual contexts in which an individual may be the subject of a medical report are life assurance and actual or possible employment. A potential life insurer or an intending employer is not entitled to obtain any medical information about the proposed insured or employee from any doctor without the consent of that person. However, if consent is withheld, the policy or employment is unlikely to proceed. In the case of those who are currently employed, the employer will only be able to call for the employee to be medically examined or for information about the employee to be disclosed by a doctor, if the contract of employment so provides. Such provisions are common.

The Access to Medical Reports Act 1988 relates to reports required for employment or insurance purposes from a doctor responsible for the clinical care of the patient; it does not cover reports from another doctor specially retained by the person requiring the report. The person requiring the report must notify the patient and give details of the patient's rights under the Act.

When giving this consent, the patient may ask to see the doctor's report before it is forwarded to the employer or insurance company. In such a case, the commissioner of the report is obliged to pass on the patient's request to the examining doctor. The patient must be informed when the report is commissioned. The doctor thus notified is obliged to let the patient see the report before sending it on to the insurance company or employer. This obligation is subject to exceptions which are similar to those under the Access to Health Records Act, unless the patient neglects to make an arrangement to see the doctor's report within twenty-one days. If the patient wants changes made to the report but the doctor disagrees, the patient may either insist that their own statement be attached to the doctor's report or may refuse to allow the report to be supplied.

SPECIFIC HIV AND AIDS LEGISLATION

There is little legislation in force specifically concerning HIV infection and disease in the United Kingdom. This in part reflects the view that the law is inappropriate to many of the issues raised. In spite of the activities of some pressure groups, the government seems to believe that the current law is adequate and gives a low political priority to the subject.

The first legislation which specifically related to AIDS was the Public Health (Infectious Diseases) Regulations 1985. These were produced in an atmosphere of near hysteria induced by ill-informed press comment at a time when medical knowledge of the causes of AIDS and the infectious nature of HIV was less advanced than it is now. It was a minimal response using what powers were available to the Secretary of State without new primary legislation, so as to stave off the calls for more draconian measures. The regulations now in force are the Public Health (Infectious Diseases) Regulations 1988.

The Regulations are made under the Public Health (Control of Disease) Act 1984. They do not make AIDS a notifiable disease but they apply sections 35 (medical examination), 37 (removal to hospital), 38 (detention in hospital), 43 (death in hospital) and 44 (isolation of the body) of the Act to AIDS. Although the Regulations are explained in some detail here, few public health experts believe they are helpful in preventing the transmission of HIV but stigmatise people with AIDS as being responsible for the spread of HIV infection.

Sections 35, 37 and 38 have common requirements for their application. In order to obtain an order applying the section concerned, the appropriate officer must make an application, which may be made without informing the person against whom the order is sought, to a magistrate who must determine whether or not to make the order.

Section 35 – medical examination

The application for an order for medical examination must be made by a medical practitioner nominated by the local authority for the district and be supported by a written certificate signed by the medical practitioner to the effect that the requirements of section 35 are satisfied.

This section applies not only to those with AIDS but to those who are HIV-infected or suspected of being so but only if it can be shown that:

* it is expedient to examine the person medically in the person's own interest or that of his family or the public generally; and
* either that the person is not under the care of a doctor or, if so, that the doctor consents.

The crucial issue is thus the question of 'interest'. Because there is at present no means either of preventing (other than by avoiding infection) or curing HIV infection and there is no cure available for HIV disease, it is difficult to argue that examination is in the interest of the person concerned or the public. The family interest is more problematical. A person having a sexual relationship with the person concerned may wish to avoid infection. Moreover, the possibility of transmission of infection from mother to child before or during birth is well known; in the case of couples where the woman is, or may become, pregnant, she may well have an even greater interest in knowing the HIV status of her male partner. However, even though it may be argued that a sexual partner has an interest, there is nothing in the legislation which permits the disclosure of the result of an examination without the consent of the person examined, so it is not an interest which can be satisfied.

Section 35 orders can be supplemented by an order under section 61 of the Act. This provides that a magistrate may issue a warrant to support the entry, if necessary by force, of an authorised officer into any premises in order to discharge the officer's duties under the Act.

Although there are penalties for failure to comply with an order for medical examination, it is notable that the legislation requires the patient to submit to treatment but there is no provision for the dispensation of consent to treatment. It is doubtful whether any doctor would proceed in the absence of consent.

Section 37 – removal to hospital

This section applies only to those who have been diagnosed as having AIDS. The magistrate before making an order on application by the local authority must be satisfied that:

- the person has AIDS;
- the person's circumstances are such that proper precautions to prevent the spread of infection cannot be or are not being taken;
- as a result there is a serious risk of infection to other people;
- there is national health service hospital accommodation available; and
- the health authority responsible for the proposed hospital of admission consents to that person's admission.

The conditions are cumulative. The implication of the section is that hospitalisation will reduce or eliminate the risk of infection. Because of the limited ways in which HIV is transmitted (see Introduction), infection can only be avoided by avoiding risk activities. It is therefore likely that, except perhaps in the case of haemorrhage, or where other large volumes of body fluids are being produced, the section will never apply.

Section 38 – detention in hospital

The local authority must show that:

- the person has AIDS;
- the person is an in-patient in hospital;
- on leaving hospital:

  - the person would not be provided with suitable lodging or accommodation to allow proper precautions to be taken to prevent the spread of infection; or
  - (the provision added by the Regulations) proper precautions will not be taken in other places to which the person might be expected to go to prevent the spread of AIDS.

The additional criterion is widely drawn and could apply to any place to which a person might go, for example, a cinema, public swimming pool, pub, club or shop, but whether the section applies is likely to be qualified by the possible activities of the person and the risk which they pose to others. Those who habitually abuse drugs administered by injection may well be caught by this provision.

It should be noted that the section refers to spreading the disease, in this case AIDS, and not the wider term 'infection' which is used in section 37.

This section has been applied once in relation to AIDS, in Manchester. The case went to appeal in the Crown Court with a High Court Judge presiding. However, because the case was dealt with by consent, no case law was created. The remarks of the Judge that the magistrate was correct in issuing the order can only be said not to be binding authority. There are grave doubts whether the person who was the subject of the order (and who was said to be explosively haemorrhaging) fell within the ambit of the section, and in particular there was no evidence that he actually had AIDS, as opposed to being HIV-antibody-positive.

Appeals

Appeals can be made against any order issued under sections 35, 37 and 38 initially to the Crown Court. Judicial review would also be available to challenge procedural errors or matters of jurisdiction.

Section 43 – removal of body of person who has died of AIDS

When a person with AIDS dies in hospital, an officer of the local authority or a doctor can certify that it is desirable, in order to prevent the spread of infection, that the body should not be removed from the hospital except for the purpose of being taken directly to a mortuary or to be cremated or buried. This section is rarely, if ever, used in respect of those who die as a result of HIV disease.

Section 44 – isolation of the body of a person who has died of AIDS

The section imposes a duty upon the person in charge or in control of the premises (for example, the hospital manager, mortician or undertaker) in which the person who has died while having a condition associated with AIDS to take such steps as are reasonably practical to prevent persons coming into contact unnecessarily with the body.

These two sections together can prohibit the body of a person who has died from AIDS lying in the home or the use of an open coffin.

The AIDS Control Act 1987 (as amended)

This Act, introduced into Parliament as a private member's bill, came into force on 15 May 1987. Essentially it provides for the collection and reporting of statistics relating to the number of people diagnosed as having AIDS, of those dying as a consequence of AIDS, of those known to be infected with HIV, the facilities and staff available for testing for HIV infection, offering counselling, treatment and other measures, in particular health education, designed to prevent the spread of HIV infection. The reports are to be drawn up by each district health authority in England and Wales and each health board in Scotland. The reports are to be produced in accordance with the requirements of the Secretary of State at least once a year. The reports are to be published.

HIV Testing Kits and Services Regulations 1992

These regulations prohibit the sale or supply of HIV-antibody testing kits to members of the public (but not to businesses). They also provide that any HIV testing kit supplied should contain a specified warning of the reliability of a positive or negative test result.

It is also a criminal offence to provide testing services other than under the direction of a registered doctor.

There are some qualifications to these offences and reference should be made to the Regulations.

The National Health Service (Charge to Overseas Visitors) (No. 2) Regulations

These Regulations impose a duty upon a health authority or board to make and recover charges for health services provided to overseas visitors.

For the purpose of the Regulations, a person is an overseas visitor if not ordinarily resident in the United Kingdom. Case law in the tax field may be relied upon where there is doubt as to residence. A person is exempt from the overseas visitors provisions if he or she:

- has been lawfully resident in the United Kingdom for the twelve months preceding the date treatment is given; or
- is an EC national; or
- is a national of a state with reciprocal health arrangements with the United Kingdom; or
- is an EC national whose need for treatment arose after arrival in the United Kingdom.

This is not a complete list of the exceptions and reference should be made to the Regulations for a complete list.

COMPLAINTS ABOUT TREATMENT OR PROFESSIONAL CONDUCT

The forum for bringing complaints relating to medical treatment varies according to the nature of the complaint, the status of the person against whom the complaint is made and the type of service involved. With the exception of damages for personal injury or death, the remedies available if the medical services concerned are shown to be at fault do not include any compensation for the patient. All that is available is the satisfaction of being vindicated and the altruistic hope that similar conduct will be less likely in the future. Against these modest benefits must be set the energy required to pursue a complaint.

Where the problem relates to a failure to provide treatment as a result of real or imagined HIV infection, rather than using the complaints procedure it may be most effective, in practice, to get in touch with the HIV officer which most health authorities have now appointed. There is a Community Health Council for each locality and assistance can be obtained free of charge with a view to obtaining treatment under the National Health Service or overcoming problems relating to such treatment and with the formal complaints procedure.

Complaints about professional conduct

Misconduct of this type may include breach of confidence, failure by a medical professional to explain or seek consent for treatment or an HIV-antibody test or failure to treat patients because they have HIV infection or disease.

If a complaint about a doctor is serious, then consideration may be given to making a formal complaint to the General Medical Council. There is no time limit for complaint to the GMC, although complaints should be made as quickly as possible. Procedure is formal and assistance should be sought from a Community Health Council.

Personal injury

Where damages are sought for personal injury or death arising out of medical treatment, the claim is based on negligence and action must be brought in the courts.

Failure of independent practitioners to provide service adequately or at all

General practitioners, dentists, opticians and retail pharmacists are all independent contractors who provide services to the National Health Service in accordance with the statutory terms and conditions for service prescribed by the relevant set of regulations.

The duties owed by a doctor are generally owed to persons including those who have been accepted on to the doctor's list drawn up by the Family Health Services Authority contracting the doctor's services. A doctor can terminate responsibilities to a particular individual by having the person removed from the doctor's list.

The primary duty imposed is for the doctor to render to patients all necessary and appropriate personal medical services of the type usually provided by general medical practitioners. Such services are to be provided at the doctor's practice premises or, if the condition of the patient otherwise requires, elsewhere within the doctor's practice area. A doctor is under no contractual duty to provide services outside that area. A doctor about to be absent, or unable to provide medical services, must ensure that patients have access to another doctor.

Complaints procedure for general practitioners

Complaints involving breach of the terms and conditions for the supply of services, such as failure to attend a patient, must be made to the relevant Family Health Services Authority.

Time limit for complaints

Complaints must be made in writing to the Family Health Services Authority and, except where the late claim provisions apply, within thirteen weeks from the event giving rise to the complaint. For dentists the complaint must be made within six months of completion of the treatment or within thirteen weeks after the event giving rise to the complaint whichever is the earlier date. The Family Health Services Authority has a discretion to accept late complaints if satisfied that illness or other reasonable cause contributed to the delay and either the person complained against or the Secretary of State consents to the admission of a late claim.

Where the Family Health Services Authority decides not to investigate the complaint, the complainant may within fourteen days make an appeal in writing setting out the grounds of appeal. If the complaint is accepted by the Family Health Services Authority, the Secretary will forward the complaint to the relevant service committee. The chair, having read the papers, will then decide whether there should be a hearing or the matter ought to be determined by the committee on the papers.

After having heard the parties and any witnesses and considering and documents submitted, the service committee draws up a report.

The Family Health Services Authority has power to:

- limit a doctor's list to a particular number;
- recommend a deduction from or withholding of remuneration;
- make representations that the practitioner's name should be removed from the list; or
- recommend that the practitioner be warned to comply with the terms and conditions for service more closely in future.

Complaints about National Health Service hospital treatment

There are no fixed legal procedures for making complaints about hospital treatment.

Many minor complaints can be resolved informally by discussing the matter with the personnel involved. Where matters cannot be dealt with in this way, the ward sister should be involved if it concerns nursing or non-medical staff. If the complaint relates to the medical staff the consultant in charge must be informed.

Where a patient wants to make a complaint to the health authority, this must be done in writing and the complaint should be addressed to the area or district administrator of the relevant authority. Information about making complaints should generally be available to all patients in the 'hospital booklet' which ought to be provided on admission and in any event at out-patient departments.

Formal complaints should usually be made within one year of the event giving rise to the complaint.

The Health Service Ombudsman

A complainant who is still dissatisfied, can seek the assistance of the appropriate

Health Service Commissioner (NHS Ombudsman). The matter, which must previously have been taken up with the NHS authority concerned, must be referred to the Ombudsman within one year of the date on which the matter came to the patient's notice.

Complaints concerning the clinical judgment of staff

Where a complaint concerns the clinical judgment of a member of staff, the consultant must deal with the issue. The member of the medical staff involved should be consulted from the outset and throughout the complaint procedure. In some cases the patient's general practitioner may be involved. If the consultant feels that litigation is likely, the consultant must also involve the district administrator who must in turn seek the advice of the authority's legal adviser. Any non-critical aspects of the complaint should be referred to the district administrator to be resolved as explained above.

The district administrator, on behalf of the authority, will send the terms of any reply to the complainant having agreed the text concerning any clinical matter with the consultant in charge.

A complainant, who is still dissatisfied with the reply, may renew the complaint either to the authority or one of its administrators or the consultant. If the complaint has not yet been reduced to writing, this will be requested. The Regional Medical Officer will now be informed by the consultant.

The Regional Medical Officer will arrange for two independent consultants in active practice in the appropriate speciality or specialities to consider all aspects of the case. These consultants will have access to all the clinical records. They will discuss the complaint with the consultant in charge, the other medical staff involved and the complainant.

On completion of the review by the independent consultants, the district administrator, on behalf of the authority, will write formally to the complainant with copies to the consultant and medical staff involved. The district administrator will explain what (if any) formal action is to be taken. The reply is treated as confidential unless the complainant seeks to make it public or prior or subsequent publicity necessitates the authority's commenting publicly.

Chapter 8

HIV, prisons and prisoners' rights

Una Padel

INTRODUCTION

The significance of prisons in the progress of the HIV pandemic has been widely acknowledged over recent years. Prisons contain a high population of people who may be particularly at risk of contracting HIV through the injection of drugs, and through participation in high risk sexual activity whilst in prison. In his address to the first world AIDS Summit in 1987, Sir Donald Acheson, who was the government's Chief Medical Officer, expressed the fear that prisons would form a bridge for the spread of HIV into the wider community. It is in these terms, the risk of HIV spreading to 'innocent' contacts of people released from prison, that the importance of prisons has usually been discussed. But this begs the question of the basic needs of those in prison to keep themselves safe, to have access to a good standard of medical care, to confidentiality and to a reasonable quality of life. Without addressing these basic needs the rhetoric about prisons as vehicles for the spread of the virus becomes nothing more than superficial scaremongering likely to stigmatise people with HIV infection in prisons yet further.

The difficulty in ensuring provision for these basic needs arises from the fact that in the British prison systems prisoners have virtually no rights. Change often comes about only as a result of test cases in either the domestic or, more frequently, the European courts. This chapter seeks to provide an overview of the situation regarding prisoner litigation and the situation of prisoners with HIV infection. The hope is that legal action may help to ensure that the worst practices in prisons are abandoned and that prisoners with HIV infection are not disadvantaged in terms of their medical care or stigmatised because they have the virus.

PRISONERS' RIGHTS

Britain's prisons are notorious for their overcrowding and squalor. This is not an entirely fair picture since many prisoners are incarcerated in relatively modern buildings which do not suffer the excesses of overcrowding, infestation or bad sanitation characteristic of the worst Victorian penal slums. One thing all prisoners have in common is a lack of rights beyond basic limited entitlements to visits, letters, food, exercise (weather permitting) and worship (as long as the prisoner belongs to a 'recognised' religious group). Almost every aspect of a prisoner's daily life consists of 'privileges' which can be easily withdrawn for administrative or punitive reasons. These include access to association with others, work, education, books and other sources of information.

Prison life in England and Wales is regulated by the Prison Rules which are made by the Secretary of State acting under the authority of the Prison Act 1952. Although partially amended in 1983, the Rules as a whole date from 1964. The Standing Orders are formulated by the Prison Service and detail the translation of the Rules into practice. Where the Rules allow the wide exercise of discretion in their application, the Standing Orders describe how that discretion should be exercised. The Standing Orders are amended fairly frequently, but are also constantly supplemented by Circular Instructions (and more recently Instructions and Advice to Governors) issued by the Prison Service, which give further detail on the interpretation and implementation of the Standing Orders.

The legal status of the Prison Rules is somewhat unclear. A breach of the Rules by prison authorities has never been recognised as grounds for judicial redress by the courts. Though the Prison Officers Training Manual states that the Rules 'are statutory rules and accordingly have the force of the law', an action for breach of statutory duty is not available in the event of an authority's non-compliance with the rules. Prisoners have generally had to resort to the assertion of general rights in order to obtain any degree of success in the courts. Even though the courts have not accepted that the Prison Rules confer any special rights on prisoners, they have generally acknowledged that prisoners retain certain rights. According to Lord Wilberforce, a prisoner 'retains all civil rights which are not taken away expressly or by implication'. In 1983 the Justice Report, *Justice in Prison*, described the situation of a prisoner thus:

> He loses his right to liberty, and his other rights are diminished so far as they are incompatible with that loss and with his obligation to live in a prison subject to its discipline. That is obvious. It is hardly less obvious that he retains other rights, subject only to that necessary diminution, and acquires new rights against the state which imprisons him.

It seems generally that prisoners' rights cases in the domestic courts have been successful only when they have related to issues of particular interest to the courts, or where the decision challenged has been quasi-judicial. In spite of its relatively narrow scope it does appear that 'prisoner litigation . . . reinforced by the success of cases taken to the European court, is becoming a significant force for change in prison policy'.

While the European Convention on Human Rights has no provisions expressly governing the conditions of imprisonment, the Council of Europe adopted Standard Minimum Rules for the Treatment of Prisoners in 1973. These were superseded by the European Prison Rules in 1987. These are intended as a guideline for EC convention organs and national administrators and courts, and the Council of

Europe recommends their eventual implementation in internal legislation and practice.

Demands for a legally enforceable code of minimum standards in prisons in England and Wales have come from diverse quarters: the Chief Inspector of Prisons, the House of Commons Education, Science and Arts Committee, the Prison Governors' branch of the Society of Civil and Public Servants and Prison Officers' Association, as well as penal reform pressure groups such as The National Association for the Care and Resettlement of Offenders (NACRO) and the Prison Reform Trust. In 1982 the Home Office announced that a code would be drawn up for publication in 1983, and would cover size and design of cells, arrangements for sharing and access to sanitation among other things. However, despite pressure to fulfil this commitment, the Home Office reneged on its promise. In 1984 it was confirmed that, apart from a set of standards for the building of new prisons, the government did not intend to publish a code of standards. Without a domestic code of standards, prisoners are left with the options of seeking redress through domestic law as it applies to general rights as mentioned above, or taking cases to the European Court. The latter is usually such a lengthy process that it is of little practical value to the majority of prisoners who are serving short sentences. In 1994, the Prison Service finally issued a Code of Standards. However, Ministers were quick to emphasise that these did not represent a legally enforceable set of minimum standards; rather, they detailed a set of facilities which prisons should provide but which could be withdrawn in the case of individual prisoners if circumstances or their behaviour warranted it.

HIV AND PRISONS

From the early days of the HIV pandemic it was clear from the experience of the United States that prisons would have a crucial role both in the care of people who had HIV-related illnesses while incarcerated, and in the education of prisoners away from high risk behaviour in or out of prison. Unfortunately it seems that these implications for policy took a long time to cross the Atlantic, and the situation was until recently handled in a rather *ad hoc* manner both in Scotland and in England and Wales. The situation in Scotland differs from that south of the border. This is probably attributable to the different profile of the epidemic in Scotland as well as the differences in prison management.

In England and Wales the last ten years have been marked by poor industrial relations in the prison service. Efforts on the part of the Home Office to curb prison officers' overtime (which averaged 16 hours per week in 1985) led to proposals for new working practices. The negotiations leading to a settlement in late 1986 were protracted and morale in the Prison Service reached a nadir. At the same time the first reported diagnoses of HIV were emerging in prisons. Prison staff were understandably worried, given the terrifying press attention HIV and AIDS had received. Furthermore, in trying to make a public case for better employment conditions, the dangerous aspects of their job, including contact with prisoners with HIV disease, were emphasised.

It was not until 1987 that a training programme designed to give prison staff a clear picture of HIV in relation to their work was introduced. Before that any attempts to provide information had been made on a very localised basis and the prevailing climate had been one of fear. The Prison Medical Service did nothing to alleviate this by announcing that the system of viral infectivity restrictions (VIR) originally formulated to protect against infection with the hepatitis B virus, should be used for prisoners diagnosed as having HIV infection.

The use of VIR has largely been phased out following a review by the Directorate of Health Care for Prisoners (formerly the Directorate of the Prison Medical Service). The restrictions permitted by VIR ranged from location in a single cell or sharing with another prisoner with a similar diagnosis to segregation from other prisoners either in the prison hospital or on a special VIR section. Prisoners categorised under VIR were also subject to discretionary limitations on their opportunities to work and participate in sport and other activities. The phasing out of VIR took some considerable time to achieve and it appears that some prisons which say they no longer use VIR are finding other ways of segregating prisoners known to have HIV infection, routinely putting them in the prison hospital, for example, when there is no medical need.

These restrictions have no practical value in terms of infection control although they were widely used. They were originally designed to reassure staff and other prisoners that there was no immediate danger to them and to protect prisoners known to have HIV infection from the negative attitudes or even violence of others. In fact, they often created a false sense of security among staff and prisoners alike, suggesting that since those with HIV infection were segregated, everyone else must be free of the virus. The Prison Officers Association called for the compulsory testing of all prisoners, although, quite apart from the infringement of civil liberties involved if such a policy had been adopted, this too would have been an ineffective method of determining who had the virus because of the 'window period' after infection but before antibodies are detectable in an antibody test. The arguments against this position were later accepted by the POA and the policy reversed.

The continued possibility of discretionary restrictions, and their use in many prisons over a period of almost seven years, perpetuated the sense that there was something to fear in contact with prisoners with HIV infection even though the educational packages developed by the Prison Medical Service made it clear that this was not so. Such fears have persisted beyond the existence of VIR and it will be important for the Directorate of Health Care to adopt a pro-active role in eliminating those fears rather than simply to wait for them to disappear.

The current Directorate of Health Care's strategy includes courses for prison medical officers, for prison staff who wish to develop HIV counselling skills and for multidisciplinary teams from prisons. The strategy is designed to develop multidisciplinary committees able to determine and oversee aspects of HIV policy and practice at a local level from HIV education to the care and management of people with HIV disease in each prison. Circular Instruction 30/91 outlined the revised HIV/AIDS organisation and procedures at establishment level and provided a checklist against which governors and multidisciplinary committees could measure their performance. Governors were also required to include a report on their progress towards developing a multidisciplinary structure and strategy in their annual report for 1991–92. In addition, the Directorate of Health Care for Prisoners has for some time been conducting a review of all aspects of HIV policy in prisons.

Considerable progress has clearly been made in policy terms and a number of prisons have successfully translated at least some of these developments into reality. At other prisons HIV education is virtually non-existent, and prisoners known to have HIV infection continue to be located in the hospital as a matter of course and their opportunities to mix with others and participate fully in the range of available activities is limited.

Prison medical services are provided by the Health Care Service for Prisoners which is separate from the National Health Service (NHS). Despite attempts to improve the Service's image many prisoners believe that prison medical staff are unlikely to be sympathetic to their needs. Prison hospital officers are usually present when prisoners see the medical officer and this too does little to inspire confidence. Convicted prisoners have no right to seek a second medical opinion or to consult a doctor of their choice. Since the HIV/AIDS field is so new it is obviously difficult for many doctors to remain abreast of developments. Many rural prisons are served by part-time medical officers who spend the rest of their time as general practitioners (GPs). Often there is no great likelihood of their encountering HIV disease in the course of the rest of their work, and they have little experience of it. There have been some instances in which prisoners have felt that this lack of experience has been reflected in the way they have been treated. Once prisoners are diagnosed as having the virus, they are usually seen by a consultant from the nearest NHS hospital, but the initial diagnosis may depend on the prison medical officer.

Day-to-day medical supervision while the prisoner is well enough to remain in the prison is also in the hands of the prison medical officer. When a prisoner is moved from one prison to another the attitude of the medical officer may be different. For example, in one instance the medical officer at the receiving prison refused to allow a prisoner to keep the supplies of AZT (Zidovudine, a drug known to slow the process of infection) he had been given at the previous prison. His treatment was thus interrupted. Although this problem was resolved quite quickly it was very distressing for the prisoner involved.

The Directorate of Health Care for Prisoners is now organising special training for medical officers about the diagnosis and care of people with HIV disease. This is a useful move, though it should have happened some time ago, as it was clear that HIV would present problems for prisons.

In the community people with HIV infection are encouraged to eat a healthy diet and avoid stress in order to remain asymptomatic for as long as possible. Some people also take advantage of a number of alternative therapies, most of which are, as yet, unresearched. Prisoners have to eat the food provided. While the Prison

Service would argue that it provides a well-balanced diet many prisoners would suggest that the nutritional value of food in prisons is often diminished by the way in which it is cooked. In particular vegetables are often overcooked, and prisoners have little access to fresh fruit. Given the lack of choice available to prisoners in terms of their medical treatment, it is hardly surprising that they are unable to try alternative therapies. Meanwhile the stress of prison life, particularly where it involves stigmatisation, segregation and few opportunities for physical exercise or social contact, may actually contribute to the onset of symptoms. A 1986 study by the New York State Commission on Correction showed that state prisoners with AIDS lived only half as long as people with AIDS in the community.

Another area which continues to cause concern is confidentiality. The Prison Service's early guidance to institutions was that staff with an 'operational need to know' should be aware which prisoners were subject to viral infectivity restrictions, though they should not be told the diagnoses of individual prisoners. The 'operational need to know' was interpreted in a very wide variety of ways so that in some prisons all staff had access to information as to which prisoners were subject to VIR. In prisons where prisoners on VIR were located on separate landings other prisoners were also aware of this. This loose confidentiality policy was bad enough, but on a number of occasions it appears to have been breached and other prisoners were told of an individual's diagnosis. In one instance a national newspaper appears to have been given the information that a prisoner about whom there had been much publicity was HIV-infected before the prisoner himself had been given the test result.

One prisoner who approached the National Council for Civil Liberties (now Liberty) was granted legal aid to seek damages for breach of confidence. When other prisoners found out he had HIV infection he had to be segregated and was unable to participate in most activities, including elements of his Open University course. Legal aid was not granted to him for an action seeking a declaration on the 'need to know' policy which would have defined its parameters.

Prison Department Circular Instruction 30/91 which updated HIV policy guidance stressed the importance of confidentiality and defined it more clearly than any previous document. It points out that medical and health care staff in prisons 'are bound by the same ethical codes of practice as their counterparts in other branches of medicine. They are not, therefore, free agents in the matter of disclosing information about inmate patients which they have obtained as a result of clinical examination and investigation.'

The Circular Instruction makes it clear that the consent of the prisoner is necessary before information about their HIV infection can be divulged to anyone other than health care staff and members of the HIV care team. Although this tightens the guidance on confidentiality considerably, glaring breaches still occur. Workers from community-based drugs and HIV agencies cite instances of individual members of prison staff entering into detailed discussions with them about named prisoners who have HIV infection, and in some prisons at multidisciplinary committee level, the names of prisoners with HIV infection seem to be mentioned almost as a matter of course.

Confidentiality does not currently appear to be a practice with which prison staff are particularly comfortable. Breaches which may have no adverse effect seem to go unchallenged and this perpetuates the situation. The guidance recognises these difficulties and suggests that it 'may also be prudent to explain to the inmate that confidentiality (medical or otherwise) is not easily achieved or maintained in prison and that while members of the care team will do everything possible to respect their wishes strict confidentiality cannot be assured'.

Information about a prisoner's HIV infection is usually included in the inmate medical record (IMR) and according to anecdotal evidence these records are sometimes handled in a manner which does little to ensure confidentiality. It seems that although it is policy that IMRs should be transferred between medical officers at different prisons in sealed envelopes, they are sometimes opened and read by escorting officers on the bus used to transport prisoners.

If the Prison Service really wishes to improve confidentiality it will have to do more than devote a few paragraphs to it in a policy document. Training of key staff may be necessary and those who breach confidentiality should be challenged by their colleagues.

It is particularly difficult for prisoners to complain about such breaches. They may be unaware that a breach has taken place immediately, and even if they do find out it may be difficult to establish the identity of the culprit or even to prove that confidentiality has been broken, since staff often justify breaches when challenged by saying that the prisoner has been free with the information. A complaint may also increase the number of people who are aware of the confidential information.

Strategic planning to provide for prisoners with HIV disease or AIDS has been through various stages in England and Wales. At one point it was feared that the numbers of prisoners becoming ill would lead to the establishment of specialised care units able to cater for people when they were not ill enough to require hospital treatment. Accommodation was set aside for this purpose but never used since it was later decided that such units would not be required. Prisoners who are ill are sent to outside hospitals and returned to prison when they are deemed to need specialised hospital care no longer. The difficulty with this is that sending prisoners to outside hospitals often necessitates a 24-hour guard or bed watch to be put on the prisoner which is extremely expensive for the prison in terms of staff time. In a time when prisons are constantly bemoaning the shortage of staff one concern is that pressure may be placed on hospitals to discharge prisoners back to prison earlier than may be advisable on the basis that some health care is available within the prison.

In Scotland similar plans to provide a residential unit at Saughton prison in Edinburgh have also been abandoned. Staffing such a unit would have involved a disproportionate amount of staff time and some staff at the prison were worried that the unit might isolate people with HIV disease. Instead Saughton offers a day centre for prisoners with HIV infection where the programme is intended to introduce prisoners to the sort of activities (creative writing, complementary therapies, relaxation) in which they could participate after release, and to provide them with information and support.

HIV AND PRISONERS' RIGHTS

Other than the prisoner mentioned earlier who attempted to claim for damages from the Prison Service for breach of confidence, there do not, so far, appear to have been any cases in either the domestic or European courts relating to the treatment of people with HIV infection in prison. This is hardly surprising. Most prisoners go through their sentences without even considering litigation, their main interest is in being released and they are surprisingly tolerant of the squalor and degradation they have to endure in prison.

The number of prisoners known to have had HIV infection in prison is of course still small (numbers in Scotland are not recorded). Prisoners are not encouraged to use the law to challenge unsatisfactory situations. Indeed it is probable that those already isolated and vulnerable because they have been found to have HIV infection would, rightly or wrongly, fear that this would add to their stigmatisation. If the individual is on remand or serving a short sentence then litigation may seem unrealistic because of the time it may take. However, it does offer one way for prisoners to apply pressure on the Prison Service to take a more pro-active stance on issues such as confidentiality.

Article 3 of the European Convention on Human Rights and Fundamental Freedoms provides that 'No-one shall be subjected to torture or degrading treatment or punishment'. In his book *AIDS and Human Rights: A UK Perspective*, Paul Sieghart raises the question whether the segregation or isolation of prisoners with HIV infection or disease might amount to inhuman or degrading treatment. 'Inhuman' treatment is regarded by the European Commission of Human Rights as being such treatment that deliberately causes severe suffering, mental or physical (*Denmark et al.* v. *Greece* [1969] *Yearbook of the European Court of Human Rights* 12; *Ireland* v. *United Kingdom*, European Court of Human Rights, series A, Judgment of 18 January 1978). The European Court stressed that a minimum, though clearly relative, level of severity must be attained in order for the treatment to be termed 'inhuman'. The circumstances of the case, including the mental and physical effects of the state of health of the victim, are crucial.

'Degrading' treatment has usually referred to physical acts, for example, inter-rogation practices. However, in the East African Asians case (3 European Human Rights Reports 1976) concerning British immigration law, it was held that any act which lowers a person in rank, position, reputation or character can be regarded as degrading treatment if it reaches a certain level of severity. Paul Sieghart concludes that:

> What is clear . . . is that, for treatment to violate the prohibition against inhuman or degrading treatment, it must reach a certain level of severity. While the

compulsory segregation or isolation of prisoners with AIDS or HIV infection would probably not, on that test, constitute 'inhuman' treatment, it might well, depending on the circumstances, amount to 'degrading' treatment, especially bearing in mind that public health experts have said they see no need for it.

CONCLUSION

Prisoners known to have HIV infection in the prisons of England and Wales are subject to a wide variety of regimes, some of them poor. At a time when they are liable to be anxious, depressed and in need of stimulation and information they may be isolated and penalised simply because they are known to have a virus. Meanwhile many other prisoners infected by the virus, who are probably unaware of the fact, continue to exist in the mainstream of prison life and this has not led to a massive epidemic among prisoners or ex-prisoners.

Although most prisoners are not particularly keen to become involved in litigation, even if they know how to go about it, this is likely to be an important tool in effecting change as it has been in other aspects of prison administration. Lawyers, civil liberties and penal reform organisations and everyone else concerned with improving the lot of prisoners with HIV infection need to be able to provide information on legal remedies to enable prisoners to choose this course, with a clear understanding of its implications, if they so wish.

Chapter 9

Legal structures and responsibilities of voluntary organisations

Timothy Costello

INTRODUCTION

If you are thinking of organising a helpline or some other group, it must have some structure. If it is to have its own funds, perhaps employ someone, it is important to ensure that the entity has the correct form, so that unnecessary difficulties are avoided and everyone is enabled to function as efficiently as possible. In this chapter the objective is to review the various alternatives and the reasons for choosing each, in order to make your decision easier. What are the issues involved?

- First of all we must consider the possible forms of organisation.
- Then we must ask how the body spends and acquires funds.
- Other important considerations are what the body will do and the level of its legal commitments and other liabilities; this will determine the appropriate form of the body.
- We should consider the advantages and drawbacks of charitable status.
- Finally we must look at the second certainty in life – taxes.

FORMS

There are a number of different forms of organisation which could be adopted. Simplest is the unincorporated association, then there is the trust, followed by the industrial and provident society and the company.

Unincorporated associations

This is like a village cricket club. It is simply a group of individuals who agree to carry out certain activities in common. As far as the law is concerned, it has no existence separate from that of its members; it has no legal personality. An unincorporated association can also be a charity but if it has any assets they must be held by trustees on behalf of the association. Such an unincorporated association will suffer from the same disadvantages as a trust.

Trust

The trust is the traditional form for a charitable body. The essence of a trust is that a person, the donor, gives property (which may be land, money, goods or rights like shares or other investments) to someone else, the trustee, who holds the property, not for the trustee's own benefit, but on condition that the trustee will give the property or the income which it produces to a third person, the beneficiary. In the case of a charitable trust there are of course usually multiple donors, and the beneficiaries are defined by description, e.g., people with HIV disease, rather than by name.

Companies

The company is a common form of organisation which is usually associated with trading activities. Most people are generally aware of the way commercial companies function. The company's business is carried on for the benefit of those who have invested in the company, namely the shareholders. The shareholders appoint the directors to manage the company's business. Non-profit-making companies are established under the same legislation. The main difference between such companies and a trading company is that, instead of having shareholders (who are often referred to in any case as members), a non-profit-making company has members who agree, in the event that the company becomes insolvent, to contribute a fixed (usually nominal) amount to its assets. Such companies are called companies limited by guarantee.

FUNDING

The common sources of funds for voluntary organisations are:

- informal gifts (the subscriptions of those involved, proceeds of fund-raising events, flag days and collecting boxes left in public places);
- central and local government grants;
- grant-making charities;
- formal giving by way of covenant, gift aid or otherwise from companies and by way of covenant or gift aid from individuals.

Of these, only the first two are generally available to bodies which are not charities. It is difficult for charities to give money to bodies which are not themselves charities. To obtain the tax advantages available for charitable gifts clearly the recipient must be a registered charity.

This is complementary to what is said below about the possibility of progressing from a relatively informal set-up to a more formal structure. As the body grows in size it will be necessary to establish it as a charity in order to make the fullest possible advantage of all possible sources of funds.

Before leaving the topic of funding, mention must be made of trading activities by the body. While minor occasional trading, such as jumble sales, will not attract the attention of the Inland Revenue, other trading will usually give rise to an income or corporation tax liability. In the case of charities only, this liability can in practice be avoided by taking the steps discussed below under Taxation.

STRUCTURES AND RESPONSIBILITIES

Unincorporated associations

Informality is the order of the day. Unlike what applies in the case of companies, the law prescribes few if any procedures which must be followed in the running of an unincorporated association. You can make your own decisions on how it should be organised. Will there be a committee of management? Will there be officers? Should they be elected and if so how often? Will there be an annual general meeting? How will accounts be kept? What are the qualifications for membership? Will the accounts be independently verified – audited? On all these questions and others you will be able to make your own decisions and the law will not force your hand, although perhaps funding bodies will have some requirements which you will need to satisfy, otherwise the body will not be eligible to receive funds.

Also as the association grows and takes on more tasks, it is very simple to change the structure to meet the increased requirements.

An unincorporated association does not have to be registered. Unless the group is very small, it is desirable to have some rules so that everyone who belongs to the organisation knows what is expected of members. All but the smallest associations will have a committee and the rules should establish how the committee is formed, what decisions it can take without consulting all the members, how often a general meeting of all the members must be held and, if the association has its own financial resources, how these are to be accounted for.

As noted above, an unincorporated association does not have a separate legal personality. Accordingly it does not have limited liability in the same way that a company does. For example, if the office manager of a limited company places an order for stationery on behalf of the company, the supplier cannot make the office manager pay for the stationery, if the company is subsequently unable to do so. In the case of an unincorporated association it is different; while the members collectively cannot usually (depending on the rules of the association) be made responsible, the individuals who placed the order can be. This is a double disadvantage: first of all it puts an unfair burden on the people who run the organisation and also traders may be unwilling to give the organisation credit; dealing with all purchases on a cash with order basis can be tiresome. If the time comes when the organisation needs premises, it will probably not be possible to continue with an unincorporated association, because the responsibilities undertaken towards the landlord by those who sign the lease or tenancy agreement on behalf of the organisation, are too heavy.

There is no reason why a body should not start as an unincorporated association and subsequently change its status as the requirements of its activities dictate. Indeed this is a common path followed by many bodies.

Trusts

A trust does not have a legal personality separate from its trustees. The trustees have no limited liability. So long as they have not committed any breach of trust, they are entitled to have recourse to the funds of the trust for any liabilities which they have incurred in their capacity as trustees. However, if the trust funds are insufficient or there is any outstanding breach of trust, the trustees will be liable to make good the shortfall from their personal assets.

Trustees must normally act unanimously and all the trustees must agree to any particular course of action. This can be inconvenient (because, for example, all the trustees must attend meetings in order that decisions can be taken) except in the case of a small organisation. The trust deed establishing a trust will provide for how new trustees are to be chosen. Trustees will remain responsible as trustees until they die or until a formal document is signed by all the trustees by which retiring trustees relinquish their responsibilities. New trustees will be appointed in a similar manner. Effectively this means that legal assistance must be sought with the preparation of these documents on each occasion when trustees retire and/or are appointed. This is cumbersome in an organisation where individuals may remain involved for a relatively short period of time. The trust is not an appropriate vehicle where democracy is to perform any role in choosing those responsible for running the organisation. In practice, the document establishing the trust cannot be changed; there is a theoretical way of doing this but it would probably be ruled out by expense. This means that it must be drafted with the maximum amount of foresight otherwise the trust may not be able to respond to changes in circumstances. Almost all trusts will need to register as charities. The Charity Commission can rightly be expected to require precision in the trust document and this may limit flexibility in the future.

Trustees must always be in a position to account for the property in their hands. This means that books of account must be kept and, for the protection of the trustees, effectively audited annually. The Charities Act 1993 obliges all charities, which are not companies, with an annual income of more than £100,000 to have their accounts audited by a qualified person; charities with a lower income need to have accounts examined by an independent examiner.

It is a cardinal principle of trust law that a trustee must not profit from the trust (unless the trustee is permitted to do so in the instrument establishing the trust). Accordingly, if the trust is proposing to buy goods or services from a trustee (or from an entity in which the trustee is interested) this cannot be done while that trustee remains a trustee; otherwise the trustee will simply have to hand back the cash or other benefit received. The position is not so stringent in the case of directors of companies.

For bodies which are passive reservoirs of funds rather than active providers of services, the trust is probably ideal. However, for the modern charity, which spends as much of its resources as possible and resorts to governmental funding for some of its activities and which needs to a be a charity not for reasons of property law but in order to obtain tax concessions, the trust is not the ideal vehicle. If it is chosen for some particular reason, it may need to have an affiliated, unincorporated association to which the individuals providing the services can belong.

The responsibilities of being a trustee are very heavy. The standard of care which a trustee is expected to exercise is much greater than that of a director of a company. If there is any breach of trust, a trustee is not permitted to resort to the trust funds for liabilities which have been incurred as a trustee rather than in a personal capacity. In practice, in the context of a large organisation minor breaches of trust may be almost impossible to avoid.

Companies

A company is regarded in law as a person separate from its members. Trustees own the property of a trust; directors do not own the property of a company – the company does.

A company exists to carry out the purposes set out in its memorandum of association (known as its objects) and for no other purpose. It has the powers specified in its memorandum of association and other powers reasonably incidental to those powers and required in order to carry out its objects.

Like the members of a trading company, the members of a non-profit-making company have a limit on their liability (i.e., the amount they agree to contribute) if the company cannot pay its debts. Similarly the directors are not responsible for the debts of a company except in certain circumstances if they let it incur additional liabilities when they know it will not be able to meet them. This advantage of limited liability cannot be stressed too much. People undertaking voluntary activities do not expect to put their personal assets at risk. The modern kind of active charity carries with it the same order of risk as a trading enterprise; the individuals concerned in it should not bear these risks.

A company can be a charity. Most of the large charities are companies. Charitable status, which is examined later in this chapter, can be a great help in obtaining funding for the activities of the organisation. The company basically has a democratic structure. Typically charitable companies have a small number of members who are admitted by the directors and hence a self-perpetuating oligarchy persists. However, if this is not desired, for instance because the company exists to provide a medium for voluntary service to the beneficiaries of the charity, the articles of association can provide for the volunteer workers and staff of the company to become members. The directors of the company are elected by the members and it is easy to reinforce this by including provisions for secret balloting in its articles.

The company is also flexible. Directors are easily appointed in between elections and they can resign simply by writing a letter of resignation. Directors normally act by majority decision at regularly convened board meetings. If there are sufficient directors present (called a quorum), a decision is validly taken. However, it would always be possible to provide that on certain matters the directors must be unanimous. It is also relatively easy to change the constitution of a company. There is almost complete freedom with regard to changes concerning the management of the company and more latitude for changing the purposes for which the company was established – its so-called objects – than there is in the case of a trust. In practice commercial companies can change their objects at will. Charitable companies, because they are subject to the tutelage of the Charity Commission and because they may be given property in such a way that they may be regarded as holding it on trust, can only change their objects with the consent of the Charity Commission. Nevertheless, changing the objects of a charitable company is much easier than is the case for a trust.

The management of the operations of a company is invariably placed by its articles of association in the hands of the board of directors as a collective body.

The board and anyone purporting to exercise powers delegated by the board must act only in the furtherance of the objects of, and using the powers contained in, the company's memorandum of association. If the directors do otherwise, the company is not bound by any commitment which may have been made and, if the assets of the company are dissipated as a result, directors can be called upon to make good the loss to the company.

The general power of the directors excludes any authority of the members of the company in general meeting. The general meeting may be asked to approve a particular course of action but it cannot initiate any conduct. If it attempts to do so the directors can ignore it. They will not be absolved from responsibility if the initiative required by the members is taken and is a breach of their duties as directors. Individual directors have no power at all in relation to a company unless particular powers have been delegated to them. The board is the fountain of all authority in a company save for matters which are reserved to the company in general meeting, such as, usually, changing the name and constitution of the company and the election of directors.

The law about the responsibilities of directors is not simple for directors of commercial companies. It is even less straightforward for directors of charitable ones. The directors owe duties to the company, to those for whose benefit the company was established (the intended beneficiaries in the case of a charitable company), to its creditors and to its employees: it is clear that the interests of the creditors prevail over those of the shareholders or charitable beneficiaries but Parliament and the courts have given no guidance as to how conflicts involving the employees and the other parties are to be resolved. Directors of a charitable company are accountable for its property as if they were trustees. This is a heavier burden than that imposed on directors of commercial companies but the advantage of limited liability is still significant.

The general duty of directors is to attend meetings of the board when not reasonably prevented from doing so. At meetings of the board and when carrying out matters delegated to a director, the director must act with reasonable care. The degree of skill required from an individual director is less than that demanded of a trustee and will depend on the experience and qualifications of that director. A higher standard will be required of an accountant or lawyer than of a teacher.

The principal obligation owed to the creditors is not to allow the company to continue to incur liabilities unless the directors are satisfied the company will be able to meet its liabilities as they fall due. Under the Insolvency Act 1986 directors of companies can be made personally responsible for some or all of the liabilities of a company if they allow it to continue in operation when there is no reasonable possibility that an insolvent liquidation can be avoided. This is known as a liability for wrongful trading. Although charitable companies do not usually trade, in the strict sense of the word, the directors could be made liable for the debts of the company and in this context 'operating' should probably be substituted for 'trading'. Such liability is not automatic and is in the discretion of the court. It will be dependent on the conduct of the individual director concerned. Resignation is not enough to exclude liability once the company is in trouble: each director must do what the director can to ensure that the interests of creditors are protected. Directors of insolvent companies are also statutorily responsible for unpaid National Insurance contributions at the date of the commencement of the liquidation. In the case of a trading company it is easier to establish when wrongful trading is likely to be occurring than it is in the case of a charitable company. A trading company knows that if it continues to do business money will flow in and it can make a reasonable prediction of the amounts which are likely to be received. On the other hand a charity must to a large extent rely on donations to maintain its cash flow and whether or not it will be able to meet future liabilities is in the hands of third parties.

Finally, directors must avoid being in a position where their own interests conflict with those of the company and, if they inevitably occur, must declare them. It is necessary for a director to declare any interest the director may have directly or indirectly in any contract to which the company is a party or in any expenditure made by the company. This must be done at a regularly convened meeting of the board even if all the directors individually are aware of the matter in question. If this is not done the director (like a trustee who would otherwise profit from the trust) becomes what is known as a constructive trustee. In other words the director is regarded as holding the money on behalf of the company and must account to it for the benefit which the director has received.

This catalogue of directors' duties may be intimidating at first sight but in fact the liability of directors is substantially less than that of trustees and less than those incurring personal liabilities on behalf of an unincorporated association.

The industrial and provident society

This is an alternative to the company limited by guarantee. It is quick to establish provided that one of the forms approved by the Registrar of Friendly Societies is used for its constitution. If one of the standard forms is not used it must be approved by the Registrar which is probably as time-consuming as having the constitution of a trust or company limited by guarantee approved by the Charity Commission (and the Inland Revenue). It seems likely that for the purposes with which readers of this book are likely to be concerned a special form of constitution will probably be necessary if only to define the beneficiaries of the body. Accordingly it is not proposed to discuss further the industrial and provident society.

Summary of legal structures

A corporate structure is the best option for substantial organisations which may wish to:

- employ staff;
- rent premises;
- make significant purchases of goods and services (rather than simply to collect and distribute money);
- obtain the income required to perform these functions.

Alternatively it may be best to start as an unincorporated association and, as and when the need arises, progress to the incorporation of a company. As will be seen below in the section on taxation, the major advantage of being a charity is the additional income which can be gained from the tax refunded on covenanted donations. Equally, however, the procedures required to collect this money are complicated. This, combined with the initial work involved in establishing a charity, may not be worthwhile for a small body which is not likely to receive significant covenant or gift aid income even if it is a charity.

A final point before we move on to consider the other aspects of establishing the body: to those who are not lawyers, a company may seem a very legalistic animal; indeed it is a creation of the law. Given the healthy suspicion about lawyers in this country, some may wonder whether it is not better to have a body with a freer form rather than one which is so hidebound. This might lead you to progress from an unincorporated association to a company later rather than sooner. This could be a mistake: apart from any inconvenience and unlooked-for personal liabilities, the great advantage of a company is its formal structure and the fact that there are rules for conducting its operations which are generally common to tens of thousands of other companies and well known. The rules of an unincorporated association are inevitably more likely to be unique to that association to a greater extent than would be the case if it were a company. Working for people living with HIV and AIDS is stressful; often the correct action in any given circumstances is open to debate and those involved may violently oppose the course proposed by those with whom they disagree. There is everything to be said for having a structure where those disputes which cannot be resolved by compromise can be disposed of cleanly and with the minimum of argument as to the correct procedure. This is more likely to apply if the structure of the body is formal.

Charitable status

It might be thought that any voluntary organisation working in the AIDS field would be eligible to be a charity but this is not necessarily the case. It will be well to review what is considered to be charitable in law but first perhaps we should look at the significance of charitable status.

Significance of charitable status

As might be expected, charitable status has advantages and disadvantages. Charities benefit from tax concessions which form a direct incentive to those who wish to give funds and which reduce the cost of operating the charity. On the other side of the ledger charities must be registered by, and are subject to the jurisdiction of, the Charity Commission and their freedom to pursue certain courses is circumscribed by law.

Once again there is a trade-off. The small organisation, which does not have the human resources to administer the reclaiming of tax on covenanted donations and which will probably not have many donors willing to make covenants or gift aid and which does not occupy premises and so cannot make use of rates relief, is probably better off not being a charity. A more substantial body may view charitable status as vital. Strictly speaking there is not a choice because there is a duty on those in charge of a charity to register with the Charity Commission but no one is likely to take the point against a small organisation which does not misrepresent itself as a charity.

Eligibility for charitable status

In order to be charitable a body must be established for one of the four 'heads of charity':

- the relief of poverty, human suffering and distress;
- the advancement of education;
- the advancement of religion;
- other purposes beneficial to the community.

There is also the overriding requirement that it should be established for the public benefit and not for a private class of people. If the beneficiaries are limited, for example, to the poor residents of a particular locality this will be charitable but not, it seems, if they are limited to the poor employees and former employees of a particular company.

Consideration of the 'heads' might lead one to think that any body formed to prevent the spread of HIV or help people with HIV infection or disease would inevitably be charitable but the Charity Commission will not necessarily agree immediately, although ultimately it is likely to be possible to convince the staff of the Commission, perhaps by specifying more precisely the objects of the proposed charity and, for example, introducing education or the relief of illness so as to come within one or both of the first two heads.

Accounts

As far as administration is concerned, even if they are not companies (which are obliged to produce periodical accounts and have them audited), charities must draw up accounts which comply with the Charities Act 1993, have them audited or examined and submit them to the Charity Commission annually. Usually this will involve the services of an accountant even if the accounts are not audited formally.

Under the Charities Act 1993 charities are also required to prepare an annual report and make an annual return to the Charity Commission.

Disposals of property

If a charity occupies property for its own purposes and wishes to dispose of it, it must comply with the Charities Act 1993.

Grants

A charity must apply its assets strictly for the purpose for which it was established and for no other purpose. There will not be a problem if one charity makes a gift to another charity having the same purpose. However, if the recipient is not a charity (although being established for the same purpose) the gift is likely to be unlawful. In relation to AIDS organisations this operates in two ways: the small body not registered as a charity may not have access to funds as a result; the larger organisation wishing to help fund a particular project may be in difficulty if the project is not being carried out by a registered charity. A possible solution is for the grant to be structured as a contract, obliging the recipient to operate the service concerned for a specified period. Then provided that the service is within the purposes of the charity providing the money there should be no breach of the law. It would be wise to try to insert in the powers of the charity a power to make grants to non-charitable bodies for the purposes only of providing services which it would be within the object of the charity to provide.

Political activities

It is often thought that a charity cannot carry on any political activities. This is not strictly true. It is true that a body established to change the law of the land is not charitable. The basic principle is that political activity must not be the prime purpose of the body either in its constitution or in practice. A charity, however, may undertake activities which can reasonably be said to be directed towards achieving the charity's purposes and which are within the powers contained in its constitution.

The Charity Commission has published some useful guidelines on what is and what is not permissible.

Fund-raising

It is beyond the scope of this book to deal in detail with the requirements of all kinds of fund-raising. However, it is worth mentioning that the Charities Act 1992 introduced provisions controlling fund-raising activities by charities and other institutions established for charitable, benevolent or philanthropic purposes. Collections in public places (which are very widely defined) require a licence from the local authority. Lotteries and competitions are also subject to control limiting the price of the ticket and the prizes which may be offered. The licensing authority is the local district council outside London, the appropriate London borough council in greater London (except the City where the licensing authority is the Common Council). Well before embarking on this kind of fund-raising and before, for example, having tickets printed, the applicable rules should be studied.

TAX

Under this heading we must consider inheritance, income and corporation tax payable by givers of money to the body, and income and corporation tax and VAT in relation to the body itself.

Taxation of donors

In the case of individuals, gifts to qualifying UK charities are now completely exempt from inheritance tax without limit and are deducted from the total amount of the estate; such gifts may take the estate out of a charge to inheritance tax altogether. Thus a gift by will or during a person's lifetime (even if shortly before death) can benefit a charity significantly more than if tax is paid on the donor's estate and the recipient then decides (independently) to make a charitable donation. There is always scope for a recipient to redirect a legacy (or other gift by will) to a charity within two years after the death and obtain the same tax-free advantage.

Gifts to charity are not deductible in establishing the taxable income of an individual for the purpose of basic rate tax, although gifts under covenants or gift aid are deductible in calculating the income of an individual subject to the higher rate of income tax. However, if the gift is made either pursuant to a deed of covenant (under which the gift will be made annually during the shorter of four years and the life of the donor or is more than £400), the charity is able to reclaim from the Inland Revenue a sum equal to tax at the basic rate of tax on the grossed up amount of the gift. Thus while the basic rate of tax is 25 per cent, if the annual amount payable by the donor is £75, this is grossed up to £100 on which the basic rate of tax is £25; this is recoverable from the Inland Revenue. Consequently the charity receives £100 in all.

Because of the treatment of higher rate taxpayers stated above, the net cost to a higher rate taxpayer of the £100 received by the charity is £60 (assuming the higher rate of income tax remains at 40 per cent).

If a company makes a payment wholly and exclusively for the purpose of its trade, this will be deductible from its gross income in establishing its taxable income. Certain payments to charities, if they secure some advantage for the company in the course of its trade, may be deductible as ordinary business expenses. The most obvious example of this is sponsorship of a particular event, which secures publicity for the company sponsor.

Value Added Tax

Like any other purchaser of goods and services, a charity must pay prices which include VAT. Generally it is in no different position from any other person in this respect. A detailed discussion of VAT in relation to charities is beyond the scope of this chapter.

Taxation of a charity

It is a commonly-held fallacy that charities are exempt from taxation. However, while they do benefit from some tax concessions, the only part of their income which is exempt from taxation is investment income and trading income in so far as it is derived from the activities for which the charity was established. To clarify this, a workshop established to provide an opportunity for paraplegics to make baskets will be exempt from tax on the profits derived from selling the baskets but a charity importing baskets from India and selling them will not. It is likely that a charity established to provide health education will be exempt from tax on the profits arising from the sale of health education literature and posters.

Much of the trading activity of charities is done for more-or-less fund-raising reasons even if the goods sold have a relationship to the activities of the charity. This kind of trading is not exempt from taxation if it is carried out by the charity itself. However, there is a mechanism whereby these profits can also effectively escape taxation. As has been mentioned, if a company enters into a deed of covenant to pay a particular amount annually for at least four years to a charity, effectively no tax is paid on the income used to fund the payment. As long as the sum to be paid is certainly ascertainable, it does not have to be expressed as a money amount. Accordingly it is possible for a company to covenant to give the whole of its net profits (after operating expenses but before tax) to a charity. If this is done, the company determines its net profits for the year. This establishes the amount due under the covenant. Because of the tax law applicable to companies, the company must deduct tax at the basic rate from the gross amount and pay this to the Inland Revenue; the remaining amount is payable to the beneficiary of the covenant. The whole amount due under the covenant (including the basic rate tax which must be deducted and paid to the Revenue) is deductible from the profits of the company in determining its taxable income, thus reducing this to zero, so that it pays no corporation tax. In addition the recipient, as a charity, is in a position to claim a refund of the amount of the tax at the basic rate withheld by the company. Accordingly no tax is payable on the profits generated by the trading. So charities which wish to raise funds by trading activities usually establish a wholly-owned subsidiary company (which is a normal commercial company limited by shares) to carry out these trading activities. The subsidiary then covenants to pay the whole of its net annual profits to the charity. One point to note is that the deduction from taxable income can only be made for amounts actually paid under the covenant during the year in question; accordingly, it is necessary before the end of the company's year to estimate the profits for that year and pay the appropriate amount under the covenant.

Charities can obtain relief from the Uniform Business Rate (but not water and sewerage charges) so that charities pay at the most one-fifth of normal rates. Local authorities can relieve charities of an even greater proportion of the Uniform Business Rate but this is at the discretion of the local authority. This means that charities will be better off paying their own rates rather than paying a rent inclusive of rates to a landlord which is not itself a charity.

PRACTICAL MATTERS

Finally we turn to considering the practical steps which must be taken in order to set up a suitable organisation.

For some bodies it will never be necessary to go beyond the stage of an unincorporated association; for others this will be an initial step to be followed in due course by a change to a more formal structure but the time taken to complete the required formalities will probably dictate starting as an unincorporated association.

Unincorporated associations

The basic idea of an unincorporated association is that it is formed by a contract between the members. The terms of the contract are set out in the rules of the association. Accordingly as soon as the decision is made to establish the association, the first thing to do is to draw up some rules.

These should deal at least with the following issues:

Purpose

- the activities which the association is established to carry out
- membership
- eligibility
- admission to membership
- obligations of members
- removal as a member

How the association is to be run

- officers' (e.g., chair, secretary and treasurer) qualifications, appointment, removal and powers
- committee (composition and powers)
- general meetings of the members
- elections
- the conduct of meetings of members and any committee (what notice is required, how many people will form a quorum, that minutes are to be kept and how they are to be published)
- accounts (bookkeeping, preparation of annual accounts, whether they are to be audited and how they are to be published to the members)
- special formalities required for changing the rules
- how the association can be dissolved

These matters should all be covered in clear everyday language. The object is to have a document to which all concerned can refer and which will give an appropriate answer to the questions which will arise in practice. Should the committee have embarked on a particular course? Was it consistent with the purposes for which the association was established? Is it right that two members of the committee can reach a decision at a meeting of which some other committee members were ignorant? Should not the accounts from two years ago now be available? How does one deal with a member who is harming the organisation?

If the rules do not provide answers in advance to these questions and the others which will come up, it will render a difficult occurrence even more troublesome. Voluntary organisations can be extremely beneficial. However, it is inevitable, human nature being what it is, that those who are giving their time do not feel as obligated as those who are being paid to do work. It is even more important to lay down what is expected in advance, so that performance can be compared with existing norms, rather than an individual's conduct being compared with a hazy notion of what is appropriate.

Time spent in formulating rules is unlikely to be wasted. As a start it will usually be possible to obtain copies of the rules of other similar bodies and to use these as a starting point. Before finally adopting any rules it is worthwhile to enquire of the funding body whether they have any requirement with regard to rules of organisations to which they provide money.

The beauty of an unincorporated association is that once the rules have been prepared and adopted, you are up and running with no more ado.

It is possible to open a bank or building society account for the association, although usually the association will need to retain a credit balance.

Companies limited by guarantee

It is possible to establish a company which is not and is not intended to be a charity. However, for this purpose we will assume that the company is intended to be charitable. If this is the case it is essential to apply for it to be registered as a charity before it has commenced its activities, although it must be in existence before it can be registered.

The constitutional documents of a company are its memorandum and articles of association. Broadly speaking, the memorandum sets out the name of the company, where it is to be registered (and incorporated), the purpose for which it is to be established, the powers it will have to achieve its objects and how any profits arising and any surplus left when it is dissolved are to be applied. The articles establish how the company is to be managed and its affairs conducted.

Drafts of these documents should be submitted to the Charity Commission for approval before the company is incorporated, together with a form setting out detailed information about the proposed charity. This form can be obtained from the Charity Commission. It will be helpful to use the memorandum and articles of an existing registered charity as a basis. The Commission is chiefly concerned with the memorandum but the draft articles of association should be submitted as well. The Commission is extremely overworked and the delay in replies to letters means that each exchange of correspondence can be expected to take six weeks as a minimum. When the Commission is satisfied with the draft it will be passed to the Inland Revenue, which may be expected to have some further observations. When the draft memorandum and articles have been approved, the company can be formed.

In order to incorporate the company, at least one of the initial members must sign the memorandum and articles of association. These documents must be sent to the Registrar of Companies together with a form setting out the initial registered office, the details of the first directors and the secretary and a statutory declaration to the effect that all the formalities required by company law have been complied with, as well as a cheque for the fee payable. About three weeks later the certificate of incorporation will be issued by the Registrar and this marks the beginning of the existence of the company.

The first meeting of the board of directors should then be held. The company will not yet be a registered charity so its activities must be limited but it is useful to proceed to open bank accounts, appoint auditors and perhaps admit additional members. The directors can then resolve to register the company as a charity. This requires the completion and signature on behalf of the company of a form obtainable from the Charity Commission. This is then sent to the Commission with a letter specifying the reference under which the Memorandum and Articles were approved. In due course the Commission will respond with confirmation that the company has been registered as a charity and will allocate a registration number.

CONCLUSION

Setting up and running an organisation requires skill and time. However, this effort will not be wasted if it enables those at the sharp end of the project to function properly and without unnecessary administrative worries and, above all, disputes.

It may be possible to obtain the services of a volunteer solicitor or accountant to assist in establishing and running the organisation. Whether or not this is possible, the National Council for Voluntary Organisations (see Appendix 1) provides advice and information for charities and voluntary bodies and publishes a number of useful guides on setting up, funding and running them. If you are embarking upon the establishment of a charity, you probably will need professional help. If this is not available on a voluntary basis, you will pay less to your professional adviser if you have thought out beforehand exactly what you want to do and are ready to give the person helping you the full details of your intentions and those involved.

Chapter 10

Powers of attorney, wills and probate

Nigel Clarke

INTRODUCTION

Preparing for death or for the possibility of being mentally or physically incapable of handling one's own affairs is something that few relish. Yet one of the few certainties of life is that all people die and, with improving medical care, increasing numbers survive longer with impaired mental or physical abilities. The legal aspects of these matters, so far as people with HIV infection and disease are concerned, are no different from those applying to any other member of the public and generally no special provisions apply. Nevertheless, a person with AIDS, and those trying to assist them, may well feel that the possibility of death, or of being mentally or physically incapable, may occur sooner rather than later and that preparation therefore ought to be made without delay.

It is hoped that the following contribution to this book will give guidance on how individuals may arrange their affairs so as to ensure that others can attend to their wishes if they are no longer mentally or physically capable of doing so, and so as to ensure that in the event of death, their wishes are carried out. In addition guidance is offered to relatives, partners, and representatives after death.

POWERS OF ATTORNEY AND THE COURT OF PROTECTION

The legal principle of agency

The principle of one person appointing another to carry out duties for such a person has long been enshrined in English Law. It is known as the principle of agency and arises whenever one person, called 'the agent', has authority to act on behalf of another, called 'the principal', and consents so to act. Thus, an infirm pensioner may arrange for a relative or friend to collect a pension from the post office by signing the requisite authority on the pension book. With a properly-signed authority by its customer, a bank may permit another to sign cheques for those unable to do so. Even the act of arranging for another to do domestic chores, such as shopping, creates in law a relationship of principal and agent. However, piecemeal arrangements may well prove unsatisfactory and having one legally-binding document will invariably prove to be more useful. This document is known as a power of attorney.

The definition of the power of attorney

A power of attorney is or may be defined as a document by which one person ('the donor') gives another person ('the attorney') the power to act on his or her behalf and in his or her name. It may be completely general, entitling the attorney to do virtually everything the donor could do, or it may be limited to certain defined objects. The donor can appoint one, two or more people to act as attorneys. Where two or more people are appointed joint attorneys they must always act together and this may prove a useful safeguard against improper acts by one attorney; if they are appointed joint and several attorneys, they may either act together or individually. The practical purpose of a power of attorney is not only to invest the attorney with power to act for the donor, but also to provide the attorney with a document defining the extent of the attorney's authority, which can be produced as evidence to third parties.

In every case a power of attorney must be in the form of a properly executed deed. The donor must also have sufficient mental capacity to grant the power and this generally coincides with the ability of the donor to enter into a binding contract; nevertheless, it has now been held that an enduring power of attorney is valid when, at the time it is made, the donor fully understands the nature and effect of the power, but on account of recurrent mental disability could not be said to be capable of managing and administering his or her property (Re K., Re F., [1988] 1 AER 358). The signature of the donor must be attested by a witness who should not be related to either the donor or the attorney and who must give his or her full name, address and occupation. The two statutes that deal in any comprehensive way with powers of attorney are the Powers of Attorney Act 1971 and the Enduring Powers of Attorney Act 1985. Unless it is proposed to use one of the forms prescribed in these Acts, the donor should always consult a solicitor in connection with the preparation of a power of attorney.

Advice on simple or limited powers of attorney

The Powers of Attorney Act 1971 simplified and codified the law relating to powers of attorney and provided a simple form which is suitable in the majority of circumstances. The prudent donor will consult a solicitor to ensure that the simple form is sufficient for the purposes required. On occasions it will not be; for example where property is owned jointly with another, a simple power of attorney will not give the attorney any right to deal with the donor's share and interest in such property (*Walia* v. *Michael Naughton Ltd* [1985]1WLR1115). In these circumstances a power must be granted under the Trustee Act 1925, and the solicitor will advise. Where it is desired to give the attorney limited powers only, such as to buy or sell a particular property or to deal with certain investments only, the advice of a solicitor should always be sought. It is much more difficult to draw up a limited power of attorney, as it must be drafted in very precise terms: if there is any ambiguity as to whether a particular power has been delegated, a court will rule that it has not been so delegated.

The advantages of such a simple power are that it is easily entered into, gives the attorney wide powers and is easily revoked if the donor no longer wishes the attorney to deal with their affairs.

The disadvantages are, first, that the power given to the attorney is extremely wide, giving the attorney almost unlimited rights over the donor's property, with the resultant possibility of irresponsible behaviour by the attorney, although the chance of this may be reduced by appointing two or more attorneys to act jointly; and secondly, in all cases involving an ordinary power of attorney, that the power is automatically revoked if the donor becomes mentally incapable. Not only is this the time when the donor might reasonably be expected to need the assistance of the attorney but it gives rise to two major inconveniences. First, it is often not clear when the donor becomes incapable, particularly in the case of the donor gradually failing with the onset of old age or illness. The validity of the power may therefore be frequently questioned. Secondly, there is no way in which a person can privately arrange in advance to give someone the authority to handle his or her affairs when, at a later date, he or she becomes incapable. The only mechanism that the law provides is an application by someone to the Court of Protection to be appointed receiver. That application is made after the patient has become incapable and without him or her having any say in the selection of the person concerned.

The enduring power of attorney

Principles and definitions

The purpose of the Enduring Powers of Attorney Act 1985 was to meet both these objections while introducing safeguards to avoid abuses. An enduring power of attorney must be granted in the prescribed form which makes it clear to the donor that the power will continue to be effective even if the donor becomes mentally incapable. It also must be executed by the attorney. This achieves two ends. It ensures that the attorney accepts that he or she should be appointed: whereas an ordinary power can be granted to an attorney who knows nothing of the appointment and may not be prepared to accept it. Further, the attorney must acknowledge the statutory duty that they may later have to register the power. That duty arises when the attorney has reason to believe that the donor is, or is becoming, mentally incapable. The attorney must then apply to the Court of Protection to register the power. The powers of an attorney appointed under an enduring power vary, depending on the status of the donor and the stages in the registration procedure. The Court of Protection has a general jurisdiction over enduring powers of attorney.

Most individuals will find the enduring power of attorney is more suitable for their needs. It is most important to note that an enduring power of attorney is only valid if completed in accordance with the strict statutory requirements and on the prescribed forms. Care should be taken not just to copy out sections of the prescribed forms since the headings and side notes form an integral part of the form. The forms can be obtained from legal stationers, although many donors will wish to consult a solicitor to ensure that all the legal formalities have been complied with, not least that the correct form has been used. Although the statute only came into force in March 1986, the initial prescribed form has already been replaced twice. The prudent donor may also consider that in the event of his or her mental incapacity the validity of the power may be called into question particularly where an unmarried partner or friend has been appointed and there might be conflict with blood relatives. In the event of there being any doubt at all as to the mental capacity of the donor, the cautious donor and attorney might also wish to obtain the opinion of the donor's doctor as to the capacity of the donor before making the power.

What acts an enduring power of attorney (or any power) authorises the attorney to do is a question of construction of the document. The donor may in completing the form both limit the powers given and also exclude powers over any particular matter. Where particular powers are to be delineated legal advice should be sought in drafting the particular clauses required. The enduring power of attorney has the additional advantage that it may be drawn in such a way that it becomes valid only when the donor becomes mentally incapable.

Duties of the attorney

Once the power of attorney has been completed and signed by the donor (and the attorney where appropriate), the attorney, if acting immediately, will usually take possession of the power and register it with any organisations the donor has dealings with: these will commonly include the donor's bank and building society and may well include government organisations such as the Department of Social Security. The attorney takes or sends the power to the organisations concerned and they will make a note of it in their registers usually stamping the power to show that it has been so registered, and return it to the attorney. The attorney will then be able to sign cheques on behalf of the donor, make withdrawals from accounts or collect pensions. In practice many attorneys will prefer to open a separate bank account in their name as attorney to pay into it the donor's income and to pay out on behalf of the donor as the donor may instruct. The basic rule is that duties are not imposed on the attorney, but that the attorney is given the power to deal with the affairs of the donor.

The Court of Protection – the administration of the affairs of a person suffering from mental incapacity

Where there is an enduring power of attorney

In the previous section it was mentioned that where an individual has created an enduring power of attorney the attorney may continue to act even when the individual becomes mentally incapable either temporarily or permanently. However, the attorney has a duty to apply to the Court of Protection to register the power as soon as practicable when they have reason to believe that the donor is, or is becoming, mentally incapable. It should be noted that for the duty to arise the attorney does not have to be sure, or have proof, that the donor is actually mentally incapable. Belief of a gradual decline into incapability should be enough (the Enduring Powers of Attorney Act 1985, s. 4[1], [2]).

Before applying to register, the attorney has to give preliminary notice of intention to do so. Written notice must be given to the donor and to the donor's relatives. At least three relatives, if there are three who qualify, must be given notice. The relatives are placed in classes, in order of priority, and if the requirement to give notice to three relatives means that any one person in a class has to be notified, then all the relatives in that class must be given notice (the Enduring Powers of Attorney Act 1985, Schedule 1, paragraph 2[4]).

The Act sets out the following classes of relatives to be given notice:

- the donor's husband or wife;
- the donor's children;
- the donor's parents;
- the donor's brothers and sisters, whether of the whole or half blood;
- the widow or widower of a child of the donor;
- the donor's grandchildren;
- the children of the donor's brothers and sisters of the whole blood;
- the children of the donor's brothers and sisters of the half blood;
- the donor's uncles and aunts of the whole blood; and
- the children of the donor's uncles and aunts of the whole blood.

No notice need be given to a relative whose name and address the attorney does not know and which cannot be reasonably obtained, or to relatives reasonably believed to be minors or mentally incapable.

The prescribed form (form EP1) of preliminary notice should be used. Registration in the court is made by letter or by completing the prescribed form (form EP2) addressed to the Court of Protection at Stewart House, 24 Kingsway, London WC2B 6JX. There are five grounds of objection set out in the Act, one or more of them if established will defeat a registration application.

The grounds are:

1 that the power purported to have been created by the instrument was not valid as an enduring power of attorney;
2 that the power created by the instrument was no longer subsisting;
3 that the application is premature because the donor is not yet becoming mentally incapable;
4 that fraud or undue pressure was used to induce the donor to create the power;
5 that, having regard to all the circumstances and in particular the attorney's relationship to or connection with the donor, the attorney is unsuitable to be the donor's attorney.

These two last grounds may be of particular concern where an unmarried partner or friend has been appointed and there are objections from blood relatives. The importance of ensuring that the power is properly created and that proof of mental capacity obtained when creating the power, can be seen.

A prudent attorney may well wish to consult a solicitor if it is necessary to consider registration. The procedural steps laid down need to be carefully and accurately followed.

Once the power has been duly registered, subject to the jurisdiction of, and any directions from, the Court of Protection, the attorney may continue to manage the affairs of the donor.

Appointment of a receiver

Where no enduring power has been entered into before mental incapacity, any person wishing to continue to assist in the management of the affairs of an individual can do so only after having been duly appointed by the Court of Protection (also known as the Public Trust Office) to be receiver of the individual, always then known as the patient. There are exceptions to this rule, the principal one being that the Department of Social Security has power to appoint individuals to receive and administer income support and other benefits for the patient; and therefore unless the patient has other assets which require an order of the Court, no application need be made. In addition, where the assets are small and the patient's needs are otherwise provided for, application need not be made.

The application for the appointment of a receiver is normally made by the nearest relative of the patient. However, if such a person is unable or unwilling to apply, another relative or friend of the patient may do so, but the reason should clearly be stated. Relatives of degree equal to or nearer than the applicant should be notified of the application and the Court must be informed that this has been done.

Printed forms for use in all proceedings in the Court are obtainable free of charge from the Court Office, Stewart House, 24 Kingsway, London WC2B 6JX. Upon written request the Court will supply a set of application forms comprising the form of application (CP1), and certificate of family and property (CP5) and the medical certificate (CP3). The applicant completes the application form and the certificate of family and property which is a lengthy form upon which the whole of the income and property of the patient is set out together with details of the patient's family and any will that might have been made. A short history of the patient is included in the form and if the applicant has any suggestions to make with regard to the disposal of the patient's property, or what ought to be done with it, such comments are again made on the form. The medical certificate is completed by the patient's general practitioner if the patient is at home, or if in hospital by the appropriate doctor having charge of the patient. The doctor will charge a fee for the report.

Although applications can be made personally and by post to the Enquiries and Applications Branch of the Court, in most cases the applicant will wish to instruct a solicitor and in particular when, for example, questions of title to property and the sale of the patient's land or house property arises, or in applications which will result in the preparation and execution of deeds. All the costs involved, including those of the solicitor and of the doctor, will be assessed by the Court and are payable out of the assets of the patient.

Once the application has been lodged at Court it will be processed by the Court and a date fixed for the consideration of it. Attendance is not required or usual in most applications. The form of application, with the hearing date endorsed, is duly returned to the applicant together with a covering letter of explanation from the Court which must be served on the patient. A copy of the letter is returned to the Court with a certificate as to service. Where a solicitor is instructed, all these steps will be dealt with by the solicitor who will complete all the forms for the applicant ready for signature

A fee is required (at present £50.00) to support the initial application and further fees become payable from time to time: these are paid out of the patient's assets. In addition, the receiver may be required to give security for their dealings with the cash passing through their hands as receiver and for their acts as receiver generally, the amount being fixed on the hearing of the application. The security is normally given by means of a fidelity guarantee bond obtained from an insurance company approved by the Court. The premium is paid out of the assets of the patient.

After the hearing the Court will send the applicant, or their solicitor, a draft of the proposed order to be made. The applicant has the opportunity of commenting on it before the Court makes the order final. The applicant, thereafter known as the receiver, may only carry out those steps that he or she is specifically authorised by the Court so to do. If at any time the receiver requires further directions, these are applied for by letter to the Court.

The receiver registers the final order, endorsed with the seal of the Court, with such organisations as may be directed by the Court, in order that the directions of the Court be carried out. Registration is effected by taking or sending the sealed office copy of the order to the organisation concerned who will enter and record the order in their registers and mark the order accordingly. Often the order will contain directions to an organisation such as a bank to lodge monies in the funds of the Supreme Court, and the bank will carry out such steps without further reference to the receiver. Normally the receiver will also be required to open a bank account as receiver of the patient.

Receivers are required to keep a careful record of all income and expenditure received or made on behalf of the patient and each year on the anniversary of the appointment a detailed statement is required to be lodged at the Court showing this information and the resultant balance in the hands of the receiver. The advantages of ensuring that all income is paid into the bank account and all expenditure paid out of the bank account will be seen. The form of account to be completed will be sent to the receiver by the Court some short time before the account is due. Many receivers instruct their solicitor to prepare the annual account and again the costs of doing so will be assessed by the Court and paid out of the assets of the patient.

The Court also has the power to make a new will for the patient upon an application being made and, in addition to next of kin, the Court will consider those for whom the patient, if in sound mind, might be expected to make some substantial provision. The Court has powers to deal with such an application on an emergency basis. Where it is proposed to consider an application the receiver should take legal advice.

Although the procedure in the Court of Protection may seem cumbersome, the Court stresses that it is trying to help those who are unable to help themselves and the officials of the Court are normally very helpful and considerate to deal with.

WILLS

What an individual should do to ensure that their affairs are in such an order so that their wishes will be carried out in the event of death.

The rules of intestacy

Any person who dies without having made a valid will, or who has made one that has been revoked either deliberately or, for example, by marriage, is known as having died intestate. All the estate of the deceased (with certain exceptions dealt with later) will be distributed in accordance with the Administration of Estates Act 1925 (as amended). Provision is made in that Act for properly married spouses of the deceased and for blood relatives. The spouse is entitled to a lump sum, known as the statutory legacy, together with the deceased's personal chattels and an interest in the balance of the estate. The amount of the statutory legacy and interest in the balance depends on whether the deceased is survived by children and/or parents. The levels vary from time to time, but at present the spouse, where there are children, would receive a statutory legacy of £125,000, where there are no children, but, say, parents, the statutory legacy is £200,000. The claims of the blood relatives are laid down in a strict table. Such statutory provision may not in any way reflect the wishes of an individual, even if married and wishing to benefit family only. Unmarried partners have no claim notwithstanding the length of any relationship that may have existed. Only by the execution of a valid will can the wishes of an individual be effectively carried out. The vital importance of making a will can therefore be appreciated.

Joint ownership

Where an individual desires another both to be in a position to handle their affairs and to benefit from their property entirely, in addition to the preparation of a valid will and an enduring power of attorney, the individual may wish to consider vesting any property, bank accounts and other assets jointly with the person it is intended to benefit.

The advantage of this is that upon death of one of the individuals such property will in most circumstances belong automatically in its entirety to the survivor. Not only can the survivor continue to operate any accounts that there may have been which have been put into joint names, but also, it may be unnecessary for the survivor ever to have to take out a grant of probate or letters of administration to the estate of the deceased partner. Nevertheless, joint property should always be carefully checked and in particular the title to joint land, houses and flats should be checked by a solicitor. The fact that the land, house or flat is in two names does not necessarily mean that the two owners hold the title 'beneficial joint tenants'. Only where property is so held does it pass to the survivor. Another, perhaps less obvious, advantage is that in a situation where there might be aggrieved blood relatives a transfer in lifetime may be more difficult to challenge than a will, the grant of probate to which can, sometimes, be held up for a considerable period of time. A solicitor should always be consulted before land, a house or flat is transferred into joint names.

The disadvantage of vesting property in joint names is that without the consent of the person to whom the property is transferred, the transfer is irrevocable. Any individual must therefore realise that unlike a will or power of attorney that, with mental capacity, may be changed at any time, the transfer into joint names, without the consent of the person to whom the transfer is made, is a once-and-for-all step.

A will – definition, preparation and advice

A will may be defined as the declaration in a prescribed manner of the intention of the person (known as the 'testator') making it with regard to matters which the testator wishes to take effect upon or after death. A will is normally made for the purpose of making dispositions of property to take effect after the testator's death, but it may also be made for the purpose of appointing executors or other persons whom the testator wishes to manage or assist in managing any part of their estate, for appointing guardians of the testator's children after death, for revoking or altering any previous will, or for any similar purpose taking effect on or after death. Every will, however, has the essential characteristic that, during the lifetime of the testator, it is a mere declaration of intention and may be freely revoked or altered in the prescribed manner. Until death it is ambulatory, or without a fixed effect, and capable of operating on property which the testator acquires after it is made.

A valid will can only be made by a person of at least 18 years of age, who has sufficient mental capacity to do so. Mental capacity is defined as having a sound disposing mind, both when giving instructions for the will and when executing it. The person making the will must understand the nature of the act and the effect of it, the extent of the property which is being disposed of, and must be able to comprehend and appreciate any claims which ought to be considered. Although mere eccentricity or foolishness does not, of itself, invalidate a will. If there is any doubt at all then the advice of the person's doctor should be obtained and if necessary the advice of a psychiatrist.

The will must be in writing and properly executed. Section 9 of the Wills Act 1837, as amended by section 17 of the Administration of Justice Act 1982, provides that a will is duly executed if: it is in writing; it is signed by the testator or by some other person in his presence and by his or her direction; it appears that the testator intended by his or her signature to give effect to the will; the signature is made or acknowledged by the testator in the presence of two or more witnesses present at the same time, with each witness either attesting and signing the will or acknowledging his or her signature in the presence of the testator (but not necessarily in the presence of any other witness).

Although, therefore, the legal requirements of a will are not particularly complex, unless the form of the document in relation to the date and signatures of the testator and witnesses is correct, difficulties will almost invariably arise when trying to prove the will after the death of the testator and an affidavit of due execution will be required to be sworn by one or both of the witnesses. Unfortunately, errors in a will are, by the very nature of the document, usually not discovered until after the death of the testator, when it is too late to attempt rectification. Further and in addition, although the contents of a will only have to be in clear and unambiguous form to express the wishes of the testator, in practice a testator may easily use words that do not have the desired effect and which cause considerable expense and difficulty to executors and beneficiaries. An individual wishing to make a will would be well advised to consult a solicitor.

Before taking legal advice and consulting a solicitor, the intending testator should consider in particular the following factors. First, the appointment of executors and trustees: there must be at least one, and where there are infants benefiting it is better that there are at least two. In preference they should be close relatives or friends, but if none are suitable, prepared to act, or the testator prefers, a bank can be appointed, or professional executors such as solicitors. Where the appointment of a bank or professional as trustee is considered, the testator should be aware of the fees that are likely to be charged: in particular some testators are surprised at the level of fees charged by banks. The duty of the executor is to administer the estate of the testator upon death. The executor may attend to the duties personally or instruct a solicitor to carry out all or some of the tasks. The burden on the executor depends on the size and complexity of the estate.

Secondly, the testator should also consider what particular powers the executors should be given and whether the testator has any particular wishes to make with regard the disposal of his or her body. Thus, for example, the testator may wish to give the executors power to advance money to minors who would not otherwise be entitled to it until attaining the age of 18 years; the testator may wish to give directions as to cremation or burial, or as to a particular type of funeral ceremony or service, although such directions do not actually bind the executor. The testator may wish to leave their personal possessions to the executor to deal with at their discretion. If the testator has children, guardians of the children may be appointed by the will, although the Children Act 1989 limits this power to:

- the mother of an illegitimate child, the father of whom does not have parental responsibility for such a child;

- mothers or fathers of legitimate children, who have separated or divorced, and obtained a residence order in court proceedings; and
- mothers or fathers, including the father of an illegitimate child who has parental responsibility for such a child, when the other parent has already died.

Thirdly, the testator should then consider how they wish the estate to be disposed of: do they wish to leave bequests to any individual or charity, and to whom is the residue left? Where there are a number of beneficiaries, because of the difficulty of establishing the balance of a testator's estate, it is normally better to express shares of the estate as percentages of the residue, rather than as fixed monetary amounts.

The individual should make their wishes very clear to the solicitor instructed, who will then be able to draw up the will in the correct form, to ensure that the wishes of the testator are carried out and that those intended to benefit actually do so.

The testator should note, as mentioned above, that he or she cannot generally give away any interest that they might have in property owned jointly with another. It is possible for alterations to be made to the legal title to land, houses and flats to enable the testator to divide his or her interest in property owned jointly with another: this is known as severing the equity in property and the advice of a solicitor should always be taken before such a step is carried out.

Provision for dependants

Every testator in making a will must consider the provisions of the Inheritance (Provision for Family and Dependants) Act 1975. This Act considerably widened the classes of those who could apply for reasonable provision to be made out of the estate of a deceased person. The Act provides the following categories of persons (applicants) who may apply to the Court on the ground that the disposition of the deceased's estate effected by their will or the law relating to intestacy, or the combination of their will and that law, is not such as to make reasonable financial provision for the applicant:

- the wife or husband of the deceased;
- a former wife or former husband of the deceased who has not remarried;
- a child of the deceased;
- any person (not being a child of the deceased) who, in the case of any marriage to which the deceased was at any time a party, was treated by the deceased as a child of the family in relation to that marriage;
- any person (not mentioned above) who immediately before the death of the deceased was being maintained, either wholly or partly, by the deceased, and it is defined that such a person shall be treated as being maintained by the deceased either, wholly or partly, as the case may be, if the deceased otherwise than for full valuable consideration was making a substantial contribution in money or money's worth towards the reasonable needs of that person.

There has been relatively little authority about claims in the last category, but decided cases clearly show that it applies in what is known as the 'mistress' type of case and it is contended that there is no reason why it should not apply where there has been dependency by one partner on another in a gay relationship. Until recently many supposed that the words 'otherwise than for full valuable consideration' might defeat claims where it could be said that the benefits the deceased gave to the applicant (such as the provision of a home) equalled the benefits the applicant gave the deceased (such as care and attention in a terminal illness). It is now clear that this is not necessarily the case and the Court need not value too finely benefits flowing between a couple (*Bishop* v. *Plumley* [1991] 1 AER 236).

Testators should therefore ensure that they have made adequate provision for dependants, otherwise the other intended beneficiaries and executors are almost bound to be met with a claim that may be expensive, lengthy and deplete the estate.

Exceptions to the rules on intestacy and wills

It should also be stated that there are a number of exceptions to the rules relating to intestacy and with regard to wills. First, assets such as National Savings certificates may have been nominated in favour of another. Such nominations take priority over the terms of a will or over intestacy and, if they are no longer desired, have to be specifically revoked in writing to the director of National Savings.

Secondly, joint property (see above) will usually pass to the survivor.

Thirdly, and perhaps most importantly, many individuals of working age are now, through their employment, members of pension or other schemes which provide for substantial death-in-service benefits, commonly two, three or four times the annual salary. It is often thought that such benefits belong to the member of the scheme and therefore may be disposed of as the member thinks fit. This is usually not the case: the benefits belong to the trustees of the scheme and do not constitute part of a testator's estate. Payment is at the discretion of the trustees. Normally, trustees invite written requests as to whom payment is to be made in the event of death; such a written request must be made to ensure that the benefit goes to the desired person. Often the request can be contained in a sealed envelope that does not need to be opened until death. Trustees, upon the death of a member of a scheme, would normally expect to pay out to spouses and blood relatives and therefore it is prudent, not only to complete the appropriate form of nomination, but also to give reasons in writing where an unmarried partner is intended to benefit. Trustees invariably will pay to the person in whose favour the request is made, but they are not bound to do so.

DEATH

Expected deaths

Death in a hospital

When a person with AIDS enters hospital particulars of next of kin will be taken. The next of kin will normally be the nearest blood relative or spouse, but may be a close friend. There is no magic in the words 'next of kin' and anyone entering hospital should not be afraid to nominate a close friend, rather than a blood relative. If the death occurs in hospital the ward sister will contact the person named as next of kin. The body will be removed to the hospital mortuary where it can be kept until the person responsible for making the funeral arrangements (the executor if there is a will or the spouse or nearest blood relative if there is not) arranges for it to be taken away. It will be noted that the persons entitled to make such arrangements are the executors of the deceased, and only where there are none do the nearest blood relatives become entitled. Normally funeral directors have a chapel of rest which can be used for a small fee, and arrangements can be made for the body to be taken there. However, if a post mortem is required the body cannot be removed from the mortuary until authorised by the pathologist. Where the deceased was a person with AIDS it may be appropriate for the body to be removed directly from the hospital mortuary to the crematorium for the funeral. Should such a situation arise it is important that legal advice is sought immediately (consult Appendix 1 for relevant advice). The ward sister will arrange for the executor or, in default, for the nearest relative to collect the dead person's possessions.

Death at home

If the death occurs at home, but was expected, the doctor who attended the dead person during their final illness should be contacted. If the cause of death can be certified immediately, the doctor will say so. The executor or nearest blood relative can then arrange for the funeral director to remove the body.

The death certificate

In both cases the doctor will give the executor or next of kin a medical certificate that shows the cause of death (this will be in a sealed envelope, addressed to the Registrar of Births and Deaths) with a formal notice stating that the doctor has signed the medical certificate and an explanation of how to register the death. Sometimes executors or next of kin are concerned that the word AIDS does not appear on the death certificate issued by the Registrar. The Registrar must enter all the causes of death given by the doctor in the medical certificate and therefore any representations must be made to the doctor certifying the death, before the medical certificate is prepared. If the death was known to be caused by a natural illness but the doctors wish to know more about the cause of death, they may ask the relatives for permission to carry out a post-mortem examination. This is a medical examination of the body which can find out more about the cause of death.

Unexpected deaths

Referral to the coroner

If the death occurs at home and is sudden or unexpected, the family doctor and the police must be advised. The doctor may be able to give a medical certificate, but in the following circumstances cannot do so and must report the death to the coroner if:

- no doctor has treated the deceased during their last illness;
- the doctor attending the patient did not see them within fourteen days before death, or after death;
- the death occurred during an operation or before recovery from the effect of an anaesthetic;
- the death was sudden or unexplained or attended by suspicious circumstances;
- the death might be due to an industrial injury or disease, or to accident, violence, neglect or to any kind of poisoning.

Post-mortem examination

The coroner may be able to ascertain that the death was due to a natural cause and that there is a doctor who is able to certify the cause of death. If this is not the case the coroner arranges to have the body removed for a post-mortem examination to be made. The examination often shows that the death was due to natural causes and in such a case there is no inquest. Instead, the coroner sends a certificate (known as the Pink Form) to the Registrar of Births and Deaths. At that stage the coroner can, if required, issue a certificate for cremation. Alternatively, after registering the death, the Registrar can issue a certificate for burial or cremation.

The inquest

If the death is not due to a natural cause, the coroner is obliged by law to hold an inquest. The inquest is not a trial, but an enquiry held to establish the facts. The coroner decides which witnesses should be asked or summoned to attend and the order in which they should give evidence. Anyone who can give evidence is entitled to come forward at an inquest, but all the evidence must be relevant to the purpose of the inquest. Only a person who has a proper interest may question a witness, but such questions must be relevant and incriminating questions may not be asked. Any person who has a proper interest may be represented by a solicitor, although legal aid is not available for such purposes. The definition of a properly interested person may not necessarily include the unmarried partner of the deceased. The decision is one for the coroner to make.

The body may be buried or cremated as soon as the coroner is satisfied that no further tests are needed and the necessary certificates have been issued. In view of the fact that the death can only be registered after the inquest, which may be some time after the death, the coroner may upon request supply a letter stating the fact of death and explaining that the death cannot be registered until the inquest has been completed.

The registration of a death

Procedure

Deaths must be registered within five days, unless referred to the coroner. The death must be registered with the Registrar of Births and Deaths for the area in which the death occurred. The registration is usually made by the nearest blood relative. If the death is to be registered by another, the entitlement to register is 'causing the body to be buried or cremated'. Some registrars insist that a blood relative, if there is one able to perform the task, attends for the registration. There may therefore be a conflict between an executor, who has the responsibility for the funeral, and a blood relative who has the responsibility of registering the death. The relevance of this is seen below.

Information to be given to the Registrar

The medical certificate showing the cause of death, together with the deceased's medical card (if available), should be taken to the Registrar. If the coroner has been involved the Pink Form also must be taken. The following information must be given to the Registrar:

- the date and place of death;
- the deceased's last address;
- the deceased's first names and surname (and maiden name in the case of a married woman);
- the deceased's date and place of birth;
- the deceased's occupation and, in the case of a woman, the name and occupation of the deceased's spouse (if any);
- whether the deceased was getting any pension or allowance from public funds;
- if the deceased was married, the date of birth of the surviving widow or widower;
- whether the deceased is to be buried or cremated.

Issue of the certificate for burial or cremation

The Registrar will supply, to the person attending to register the death, the certificate for burial or cremation (the Green Form) unless the coroner has given an order or certificate for the purpose, together with a short certificate of death for the Department of Social Security only: this is completed and handed in to the Department if appropriate. The death itself is entered into the register, but a certified copy (known as a certified copy death certificate), although available, is not supplied unless requested and the appropriate fee paid. In almost all circumstances a certified copy of the entry should be obtained.

The funeral

Most funerals are arranged by a funeral director and it is a good idea to choose a member of the National Association of Funeral Directors. It is important to ensure that the funeral director is sympathetic. Executors should tell the funeral director what has caused or contributed towards the death. The Terrence Higgins Trust helpline or local AIDS helpline may be able to assist.

Estimates will be given, if asked, but the funeral director's fee will not cover things like the church or crematorium fees, flowers or notices in the local paper. In cases of hardship an application may be made for financial assistance towards the funeral to the Department of Social Security. The financial hardship is that of the person responsible for arranging the funeral, not the deceased. It should be noted that the Department of Social Security may later require repayment from the estate of the deceased, e.g., if the deceased has property which is later sold.

The funeral director should be instructed as soon as possible and the Green Form supplied by the Registrar handed over. The decisions as to burial or cremation and as to the type of funeral are for the deceased's executor or where there is none the nearest blood relative. The funeral director will make all the appropriate arrangements in accordance with instructions given, including the removal of the body to the chapel of rest and completing the forms necessary to enable cremation to go ahead.

It should be noted that the funeral director cannot proceed without the Green Form. Conflict may arise where there are differences between the blood relatives, who have registered the death and therefore have the Green Form, and the executor who is responsible for the arrangements. In such a situation legal advice should be sought without delay.

PROBATE AND THE ADMINISTRATION OF THE ESTATE

Obtaining the grant

When a person dies somebody has to deal with the money property and possessions left, known as the estate, by collecting in all the money, paying any debts and distributing the estate to those entitled to it. The term probate often means the issuing of a legal document to one or more people authorising them to do this.

Property not in the estate

Some property does not belong to the estate of the deceased, or does not pass under the terms of the deceased's will or intestacy. Thus where the deceased owned property jointly with another it passes in most cases to the survivor. A certified copy death certificate is produced to the bank or building society to enable the deceased's name to be removed from the account and permit the survivor to continue to operate it.

So far as land, houses and flats are concerned, the advice of a solicitor should be sought: if the joint owners hold the property as beneficial joint tenants it will pass to the survivor; if the title is not registered a certified copy death certificate merely needs to be placed with the title deeds; if the title is registered, the land or charge certificate will have to be submitted to HM Land Registry for amendment. If the property is held by the deceased and another as tenants-in-common, then the deceased's share falls in to be administered with the remainder of the estate and a grant of probate or administration is usually required.

As far as nominations of Savings Certificates are concerned, a certified copy death certificate is sent to the Director of National Savings, who will then send any form that needs to be completed with regard to encashment in favour of the nominated person.

So far as death-in-service benefits relating to occupational pension schemes are concerned, the certified copy death certificate is sent to the trustees who will usually make enquiries as to any will made, as to what blood relatives there are, and in particular to any request made to them by the deceased. The trustees will then make their distribution in accordance with their discretion and the rules of the scheme.

Applying for a grant

The legal document issued to enable the estate to be dealt with is known as a grant of representation. First, it has to be considered whether it is necessary to make any application for a grant. In the previous paragraph circumstances were set out where no grant is necessary. Further, if the whole estate of the deceased comprises less than £5,000 in value, it may be possible for it to be released without a grant. In such circumstances enquiries should be made of the organisations such as insurance companies, banks and building societies, to see if they will release the money without a grant. They are not bound to do so as releasing money without a grant is entirely at their discretion. The authority for this is the Administration of Estates (Small Payments) Act 1965 as amended by the Administration of Estates (Small Payments) (Increase of Limit) Order 1984, SI 1984/539, which should be stated when a request in writing is made.

Where there are other assets such as shareholdings, experience shows that it is probably easier, and cheaper, to apply for a grant in any event as the forms to be completed, without a grant, are often complex and require guarantees by banks, which have to be paid for. The person making the application to deal with the assets without the necessity of obtaining a grant must still be the executor named in the will, the principal beneficiary if the executor has died or the nearest blood relative if there is no will. The person retains all the responsibilities with regard to the administration of the estate that are referred to below.

In other circumstances a grant of representation is required; if there is a will, this consists of a grant of Probate to the executors named in the will, or if there is no will, a grant of Letters of Administration to the spouse or nearest blood relatives. Where there is a will and either the executors have already died, or none are named, a grant of Letters of Administration is made to the principal beneficiaries. The grant is issued by the Probate Registry of the Family Division of the High Court. In London personal enquiries can be made at Room 526, 5th Floor, Golden Cross House, Duncannon Street, London WC2N 4JF. There are local probate registries and offices in most cities and major towns.

Excepted estates

There are two categories of estate to consider when applying to obtain a grant.

First, those estates known as 'excepted estates', broadly comprising estates with a net worth of less than £125,000 (for deaths after 1 July 1991) and where no Inland Revenue account has to be delivered. The net worth is calculated by taking the total of all assets (the gross estate) and deducting the funeral expenses and any debts.

Secondly, other estates, generally exceeding £125,000 in value, where a complex Inland Revenue form IHT 200, or less complex form IHT 202, is required. In computing the value of the estate the total assets of the deceased including personal items and any share in jointly owned property are taken.

Inheritance Tax is not payable until the value of the estate exceeds £154,000. The tax is then payable at a fixed rate of 40 per cent on the excess.

Who may apply

At most, four persons may apply for a grant of Probate or Letters of Administration. In an application for Letters of Administration, where there are infant beneficiaries, at least two must apply, otherwise one person may apply. If there is a will, the applicants will be the executors named. If no executors are named or those named have died or refuse to act, the applicant will be the principal or residuary beneficiary. If there is no will a strict table is laid down, commencing with the spouse, then in order and in default of any category, the children, the grandchildren, the parents, the brothers and sisters of the whole or half blood and their issue, grandparents, and uncles or aunts of the whole or half blood and their issue.

Procedure

Applicants may wish to instruct a solicitor, but where they wish to deal with matters personally, they have to obtain and complete the application forms, return them with the certified copy death certificate and the original will, if any, to the appropriate Probate Registry, and attend an interview.

The appropriate forms can be obtained from the Principal Registry or from local registries and offices. The probate application asks for details of the deceased and the applicants. Where the estate is not an excepted estate, a detailed account of the estate for the Inland Revenue must be completed. The completed forms, together with the certified copy death certificate and original will (if any), are sent to the Probate Registry chosen by the applicant as being most convenient. Applicants must attend one interview at the Registry to confirm the details and to answer any necessary questions. A fee may be payable, and if inheritance tax is due, payment must be usually made (with certain exceptions) to the Inland Revenue, Finance Division (Cashiers), Barrington Road, Worthing, West Sussex BN12 4XH. A receipt is given which must be lodged at the Probate Registry before the grant can be issued. It may be necessary to arrange a bridging loan to pay the inheritance tax. In due course the grant of Probate or Letters of Administration will be sent to the executors or administrators respectively. The executors may also ask the registry for sealed office copies of the grant for use in the administration. The responsibility of the Probate Registry ends when the grant is issued.

Administering the estate

Gathering in the assets

Once the grant has been obtained by the executors they must proceed to administer the estate. The first responsibility is to gather in all the assets. This is done by producing and registering the original grant or one of the sealed office copies with all the organisations concerned, such as banks, building societies and insurance companies. They in turn will supply the executors with forms to be completed and signed to enable the accounts to be closed and policies cashed. Personal items and furnishings may well have to be disposed of and any home owned by the deceased sold, or transferred.

Settlement of debts

Once the monies have been gathered in, the executors should start to settle the debts. These will include the cost of the funeral and usual household bills of the deceased. Reasonable enquiries must be made to ensure that all the debts of the deceased have been discovered; the executors can only ensure that they have protected themselves in this duty by advertising for claims. The deceased's last employer should be contacted to ensure that no other monies are due to an estate as should the Department of Social Security to ensure that all benefits have been paid up to date.

Tax liability

Executors should also remember that they are responsible for any tax liabilities of the deceased and the grant should therefore be registered with the local tax office of the deceased. Tax returns up to the date of death must be made, necessitating enquiries as to income, sometimes over a number of years. Executors are also responsible for making a return to the Inland Revenue of income arising during the course of the administration, that is after the date of death, but before distribution. Whenever inheritance tax has arisen, the executors have to ascertain whether the values realised for any items differ from those originally estimated in the Inland Revenue Account; if so, a corrective account will need to be filled. All correspondence is with the Capital Taxes Office, Inland Revenue, Minford House, Rockley Road, London W14 0DF. If property is not sold, the Capital Transfer Taxes office may well ask the district valuer, an officer of the Inland Revenue, to check the estimates given and if there is any disagreement the executors may need to instruct their own valuers. Finally a clearance certificate (Cap 30) from the Capital Taxes Office must be obtained to confirm that the executors have cleared all the liabilities of the estate for inheritance tax.

Residuary beneficiaries

When the executors are satisfied that they have completed these steps and that the estate is therefore solvent, they should proceed to pay out any legacies and finally make the distribution to the residuary beneficiaries.

Is it necessary to obtain the services of a solicitor?

Where the estate is small and no grant is required those responsible for the affairs of the deceased may well feel confident to deal with the administration in person. Similarly, where the estate is relatively simple and is an 'excepted estate', executors and administrators may feel able to deal with matters themselves, particularly where the executor and beneficiary is one and the same person.

Nevertheless, the period following the death of the deceased can be a distressing time for the executors and beneficiaries and they may feel overwhelmed by the sheer volume of work in the administration, by the many letters to be written and forms to be completed. Where the assets are large and the estate complex, or the estate includes property such as land, a house, or flat, legal assistance should be sought. The executors can leave all the work to a solicitor.

The solicitor completes all the forms relating to the grant including any Inland Revenue accounts that may have to be completed. The prospective executor or administrator will only have to go to the solicitor's office to sign and swear the papers. Once the grant has been obtained, the solicitor will deal with the administration and ensure that all the debts have been paid. They will at the completion of the administration provide a complete financial account known as the estate account. Where there are a substantial number of beneficiaries (who are not the executors), the executors may prefer to appoint a solicitor to administer the estate, the solicitor's charges being deducted from the estate before distribution. The executors may also therefore be able to protect themselves if they then find that there are other liabilities to meet, for example, a back claim from the Department of Social Security for overpaid benefits. The solicitors will have to accept responsibility for any error made by them.

Appendices

APPENDIX 1 – ADVICE AGENCIES

A list of organisations who will either be able to advise or suggest where you can obtain advice on HIV/AIDS or related legal, welfare rights or housing issues.

1   General advice about HIV and AIDS

National AIDS Helpline, for all of the UK.
Freephone 24 Hour Helpline: 0800 567123

The Terrence Higgins Trust
52–54 Gray's Inn Road, London WCIX 8JU
General number: 0171 831 0330. Mon. – Fri. 9.30–5.30p.m.
Helpline: 0171 242 1010. 12 noon – 10p.m.

2   Legal, housing and welfare rights advice on HIV and AIDS

The Terrence Higgins Trust Advice Centre
Tel. 0171 831 0330
Legal Advice: Mon. – Fri. 9.30–5.30p.m.
Legal Line: 0171 405 2381. Mon. and Wed. 7–9p.m.

Housing advice –   north of the river, Mon. – Wed. and Fri. 10 – 5p.m.
                                 south of the river, phone *The Landmark*: 0171 737 2733

Welfare rights – opening hours: Mon. Thurs. and Fri. 10–12.30p.m. and 2–5p.m.
                                                   Wed. 10–1p.m. and 2.30–5p.m.

Immunity
Tel. 0171 388 6776. Mon. – Fri. 10–1p.m. and 2–5p.m.
32–38 Osnaburgh Street, London NW1 3ND

Apart from these organisations, advice can be obtained from a Citizens Advice Bureau or Law Centre, but first contact your local HIV co-ordinator or a local HIV/AIDS group – who may know of a lawyer or welfare rights/housing adviser who advises on HIV/AIDS issues.
Details of Citizens Advice Bureaux are obtainable from:
The National Association of Citizens Advice Bureaux, Tel. 0171 833 2181
and Law Centres: Tel. 0171 387 8570.

If these agencies cannot help, phone The National AIDS Helpline or local AIDS Helpline who will have access to the National AIDS Manual or an up-to-date list of advice and help organisations in your area.

APPENDIX 2 – REFERENCES AND FURTHER READING

An up-to-date list of legal and related authorities is available from The Terrence Higgins Trust Legal Centre.

Medico-legal authorities

Major statutory and case material: Aspects of treatment and consent

Sidaway v. *Bethlem Royal Hospital Governors et al.* [1985] 2 WLR 480
Chatterton v. *Gershon* [1981] QB 432
Bolam v. *Friern Barnet Hospital Management Committee* [1957] 2 AER 118
GMC Guidance British Medical Journal (*BMJ*) 30.5.87, p.1436; *BMJ* 295 p. 1500; and *BMJ* p. 1613.

Confidentiality of medical records

Stephens v. *Avery* [1988] 2 AER 477
X v. *Y* [1988] 2 AER 648

Specific AIDS legislation

AIDS (Control) (Contents of Reports) Order 1988. SI 1988/117. Amendments to NHS (Charges to Overseas Visitors) (No. 2) Regulations SI 1982/863 have been made by SI 1983/302, 1987/371, 1988/8, and 1988/472.

Housing and people with HIV

Association of London Authorities, *AIDS: A Model Policy for Local Government*, available from The Association of London Authorities, 36 Old Queen Street, London SW1H 9JF, price £3.50
Department of the Environment, *The Housing Aspects of AIDS and HIV Infection: A Housing Research Report; A Manual for Housing Professionals; A Manual for Health and Social Care Professionals*, available from HMSO, price £11, £9 and £8.50 respectively.
Housing Corporation circular HC 40/87, *Housing for People with AIDS*, available from the Housing Corporation, 149 Tottenham Court Road, London W1P 0BN
Resource Information Service, *AIDS: The Issues for Housing*, available from RIS, The Basement, 38 Great Pultney Street, London W1R 3DE, price £4.50.
Resource Information Service, *Roads Home: Housing Advice for People Living with HIV*, available from RIS (address above), price £7.50.
The Terrence Higgins Trust and the Landmark Trust, *The Housing Leaflet: For People Living with HIV and AIDS*, available from The Terrence Higgins Trust, price 50p.

Employment law

Department of Employment and Health and Safety Executive, 'AIDS and employment'.
Southam, C. and Howard, G. (1988) *AIDS and Employment Law*, Financial Trading Publications Ltd.

On employment law

Tolley's Employment Handbook (1988), Tolley Publishing Co. Ltd.

Immigration law

Bender, M. *Immigration Law and Procedure*, New York (1988 supplement).
Fransman, L. (1989) *British Nationality Law*, Format.
Fransman, L. and Webb, D. (1986) *Immigration Emergency Procedures*, Legal Action Group, London.
Hartley, T. (1978) *EEC Immigration Law*, North-Holland, London.
Macdonald, I. (QC) (1987) *Immigration Law and Practice in the United Kingdom*, 2nd edn, Butterworths, London.
Mole, N. (1987) *Immigration – Family Entry and Settlement*, Family Law, Bristol.
Nakonechny, E. (1987) 'The International Civil Liberties Implications of AIDS', unpublished study, University of Essex.
Plender, Dr R. (QC) (1988) *International Migration Law*, 2nd edn, 2 vols, Martinus Nijhoff, London and Dordrecht.
Stonewall (1994) *United Kingdom Immigration Law and Rules As They Affect Same-Sex Couples*, Stonewall, 1 Greycoat Place, London SW1P 1SB. Tel. 0171 222 9007
Supperstone, M. (1988) *Immigration: The Law and Practice*, 2nd edn, Oyez Longman, London.

Powers of attorney, wills and probate

Aldridge, Trevor (1986) *Powers of Attorney*, Oyez/Longman.
Citizens Advice Bureaux, *Information on Powers of Attorney*.
Cretney, Stephen (1991) *Enduring Powers of Attorney*, Jordans.
Department of Health and Social Security, *What To Do After Death*, HMSO, London.
Home Office, *The Work of the Coroner, a Guide*, HMSO, London.
Lord Chancellor's Department, 'How to obtain Probate'.
Maurice, Spencer G., *Family Provision Practice*, Oyez/Longman.
Whitehorn, Norman (1986) *Court of Protection*, Oyez/Longman.

APPENDIX 3 – A BILL TO OUTLAW DISCRIMINATION IN EMPLOYMENT

Employment Protection on AIDS (Amendment) Bill 1987

A BILL TO MAKE PROVISION FOR THE EMPLOYMENT PROTECTION OF PEOPLE WITH AIDS AND THOSE WHO ARE INFECTED BY HIV, BY AMENDMENT TO THE EMPLOYMENT PROTECTION (CONSOLIDATION) ACT 1978, AND BY MAKING THE DISMISSAL OF A PERSON WITH AIDS

OR WITH HIV INFECTION AN UNFAIR DISMISSAL AND INADMISSIBLE REASON FOR THE PURPOSES OF THAT ACT.

1. – (1)   After Section 58A of the 1978 Act, as amended by Section 7 of the 1980 Employment Act there shall be inserted –

Dismissal of a person
with AIDS or HIV

58B. (1)   An employee shall be treated for the purposes of this Part as unfairly dismissed if the reason or principal reason for his dismissal is that he has AIDS or is infected with HIV, or is for any other reason connected with being infected by HIV except one of the following reasons –

(a)   that at the effective date of termination of his employment he is incapable of adequately complying with his terms and conditions of employment;

(b)   that because of his medical condition his employer cannot continue to employ him without a contravention or restriction imposed under any enactment.

(2)   For the purposes of subsection (1) a person with AIDS shall include an employee whose employer or other employees regard as having AIDS and a person with HIV shall include an employee whose employer or other employees regard as having been infected by Human Immuno-deficiency Virus (HIV), notwithstanding the fact that such employee may have had no medical diagnosis of AIDS or HIV antibody test performed by a fully registered medical practitioner.

(3)   Any reason by virtue of which a dismissal is regarded to be unfair in consequence of sub-section (1) or (2) is in this Part referred to as an inadmissible reason.

Index